THE ORIGINAL HITCHHIKER RADIO SCRIPTS

An epic adventure in time and space,
including some helpful advice on how to see the Universe
for less than thirty Altairian dollars a day

D1293753

ALSO BY DOUGLAS ADAMS

THE HITCHHIKER'S GUIDE TO THE GALAXY

THE RESTAURANT AT THE END OF THE UNIVERSE

LIFE, THE UNIVERSE AND EVERYTHING

SO LONG, AND THANKS FOR ALL THE FISH

MOSTLY HARMLESS

DIRK GENTLY'S HOLISTIC DETECTIVE AGENCY

THE LONG DARK TEA-TIME OF THE SOUL

THE MEANING OF LIFF (with John Lloyd)

THE DEEPER MEANING OF LIFF (with John Lloyd)

LAST CHANCE TO SEE (with Mark Carwardine)

THE ILLUSTRATED HITCHHIKER'S GUIDE TO THE GALAXY

The Original HITCHHIKER Radio Scripts

By
DOUGLAS ADAMS

Edited and with an introduction by
GEOFFREY PERKINS
(who produced it),
With another introduction by
DOUGLAS ADAMS,
largely contradicting the one by

GEOFFREY PERKINS

Harmony Books/New York

Published by Harmony Books, a division of Crown Publishers, Inc., 201 East 50th Street,
New York, New York 10022. Member of the Crown Publishing Group.

Random House, Inc. New York, Toronto, London, Sydney, Auckland

HARMONY and colophon are trademarks of Crown Publishers, Inc.

Originally published in Great Britain by Pan Books, Ltd., Cavaye Place, London
SW10 9PG, under the title *The Hitch-hikers Guide to the Galaxy: The
Original Radio Scripts*, and in the United States by Harmony Books, New York, 1985.

Manufactured in the United States of America

Library of Congress Cataloging-in-Publication Data

Adams, Douglas, 1952–
The original Hitchhiker.

1. Radio plays, English. 2. Science Fiction, English. I. Perkins, Geoffrey.
II. Hitchhiker (Radio Program). 1985. III. Title.
PR6051.D335207 1985   822'.914 85-13947

ISBN 0-517-88384-8

10 9 8 7 6 5 4 3 2 1

First American Paperback Edition

To the BBC Radio Station Manager

Introduction

The first time I can remember coming across Douglas Adams he was standing on a rickety chair making a speech, and the thing I remember most about that was that it was really a rather strange thing to do, since he was already some six inches taller than anyone else in the room. He also pressed on with his speech despite being aggressively heckled by members of the cast of the Cambridge Footlights show that he had just directed.

It was plain here was someone prepared to stick his neck out more further than most people, someone who would carry on in the face of adversity, and someone who would shortly fall off a chair. I was right on all three counts.

Some years later when I was producing the radio series of *The Hitch-Hiker's Guide to the Galaxy* I was also to learn that he was an amazingly imaginative comic writer whose desire to push back the barriers of radio comedy was only matched by his desire for large meals in restaurants.

I came to work for BBC Radio from a shipping company in Liverpool. I only went there because when I told the University appointment board that I didn't know what I wanted to do they immediately told me to go into shipping. It was only afterwards that I realised they probably recommend everyone who comes in on a Wednesday and doesn't know what they want to do to go into shipping. On Thursdays it's probably accountancy, and so on. I sat around wondering what I was doing there for six months until I was recommended to the BBC as a potential producer by Simon Brett, who also started Douglas off with *Hitch-Hiker's*. We both owe him an enormous debt.

Prior to the shipping company I had been at Oxford and directed the University revue at the Edinburgh Festival for the previous two years. This made me an unlikely person to work with Douglas, he being a Cambridge man, not to mention nearly twice my size. If you saw us together you would immediately think of Simon and Garfunkel. Except that I don't write songs and Douglas doesn't sing. Well, he does, but he shouldn't. He is, however, a very good guitarist (unlike Art Garfunkel) and is very keen on Paul Simon, whom he exactly resembles in no way at all. In fact Paul Simon actively refused to meet Douglas in New York when he heard how tall he was. This may have been because he had heard that Douglas was prone to falling off rickety chairs and to breaking his nose with his own knee and so was liable to step on him accidentally and squash him.

Douglas is also the only person I know who can write backwards. Four days before one of the *Hitch-Hiker's* recordings he had written only eight pages of script. He assured me he could finish it in time. On the day of the recording, after four days of furious writing, the eight pages had shrunk to six. Some people would think this was a pretty clever trick but I've been with Douglas when he's writing and I know how he does it. When he wants to change anything, a word or a comma, he doesn't just cross it out and carry on; he takes the whole page out of the typewriter and starts all over again from the top. Yes, he is something of a perfectionist but he would also do almost anything to avoid having to write the next bit. His other favourite way of putting off writing the next bit is to have a bath. When a deadline is really pressing he can have as many as five baths a day. Consequently, the later the script the cleaner he gets. You can't fault him for personal hygiene in a crisis.

But of course much of the strength of *Hitch-Hiker's* comes from the fact that Douglas has sweated over every word of it. It's not just funny, it is also very good writing; and one of the few comedy shows where people don't think that the actors have made it all up as they went along. And at least Douglas was never quite as bad at overrunning deadlines as Godfrey Harrison, who wrote the popular 50s radio comedy show *The Life of Bliss*, who often finished the script some hours after the audience had all gone home.

Fortunately we didn't have to worry about the audience leaving. Amazingly there was some debate when the programme started about whether we should have a studio audience, since at that time nearly all radio comedy shows had one. In fact an audience for *Hitch-Hiker's* would have needed about a week of spare time, since that's about how long it took to make each show.

They'd also have been thoroughly confused by the whole thing, since much of the time the show was recorded out of order, rather like a film, and only half the actors in any scene would actually be visible on stage. In fact we evolved a whole new form of radio performance which Mark Wing-Davey called 'cupboard acting'. All the various robots, computers, Vogons and so on, had their voice treatments added after the recordings, so it was necessary to separate them from the other actors, and this we did by putting them in cupboards. During the series several elderly and very distinguished actors were reluctantly shut up in cupboards and only got to talk to the other actors through a set of headphones. Sometimes we would forget all about them and long after their scenes had finished a plaintive voice would be heard in the control box, saying 'Can I come out now?' The experience was all the odder because we recorded the shows in the Paris, BBC Radio's main audience studio in London's Lower Regent Street, since at the time it was the only stereo studio with a multi-track tape recorder (albeit only eight tracks). The actors would consequently perform in front of rows and rows of empty seats, and sometimes when three or four aliens were taking part in a scene you could look out of the control box and there would be nobody on the stage at all. They'd all be in various cupboards dotted around the studio. Sometimes the actors played more than one part, sometimes as many as five parts. This of course was so that they could show off their versatility. It was also so that we could manage to bring the show in somewhere in the region of the budget.

The actors were recorded without all the backgrounds and effects which were put on afterwards. Contrary to many people's beliefs most of the sounds are not pure 'radiophonic sound' but were made up by playing around with some of the thousands of ordinary BBC effects discs. Most of the synthesised effects and music were done on an ARP Odyssey, which sounds impressive unless you happen to know that it is in fact a tacky little machine which can be found irritating people in cocktail bars all over the world. The Radiophonic Workshop itself (housed in a pink painted converted ice rink in Maida Vale) is a marvellous lash up of bits and pieces of gadgetry gradually picked up over the years. When we started the series we spent many hours just finding out what some of the equipment could do (or not do in the case of their vocoder, which must have been one of the first ones around, took up a whole room and stubbornly refused to do anything other than emit various vaguely unpleasant hums). However, if we had known how all the equipment worked we'd have missed all the fun of playing around with it, and I'd have missed all the fun of finding out what the pubs are like in Maida Vale.

More playing around went on in the Paris studio where most of the shows were put together. Many of the backgrounds and incidental noises (like Marvin's walk) were put on loops of tape which went round endlessly. Sometimes we would have three or four of these loops on the go at any one time and the cubicle would look as if it had been strewn with grim black Christmas decorations. But I can't speak too highly of the efforts of the technical team led by Alick Hale-Munro. I particularly remember one occasion when, after we'd overrun our mixing session for the umpteenth time, I received a stern phone call strictly forbidding me from incurring any more overtime for the studio managers. So at six o clock sharp I said 'Right, that's it', whereupon they all looked at me rather incredulously and said 'But we're half way through this scene'. When I explained I wasn't allowed to let them run over they insisted on finishing the scene and said they had no intention of claiming any overtime. That sort of attitude was undoubtedly a great factor in the success of the show.

The first time that we realized the show might not just be different but also successful was probably when a letter managed to find its way to my office addressed simply to Megadodo Publications, Megadodo House, Ursa Minor. Now if the British Post Office knew about the show then we really must be on to something.

Hitch-Hikers became rather a freak success for a radio show; after all, good as it was, *Under Milk Wood* didn't go on to spawn a spin-off towel. Feeling, however, that radio shows were not big money spinners, BBC Enterprises turned down the suggestion of doing a book or a record of the show and the last I heard they were fiercely trying to win back lost ground by obtaining the soft toy rights. We were soon deluged by letters, some of which are quoted from in the footnotes, (and some of which sadly seem to have disappeared somewhere between the BBC and Original Records with whom we made the two *Hitch-Hiker's* albums).

The show was lavishly praised by all of the radio critics (except one who found it 'noisy and confused') and it went on to win a variety of radio awards (though it failed to win a European award, possibly because of a rather erratic translation into French).

The show was also a big hit when it was transmitted on the BBC World Service, though there were one or two interesting criticisms. One listener in Belgium (excuse my language) asked 'Why should humour be frantic? Do we have to get it over quick, so that the smile can appear on the face, like when a doctor swiftly jabs a hyperdermic into the bottom of a luckless child?' A listener in Sierra Leone thought that 'as a source of information it is misleading' and asked if it could be 'replaced by something more educative, such as a programme on National Anthems of the world', and a listener in India strongly objected to 'Robots taking part in a comedy show'. Who knows, we may start receiving messages from beings who have picked it up on the other side of the galaxy complaining about our inaccurate portrayal of the Vogons and saying how much they prefer their own comedy spectacular, *Eg Twonkwarth El Ploonikon.*

The people who heard the show on BBC World Service will have heard a slightly different version from the original BBC Radio 4 transmission. Those people who heard the BBC transcription service disc will have heard another version and those who heard the commercial records will have heard another version again. Those people who saw the television show will have seen another different version, and those people who have read the books will have come across yet another different version. But this book contains the original radio scripts, *Hitch-Hiker's* as it was originally written, and exactly as it appeared for the very first time.

Well, all right, like everything else involving *Hitch-Hiker's* that is not exactly what it seems. These scripts include numerous alterations, amendments and additions, often made during recording, which helped to make a little more sense of the whole thing and gave us something to do while we were waiting for Douglas to come up with the next page. In addition some bits have been restored which were cut from the original transmission. Some of these bits were cut because, although they read well they slowed down the dramatic pace of a scene. Some were cut simply for reasons of time, since each show had to be exactly twenty eight minutes and thirty seconds and unfortunately twenty eight minutes and thirty seconds is not a magically perfect length for every single show that is made. The pieces that have been restored are indicated in the script in italics.

The short captions at the start of each episode, or fits as they were called (from Lewis Carroll's *Hunting of the Snark*) are the original billings from the Radio Times, and the Announcer lines appeared at the end of the programme credits and were thought up either by me or Douglas.

I have added some footnotes at the end of each episode which are not in any way intended to be comprehensive but simply contain one or two things that might interest people. They may not always be absolutely true or accurate, but where they are inaccurate I hope that (to quote the *Guide)* they are at least 'definitively inaccurate'.

I was aware of the sort of things people might be interested in by some of the letters. About half of them asked what the signature tune was, and since one person said they would 'like to be able to hear the excellent background music without the annoying intrusion of the voices', I have included details of the main pieces of music that we used in the series.

Most of the effects (called FX) directions that Douglas wrote have been retained. One critic wrote that *Hitch-Hiker's* often sounded like somebody thinking out loud, and nowhere does Douglas do that more evidently than in these notes.

My warmest thanks to the cast, who are all named in the footnotes, to Simon Brett who has helped me to be accurate about the early days, to Paddy Kingsland for great help and moral support at the time and some memory jogging lunches that helped me with the footnotes, to Alick Hale-Munro for his fantastic hard work on the shows and his magnificent door clunks, to Paul Hawdon, Lisa Braun and Colin Duff who helped him, to Dick Mills and Harry Parker at the Radiophonic Workshop, to my then head of department David Hatch who helped me make the impossible deadline of the second series, to Richard Wade who kept repeating the show on Radio 4 at all hours of the day and night, to Deborah Amos, Larry Josephson and others whose enthusiasm helped to get the show played on American radio, to my ex-secretary Anne Ling, who was superbly unflappable at the time, who typed the script whenever she was given a chance and who has been of great assistance in getting various bits and pieces together for this book, and finally to Douglas for giving me such a tremendous opportunity as a producer. May we share many more large meals.

Geoffrey Perkins
July 1985

'Where do you get all your ideas from?'

The story goes that I first had the idea for *The Hitch-Hiker's Guide to the Galaxy* while lying drunk in a field in Innsbruck (or 'Spain' as the BBC TV publicity department authoratitively has it, probably because it's easier to spell).

Apparently I was hitch-hiking around Europe at the time, and had a copy of *The Hitch-Hiker's Guide to Europe* (by Ken Walsh, also published by Pan Books) with me at the time. I didn't have *Europe On* (as it was then) *Five Dollars A Day* because I simply wasn't in that kind of financial league.

My condition was brought on not so much by having had too much drink, so much as having had a bit to drink and nothing to eat for two days. So as I lay there in this field, the stars span lazily around my head, and just before I nodded off, it occurred to me that someone ought to write a *Hitch-Hiker's Guide to the Galaxy* as well.

Now, this may well be true.

It sounds plausible. It certainly has a familiar kind of ring to it. Unfortunately, I've only got my own word for it now, because the constant need to repeat the story ('Tell me Douglas, how did it all *start* . . .?') has now completely obliterated my memory of the actual event. All I can remember now is the sequence of words which makes up the story – ('Well, it's very interesting you should ask that, Brian. I was lying in this field . . .'), and if I ever forget that, then the whole thing will have vanished from my mind forever.

If I then come across a BBC press release which says that I thought of the idea in Spain, I'll probably think it must be true. After all, they are the BBC aren't they?

However, I wouldn't like to create the impression that all a writer has to do is sit in a field cramming himself with a couple of Stella Artoises whereupon a passing idea will instantly pounce on him, and then it's all over bar the typing. An idea is only an idea.

An actual script, on the other hand, is hundreds of ideas bashed around, screwed up, thrown into the bin, fished out of the bin an hour later and folded up into thick wads and put under the leg of a table to stop it wobbling. And then the same again for the next line, and the the next, and so on, until you have a whole page or the table finally keels over.

The problem is that you can't go off and rave it up in a field every time you need an idea, so you just have to sit there and think of the little bastards. And if you can't think of them you just have to sit there. Or think of an excuse for doing something else. That's quite easy. I'm very good at thinking of reasons for suddenly having a quick bath or a Bovril sandwich. Which is why truthful explanations of how writers get ideas tend to be rather dull:

> I sat and stared out of the window for a while, trying to think of a good name for a character. I told myself that, as a reward, I would let myself go and make a Bovril sandwich once I'd thought of it.
>
> I stared out of the window some more and thought that probably what I really needed to help get the creative juices going was to have a Bovril sandwich now, which presented me with a problem that I could only successfully resolve by thinking it over in the bath.
>
> An hour, a bath, three Bovril sandwiches, another bath and a cup of coffee later, I realised that I still hadn't thought of a good name for a character, and decided that I would try calling him Zaphod Beeblebrox and see if that worked.
>
> I sat and stared out of the window for a while, trying to think of something for him to say . . .

Zaphod was definitely a three sandwich idea. Arthur Dent came quite easily after a couple of biscuits and a cup of tea. Vogon poetry I remember was a tough one, and only came after several miles of rampaging round the country lanes of Stalbridge, Dorset, in a track suit trying to work off the effects of thinking up the Babel Fish (six slices of toast and peanut butter, a packet of crisps and a shower). Marvin was . . .

Marvin was different. Marvin was actually based on a real person, but the person concerned tends to get annoyed if I go around telling people it was him. However he gets even more annoyed if I don't go around telling people it was him because then he has to tell people himself before he can tell them how annoyed he is about it, and I think he finds that particularly irritating.

There is a rumour to the effect that the person I'm referring to here is the comedy writer Andrew Marshall, who co-wrote *The Burkiss Way, End of Part One*, and *Whoops, Apocalypse*, but I would like to emphasize that it is only a rumour. I know that for a fact because I started it.

Is there any evidence to support the rumour? Well, it is true that when I used to know Andrew well, he was the sort of person you would feel rather nervous about introducing to people. Suppose you were with a group of people in a pub and he joined you. You would say 'Andrew, meet . . .' whoever it was, and everyone would say hello to him. There would be a slight pause, and then Andrew would say something so devastatingly rude to them that they would be absolutely stunned rigid. In the silence that followed Andrew would then wander off into a corner and sit hunched over a pint of beer. I would go over and say 'Andrew, what on earth was the point of saying that?' and Andrew would say 'What's the point of not saying it? What's the point of being here? What's the point of anything? Including being alive at all? That seems particularly pointless to me.'

However, this is all purely circumstantial evidence, because in fact all comedy writers are like that.

Reading through what I've written so far, I feel I must correct the impression that it's all done with sandwiches, because there's also a lot of playing the guitar very loudly involved as well.

This used only mildly to irritate the neighbours when I just had an acoustic guitar which I would practise intricate fingerpicking styles on when suffering from writer's block. However, since I bought a Fender Stratocaster a couple of years ago even a mild case of searching for *le mot juste* can now cause pain and anger along most of Upper Street.

I also suffer from the fallacy of thinking that playing records will help you work. It doesn't. You end up listening to the record and then you have to start work all over again when it's finished. However, this did in the end have a lot to do with how *Hitch-Hiker's* was actually produced.

Though it was now ten years since *Sergeant Pepper* had revolutionised the way that people in the rock world thought about sound production, it seemed to me, listening to radio comedy at the time, that we still hadn't progressed much beyond Door Slam A, Door Slam B, Footsteps On a Gravel Path and the odd Comic Boing. This wasn't so much lack of imagination, as a perfectly reasonable worry that an overindulgence in sound effects easily creates irritating mish mash which detracts from a strong script and fails to disguise a weak one. Also it took time, which, it was felt, could be better used making more programmes.

However, long-standing rules are made to be broken, and I wanted *Hitch-Hiker's* to sound like a rock album. I wanted the voices and the effects and the music to be so seamlessly orchestrated as to create a coherent picture of a whole other world – and I said this and many similar sorts of things and waved my hands around a lot, while people nodded patiently and said 'Yes, Douglas, but what's it actually *about*?'

We never did clear that one up, of course, but I think we can fairly claim to have made some good noises. In fact recording these shows was some of the best and most nerve-racking fun I've ever had. Were we doing something extraordinary, or were we simply going mad? It was mostly very hard to tell. Because the BBC Light Entertainment Department had simply never attempted anything like this before, we were largely having to invent the process by which we worked as we went along. Geoffrey Perkins has explained a lot of how the production techniques gradually evolved elsewhere in this book, and I only want to add one thing – which is to say to him and to Simon Brett and Paddy Kingsland and John Lloyd and all the studio managers who worked so incredibly hard and inventively on the show, that the way you really get good ideas is from working with talented people you have fun with.

Douglas Adams
London July 1985

Yet Another Introduction

I do enjoy having these little chats at the front of books. This is a complete lie in fact. What actually happens is that you are battling away trying to finish, or at least start, a book you promised to deliver seven months ago and faxes start arriving asking you if you could possibly write yet another short little introduction to a book that you clearly remember writing 'The End' to in 1981. It won't, promises the fax, take you two minutes. Damn right it won't take you two minutes. It actually takes about thirteen hours and you miss another dinner party and your wife won't speak to you, and the book gets so late that you start missing entire camping holidays in the Pyrenees and your wife won't talk to you, particularly since the camping holiday was your idea and not hers and she was only going on it because you wanted to and now she has to go and do it by herself when you know perfectly well that she hates camping. (So do I, incidentally. I am making this bit up.)

And then more faxes come in demanding more introductions, this time for omnibus editions of books, each of which I have already written individual introductions to. After a while I find I have written so many introductions that someone collects them all together and puts them in a book and asks me to write an introduction to it. So I miss another dinner party and also a scuba-diving trip to the Azores and I discover that the reason my wife isn't talking to me is that she is now in fact married to someone else. (I am making this bit up as well, as far as I know.)

In the days when I used to be able to go to parties, in other words, in the days when I had only written a couple of books and the business of writing introductions to them had yet to become a full-time activity, it used to save a lot of time when you discovered that two of your friends didn't know each other, just to say to them, 'This is Peter, this is Paula, why don't you introduce yourselves?' This usually worked fantastically well, and before you knew it Peter and Paula would be a happy couple going off on joint skiing holidays in the French Alps with your wife and her second husband.

So, dear reader, this is the tenth anniversary reissue of *The Original Hitch-Hiker Radio Scripts*. Why don't you introduce yourselves?

I have enjoyed this little chat.

Douglas Adams
London, February 1995

Complete cast list

THE BOOK	Peter Jones
ARTHUR DENT	Simon Jones
FORD PREFECT	Geoffrey McGivern
PROSSER and PROSTETNIC VOGON JELTZ	Bill Wallis
LADY CYNTHIA FITZMELTON	Jo Kendall
THE BARMAN	David Gooderson
EDDIE THE COMPUTER AND THE VOGON GUARD	David Tate
MARVIN, THE PARANOID ANDROID	Stephen Moore
ZAPHOD BEEBLEBROX	Mark Wing-Davey
TRILLIAN	Susan Sheridan
SLARTIBARTFAST	Richard Vernon
DEEP THOUGHT	Geoffrey McGivern
MAJIKTHISE AND THE CHEERLEADER	Jo Nathan Adams
FIRST COMPUTER PROGRAMMER and BANG BANG	Ray Hassett
SECOND COMPUTER PROGRAMMER	Jeremy Browne
VROOMFONDEL AND SHOOTY	Jim Broadbent
FRANKIE MOUSE	Peter Hawkins
BENJY MOUSE	David Tate
GARKBIT THE WAITER and ZARQUON THE PROPHET	Anthony Sharp
MAX QUORDLEPLEEN	Roy Hudd
'B' ARK NUMER TWO, HAGGUNENONN UNDERFLEET COMMANDER and HAIRDRESSER	Aubrey Woods
'B' ARK NUMBER ONE AND MANAGEMENT CONSULTANT	Jonathan Cecil
CAPTAIN and THE CAVEMAN	David Jason
MARKETING GIRL	Beth Porter
GAG HALFRUNT	Stephen Moore
ARCTURAN NUMBER ONE	Bill Paterson
ARCTURAN CAPTAIN, RADIO VOICE, RECEPTIONIST and LIFT	David Tate
FROGSTAR ROBOT and AIR TRAFFIC CONTROLLER	Geoffrey McGivern
ROOSTA	Alan Ford
FROGSTAR PRISON RELATION OFFICER	David Tate
GARGRA VARR	Valentine Dyall
THE VENTILATION SYSTEM	Geoffrey McGivern
THE NUTRIMAT MACHINE	Leueen Willoughby
ZAPHOD BEEBLEBROX THE FOURTH	Richard Goolden

BIRD ONE ....Ronald Baddiley
BIRD TWO and THE FOOTWARRIOR ....John Baddeley
THE WISE OLD BIRD ....John Le Mesurier
LINTILLA (AND HER CLONES) ....Rula Lenska
THE FILM COMMENTATOR and THE COMPUTEACH ....David Tate
THE PUPIL ....Stephen Moore
HIG HURTENFLURST ....Mark Smith
VARNTVAR THE PRIEST..Geoffrey McGivern
THE ALLITNILS..David Tate
POODOO ....Ken Campbell
AIRLINE STEWARDESS...Rula Lenska
AUTOPILOT and ZARNIWOOP ....Jonathan Pryce
THE MAN IN THE SHACK...Stephen Moore

FIT THE FIRST

In which the Earth is unexpectedly destroyed and the great
Hitch-Hike begins.

NARRATOR **(Over music. Matter of fact, characterless voice)**

This is the story of *The Hitch-Hiker's Guide to the Galaxy*, perhaps the most remarkable, certainly the most successful book ever to come out of the great publishing corporations of Ursa Minor – more popular than the *Celestial Home Care Omnibus*, better selling than *53 More Things To Do In Zero Gravity*, and more controversial than Oolon Coluphid's trilogy of philosophical blockbusters: *Where God Went Wrong, Some More of God's Greatest Mistakes* and *Who is This God Person Anyway?*

And in many of the more relaxed civilizations on the outer Eastern rim of the Galaxy, the Hitch-Hiker's Guide has already supplanted the great Encyclopaedia Galactica as the standard repository of all knowledge and wisdom, because although it has many omissions, contains much that is apocryphal, or at least wildly inaccurate, it scores over the older, more pedestrian work in two important ways. First, it is slightly cheaper, and second it has the words 'DON'T PANIC' inscribed in large, friendly letters on the cover.

To tell the story of the book, it is best to tell the story of some of the minds behind it. A human from the planet Earth was one of them, though as our story opens he no more knows his destiny than a tea leaf knows the history of the East India Company. His name is Arthur Dent, he is a six foot tall ape descendant, and someone is trying to drive a bypass through his home.

F/X GENERAL ROAD BUILDING NOISES. BULLDOZERS, PNEUMATIC DRILLS, ETC.

(The following conversation is carried out over this noise. The man from the Council, Mr Prosser, is being dictatorial through a megaphone, and Arthur is shouting his answers rather faintly in the distance.)

PROSSER Come off it Mr Dent, you can't win you know. There's no point in lying down in the path of progress.

ARTHUR I've gone off the idea of progress. It's overrated.

PROSSER But you must realize that you can't lie in front of the bulldozers indefinitely.

ARTHUR I'm game, we'll see who rusts first.

PROSSER I'm afraid you're going to have to accept it. This bypass has got to be built, and it's going to be built. Nothing you can say or do . . .

ARTHUR Why's it got to be built?

PROSSER What do you mean, why's it got to be built? It's a bypass, you've got to build bypasses.

ARTHUR Didn't anyone consider the alternatives?

PROSSER There aren't any alternatives. Look, you were quite entitled to make any suggestions or protests at the appropriate time.

ARTHUR Appropriate time? The first I knew about it was when a workman arrived at the door yesterday. I asked him if he'd come to clean the windows and he said he'd come to demolish the house. He didn't tell me straight away of course. No, first he wiped a couple of windows and charged me a fiver. Then he told me.

PROSSER **(Ordinary voice, but he is still clearly audible. In other words, he was standing next to Arthur anyway.)**

But Mr Dent, the plans have been available in the planning office for the last nine months.

ARTHUR Yes. I went round to find them yesterday afternoon. You hadn't exactly gone out of your way to call much attention to them had you? I mean, like actually telling anybody or anything.

PROSSER The plans were on display.

ARTHUR And how many average members of the public are in the habit of casually dropping round at the local planning office of an evening? It's not exactly a noted social venue is it? And even if you had popped in on the off-chance that some raving bureaucrat wanted to knock your house down, the plans weren't immediately obvious to the eye, were they?

PROSSER That depends where you were looking.

ARTHUR I eventually had to go down to the cellar . . .

PROSSER That's the display department.

ARTHUR . . . with a torch.

PROSSER Ah, the lights had probably gone.

ARTHUR So had the stairs.

PROSSER But you found the notice didn't you?

ARTHUR Yes. It was on display in the bottom of a locked filing cabinet stuck in a disused lavatory with a sign on the door saying 'Beware of the Leopard'. Ever thought of going into advertising?

PROSSER It's not as if it's a particularly nice house anyway.

ARTHUR I happen rather to like it.

PROSSER Mr Dent!

ARTHUR Hello? Yes?

PROSSER Have you any idea how much damage that bulldozer would suffer if I just let it roll straight over you?

ARTHUR How much?

PROSSER None at all.

GRAMS NARRATOR BACKGROUND

NARRATOR By a strange coincidence, 'None at all' is exactly how much suspicion the ape descendant Arthur Dent had that one of his closest friends was not descended from an ape, but was in fact from a small planet somewhere in the vicinity of Betelgeuse. Arthur Dent's failure to suspect this reflects the care with which his friend blended himself into human society after a fairly shaky start. When he first arrived fifteen years ago the minimal research he had done suggested to him that the name Ford Prefect would be nicely inconspicuous. He will enter our story in 35 seconds and say 'Hello Arthur'. The ape descendant will greet him in return, but in deference to a million years of evolution he will not attempt to pick fleas off him. Earthmen are not proud of their ancestors and never invite them round to dinner.

FORD   (**Arriving**) Hello Arthur.

ARTHUR   Ford, hi, how are you?

FORD   Fine, look, are you busy?

ARTHUR   Well, I've just got this bulldozer to lie in front of, otherwise no, not especially.

FORD   There's a pub down the road. Let's have a drink and we can talk.

ARTHUR   Look, don't you understand?

PROSSER   Mr Dent, We're waiting.

ARTHUR   Ford, that man wants to knock my house down!

FORD   Well, he can do it whilst you're away can't he?

ARTHUR   But I don't want him to!

FORD   Well just ask him to wait till you get back.

ARTHUR   Ford . . .

FORD   Arthur! Will you please just listen to me, I'm not fooling. I have got to tell you the most important thing you've ever heard, I've got to tell you now, and I've got to tell you in that pub there.

ARTHUR   Why?

FORD   Because you're going to need a very stiff drink. Now, just trust me.

ARTHUR   (**Reluctantly**) I'll see what I can do. It'd better be good. (**Calls**) Hello! Mr Prosser!

PROSSER   Yes Mr Dent? Have you come to your senses yet?

ARTHUR   Can we just for a moment assume for the moment that I haven't?

PROSSER   Well?

ARTHUR   And that I'm going to be staying put here till you go away?

PROSSER   So?

ARTHUR   So you're going to be standing around all day doing nothing.

PROSSER   Could be.

ARTHUR Well, if you're resigned to standing around doing nothing all day you don't actually need me here all the time do you?

PROSSER Er, no. Not as such.

ARTHUR So if you can just take it as read that I am actually here, I could just slip off down to the pub for half an hour. How does that sound?

PROSSER Er . . . that sounds . . . very er, reasonable I think Mr Dent. I'm sure we don't actually need you there for the *whole* time. We can just hold up our end of the confrontation.

ARTHUR And if you want to pop off for a bit later on I can always cover for you in return.

PROSSER Oh, thank you. Yes. That'll be fine Mr Dent. Very kind.

ARTHUR And of course it goes without saying that you don't try and knock my house over whilst I'm away.

PROSSER What? Good Lord no Mr Dent. *The mere thought hadn't even begun to speculate about the merest possibility of crossing my mind.*

ARTHUR Do you think we can trust him?

FORD Myself, I'd trust him to the end of the Earth.

ARTHUR Yes, but how far's that?

FORD About twelve minutes away. Come on, I need a drink.

GRAMS NARRATOR BACKGROUND

NARRATOR By drink Ford Prefect meant alcohol. The *Encyclopaedia Galactica* describes alcohol as a colourless, volatile liquid formed by the fermentation of sugars, and also notes its intoxicating effect on certain carbon-based life forms. *The Hitch-Hiker's Guide to the Galaxy* also mentions alcohol. It says that the best drink in existence is the Pan Galactic Gargle Blaster, the effect of which is like having your brains smashed out with a slice of lemon wrapped round a large gold brick. The *Guide* also tells you on which planets the best Pan Galactic Gargle Blasters are mixed, how much you can expect to pay for one, and what voluntary organizations exist to help you rehabilitate.

The man who invented this mind-pummelling drink also invented the wisest remark ever made, which was this: 'Never drink more than two Pan Galactic Gargle Blasters unless you are a thirty ton elephant with bronchial pneumonia.' His name is Zaphod Beeblebrox and we shall learn more of his wisdom later.

F/X PUB INTERIOR. GENERAL CONVERSATION CHATTER, CLINK OF GLASSES, JUKEBOX, ETC.

FORD Six pints of bitter. And quickly please, the world's about to end.

BARMAN Oh yes, sir? Nice weather for it. Going to watch the match this afternoon sir?

FORD No. No point.

BARMAN	Foregone conclusion that, you reckon sir? Arsenal without a chance?
FORD	No, it's just that the world's going to end.
BARMAN	Of yes, sir, so you said. Lucky escape for Arsenal if it did.
FORD	No, not really.
BARMAN	There you are sir, six pints.
F/X	DRINKS BEING PUT ON BAR. RUSTLE OF BANK NOTES
FORD	Keep the change.
BARMAN	What, from a fiver? Thank you, sir.
FORD	You've got ten minutes left to spend it.
ARTHUR	Ford, would you please tell me what the hell is going on? *I think I'm beginning to lose my grip on the day.*
FORD	Drink up, you've got three pints to get through.
ARTHUR	Three? At lunchtime?
FORD	Time is an illusion. Lunchtime doubly so.
ARTHUR	Very deep. You should send that in to the *Reader's Digest*. They've got a page for people like you.
FORD	Drink up.
ARTHUR	Why three pints?
FORD	Muscle relaxant. You'll need it.
ARTHUR	Did I do something wrong today, or has the world always been like this and I've been too wrapped up in myself to notice?
FORD	All right. I'll try to explain. How long have we known each other Arthur?
ARTHUR	Er . . . five years, maybe six. Most of it seemed to make some kind of sense at the time.
FORD	All right. How would you react if I said that I'm not from Guildford after all, but from a small planet somewhere in the vicinity of Betelgeuse?
ARTHUR	**(Really baffled now)** I don't know. Why, do you think it's the sort of thing you feel you're likely to say?
FORD	Drink up, the world's about to end.
ARTHUR	This must be Thursday. I never could get the hang of Thursdays.
F/X: GRAMS	NARRATOR BACKGROUND
NARRATOR	On this particular Thursday, something was moving quietly through the ionosphere miles above the surface of the planet. But few people on the surface of the planet were aware of it. One of the six thousand million people who hadn't glanced into the ionosphere recently was called Lady Cynthia Fitzmelton. She was at that moment standing in front of Arthur

Dent's house in Cottington. Many of those listening to her speech would probably have experienced great satisfaction to know that in four minutes time she would evaporate into a whiff of hydrogen, ozone and carbon monoxide. However, when the moment came they would hardly notice because they would be too busy evaporating themselves.

(Lady Cynthia Fitzmelton is a sort of Margaret Thatcher, Penelope Keith character, who delivers this speech with dignity and utter conviction through a barrage of enraged boos and catcalls.)

LADY CYNTHIA   I have been asked to come here to say a few words to mark the beginning of work on the very splendid and worthwhile new Bevingford bypass. And I must say immediately what a great honour and a great privilege I think it must be for you, the people of Cottington, to have this gleaming new motorway going through your cruddy little village . . . I'm sorry, your little country village of cruddy Cottington. **(Shouts from annoyed crowd)** I know how proud you must feel at this moment to know that your obscure and unsung hamlet will now arise reborn as the very splendid and worthwhile Cottington Service Station, providing welcome refreshment and sanitary relief for every weary traveller on his way.

VOICE 1   Why don't you push off, you crud-faced old bat?

VOICE 2   What about our bloody homes?

LADY CYNTHIA   And for myself, it gives me great pleasure to take this bottle of very splendid and worthwhile champagne and break it against the noble prow of this very splendid and worthwhile yellow bulldozer.

F/X   BOTTLE SMASHING AGAINST BULLDOZER, WHICH BEGINS TO RUMBLE FORWARD

F/X: CAST   LOUD JEERS AND ALSO A PERFUNCTORY RIPPLE OF APPLAUSE FROM ONE OR TWO HIRED LACKEYS

F/X   SWITCH BACK TO PUB INTERIOR ATMOS. THE MUFFLED SOUND OF THE HOUSE BEING KNOCKED DOWN FILTERS THROUGH

ARTHUR   What's that?

FORD   Don't worry, they haven't started yet.

ARTHUR   Oh good.

FORD   It's probably just your house being knocked down.

ARTHUR   What?

FORD   It hardly makes any difference at this stage.

ARTHUR   My God it is! What the hell are they doing! We had an agreement!

FORD   Let 'em have their fun.

ARTHUR   Damn you and your fairy stories, they're smashing up my home!

F/X   HE RUNS OUT OF THE PUB

ARTHUR (**Shouting**) Stop you vandals! You home wreckers! You half-crazed visigoths, stop will you!

FORD Arthur! Come back. It's pointless! Hell, I'd better go after him. Barman, quickly, can you just give me four packets of peanuts?

BARMAN Certainly, sir. There you are, twenty eight pence.

F/X NOTE SLAPPED ON TABLE

FORD Keep the change.

BARMAN Are you serious sir? I mean, do you really think the world's going to end this afternoon?

FORD Yes, in just over one minute and thirty five seconds.

BARMAN Well, isn't there anything we can do?

FORD No, nothing.

BARMAN I always thought we were meant to lie down or put a paper bag over our head or something.

FORD If you like, yes.

BARMAN Will that help?

FORD No. Excuse me, I've got to find my friend. (**Goes**)

BARMAN Oh well then, last orders please!

F/X OUTSIDE ATMOS.

ARTHUR (**Yelling**) You pinstriped barbarians! I'll sue the council for every penny it's got! I'll have you hung, drawn and quartered, and whipped and boiled, and then I'll chop you up into little bits until . . . until . . . until you've had enough!

FORD Arthur, don't bother, there isn't time, get over here, there's only ten seconds left!

ARTHUR (**Oblivious**) And then I'll do it some more! And when I've finished I will take all the little bits . . . and I will *jump* on them! And I will carry on jumping on them until I get blisters or I can think of something even more unpleasant to do, and then I'll . . . WHAT THE HELL'S THAT????

F/X AN UNEARTHLY SCREAM OF JETS THUNDERS ACROSS THE SKY. MASS PANDEMONIUM BREAKS OUT, WITH PEOPLE SHOUTING, RUNNING IN EVERY DIRECTION

FORD Arthur! Quick, over here!

ARTHUR What the hell is it?

FORD It's a fleet of flying saucers, what do you think it is? Quick, you've got to get hold of this rod!

ARTHUR What do you mean, flying saucers?

FORD   Just that, it's a Vogon constructor fleet.

ARTHUR   A what?

FORD   A Vogon constructor fleet, I picked up news of their arrival a few hours ago on my sub-ether radio.

ARTHUR   (**Still yelling to be heard over din**) Ford, I don't think I can cope with any more of this. I think I'll just go and have a little lie down somewhere.

FORD   No! Just stay here! Keep calm . . . and just take hold of . . . (**lost in din**).

F/X   CLICK OF A P.A. CHANNEL OPENING. ALIEN VOICE REVERBERATES ACROSS THE LAND:-

ALIEN   People of Earth, your attention please. This is Prostetnic Vogon Jeltz of the Galactic Hyperspace Planning Council. As you will no doubt be aware, the plans for the development of the outlying regions of the Western Spiral arm of the Galaxy require the building of a hyperspace express route through your star system and, regrettably, your planet is one of those scheduled for demolition. The process will take slightly less than two of your Earth minutes. Thank you very much.

F/X   CLICK OF CHANNEL TURNING OFF. WILD HUBBUB OF PROTEST AS PANIC BREAKS OUT. CLICK AS CHANNEL OPENS AGAIN

ALIEN   There's no point in acting all surprised about it. All the planning charts and demolition orders have been on display at your local planning department in Alpha Centauri for fifty of your Earth years, so you've had plenty of time to lodge any formal complaints, and it's far too late to start making a fuss about it now.

F/X   MORE PROTESTING HUBBUB

ALIEN   What do you mean you've never been to Alpha Centauri? Oh, for heaven's sake mankind it's only four light years away you know. I'm sorry, but if you can't be bothered to take an interest in local affairs that's your own lookout. Energize the demolition beams. (**To himself**) God, I don't know, apathetic bloody planet, I've no sympathy at all . . .

F/X   A LOW THROBBING HUM WHICH BUILDS QUICKLY IN INTENSITY AND PITCH. WIND & THUNDER, RENDING, GRINDING CRASHES. ALL THE NIGGLING LITTLE FRUSTRATIONS THAT THE BBC SOUND EFFECTS ENGINEERS HAVE EVER HAD CAN ALL COME OUT IN A FINAL DEVASTATING EXPLOSION WHICH THEN DIES AWAY INTO SILENCE

(**Longish pause. Then:**)
A FAINT BUT CLEAR BACKGROUND HUM STARTS UP. VARIOUS QUIET ELECTRONIC MECHANISMS. A FEW VAGUE RUSTLES OF MOVEMENT. SOME SOFTLY PADDING FOOTSTEPS

(A pause – just long enough to build up the suspense, then:)

FORD I bought some peanuts.

ARTHUR Whhhrrr?

(This conversation mostly in hushed tones)

FORD If you've never been through a matter transference beam before you've probably lost some salt and protein. The beer you had should have cushioned your system a bit. How are you feeling?

ARTHUR Like a military academy – bits of me keep on passing out. If I asked you where the hell we were would I regret it?

FORD We're safe.

ARTHUR Good.

FORD We're in a small galley cabin in one of the spaceships of the Vogon Constructor Fleet.

ARTHUR Ah, this is obviously some strange usage of the word safe that I wasn't previously aware of.

FORD I'll have a look for the light.

ARTHUR All right. How did we get here?

FORD We hitched a lift.

ARTHUR Excuse me, are you trying to tell me that we just stuck out our thumbs and some bug-eyed monster stuck his head out and said 'Hi, fellas, hop right in, I can take you as far as the Basingstoke roundabout'?

FORD Well, the thumb's an electronic sub-ether device, the roundabout's at Barnard's Star six light years away, but otherwise that's more or less right.

ARTHUR And the bug-eyed monster?

FORD Is green, yes.

ARTHUR Fine. When can I go home?

FORD You can't. Ah, I've found the light.

F/X THE SOUND OF LIGHT GOING ON IN A VOGON SPACESHIP

ARTHUR (**Wonderment**) Good grief! Is this really the interior of a flying saucer?

FORD It certainly is. What do you think?

ARTHUR It's a bit squalid, isn't it?

FORD What did you expect?

ARTHUR Well I don't know. Gleaming control panels, flashing lights, computer screens. Not old mattresses.

FORD These are the Dentrassi sleeping quarters.

ARTHUR I thought you said they were called Vogons or something.

FORD   The Vogons run the ship. The Dentrassi are the cooks. They let us on board.

ARTHUR   I'm confused.

FORD   Here, have a look at this.

ARTHUR   What is it?

FORD   *The Hitch-Hiker's Guide to the Galaxy.* It's a sort of electronic book. It'll tell you everything you want to know. That's its job.

ARTHUR   I like the cover. 'DON'T PANIC'. It's the first helpful or intelligible thing anybody's said to me all day.

FORD   That's why it sells so well. Here, press this button and the screen will give you the index, several million entries, fast wind through the index to 'V'. There you are, Vogon Constructor Fleets. Enter that code on the tabulator and read what it says.

NARRATOR   Vogon Constructor Fleets.

Here is what to do if you want to get a lift from a Vogon: Forget it. They are one of the most unpleasant races in the Galaxy – not actually evil, but bad-tempered, bureaucratic, officious and callous. They wouldn't even lift a finger to save their own grandmothers from the Ravenous Bugblatter Beast of Traal without orders signed in triplicate, sent in, sent back, queried, lost, found, subjected to public inquiry, lost again, and finally buried in soft peat for three months and recycled as fire lighters. The best way to get a drink out of a Vogon is stick your finger down his throat, and the best way to irritate him is to feed his grandmother to the Ravenous Bugblatter Beast of Traal.

ARTHUR   What a strange book. How did we get a lift then?

FORD   That's the point, it's out of date now. I'm doing the field research for the new revised edition of the *Guide*. So, for instance, I will have to include a revision pointing out that since the Vogons have made so much money being professionally unpleasant, they can now afford to employ Dentrassi cooks. Which gives us a rather useful little loophole.

ARTHUR   Who are the Dentrassi?

FORD   The best cooks and the best drinks mixers, and they don't give a wet slap about anything else. And they will always help hitch-hikers on board, partly because they like the company, but mostly because it annoys the Vogons. Which is exactly the sort of thing you need to know if you're an impoverished hitch-hiker trying to see the marvels of the Galaxy for less than thirty Altairian dollars a day. And that's my job. Fun, isn't it?

ARTHUR   It's amazing.

FORD   Unfortunately I got stuck on the Earth for rather longer than I intended. I came for a week and was stranded for fifteen years.

ARTHUR   But how did you get there in the first place?

FORD   Easy, I got a lift with a teaser. You don't know what a teaser is, I'll tell you. Teasers are usually rich kids with nothing to do. They cruise around looking for planets which haven't made interstellar contact yet, and buzz them.

ARTHUR   Buzz them?

FORD   Yes. They find some isolated spot with very few people around, then land right by some poor unsuspecting soul whom no one's ever going to believe and then strut up and down in front of him wearing silly antennae on their head and making beep beep noises. Rather childish really.

ARTHUR   Ford, I don't know if this sounds like a silly question, but what am I doing here?

FORD   Well, you know that. I rescued you from the Earth.

ARTHUR   And what has happened to the Earth?

FORD   It's been disintegrated.

ARTHUR   Has it?

FORD   Yes, it just boiled away into space.

ARTHUR   Look. I'm a bit upset about that.

FORD   Yes, I can understand.

ARTHUR   So what do I do?

FORD   You come along with me and enjoy yourself. You'll need to have this fish in your ear.

ARTHUR   I beg your pardon?

F/X   A RATHER EXTRAORDINARY NOISE STARTS UP. IT SOUNDS LIKE A COMBINATION OF GARGLING, HOWLING, SNIFFING AND FIGHTING OFF A PACK OF WOLVES

ARTHUR   What's the devil's that?

FORD   Listen, it might be important.

ARTHUR   What?

FORD   It's the Vogon Captain making an announcement on the PA.

ARTHUR   But I can't speak Vogon!

FORD   You don't need to. Just put the fish in your ear, come on, it's only a little one.

ARTHUR   Uuuuuuuuggh!

F/X   THE CACOPHONOUS AND HIGHLY IMAGINATIVE SOUNDS DESCRIBED ABOVE ABRUPTLY TRANSFORM INTO THE VOICE OF THE ALIEN WHO ADDRESSED THE EARTH

ALIEN   . . . should have a good time. Message repeat. This is your Captain speaking so stop whatever you're doing and pay attention. First of all I see from our instruments that we have a couple of hitch-hikers aboard our ship. Hello wherever you are, I just want to make it totally clear that you are not at all welcome. I worked hard to get where I am today, and I didn't become Captain of a Vogon Constructor ship simply so that I could turn it into a taxi service for degenerate freeloaders. I have sent out a search party, and as soon as they find you I will put you off the ship. If you're very lucky I might read you some of my poetry first.

Secondly, we are about to jump into hyperspace for the journey to Barnard's Star. On arrival we will stay in dock for a seventy two hour refit, and no-one's to leave the ship during that time. I repeat, all planet leave is cancelled. I've just had an unhappy love affair, so I don't see why anyone else should have a good time. Message ends.

ARTHUR   Charming these Vogons. I wish I had a daughter so I could forbid her to marry one.

FORD   You wouldn't need to. They've got as much sex appeal as a road accident. And you'd better be prepared for the jump into hyperspace. It's unpleasantly like being drunk.

ARTHUR   Well what's so unpleasant about being drunk?

FORD   You ask a glass of water.

ARTHUR   Ford.

FORD   Yes?

ARTHUR   What's this fish doing in my ear?

FORD   Translating for you. Look under Babel Fish in the book.

F/X   BOOK MOTIF, INTERRUPTED BY A SUDDEN SWELLING SOUND OF FANTASTIC ACCELERATION . . .

ARTHUR   (**A slurring distort**) What's happening?

FORD   (**A slurring distort**) We're going into hyperspace.

ARTHUR   Ugggh! I'll never be cruel to a gin and tonic again.

F/X   SOUND DISTORTS TOTALLY. THE NARRATOR'S VOICE CUTS ACROSS IT

GRAMS   NARRATOR BACKGROUND

NARRATOR   The Babel Fish is small, yellow, leechlike, and probably the oddest thing in the Universe. It feeds on brainwave energy, absorbing all unconscious frequencies and then excreting telepathically a matrix formed from the conscious frequencies and nerve signals picked up from the speech centres of the brain; the practical upshot of which is that if you stick one in your ear you can instantly understand anything said to you in any form of language – the speech you hear decodes the brainwave matrix. Now it is such a bizarrely improbable coincidence that anything so mindbogglingly useful could evolve purely by chance that some thinkers have chosen to see it as a final clinching proof of the non-existence of God.

The argument goes something like this:

'I refuse to prove that I exist' says God, 'for proof denies faith, and without faith I am nothing'. 'But', says Man, 'the Babel Fish is a dead giveaway isn't it? It proves you exist, and so therefore you don't. QED'. 'Oh dear', says God, 'I hadn't thought of that' and promptly vanishes in a puff of logic. 'Oh, that was easy' says Man, and for an encore he proves that black is white and gets killed on the next zebra crossing.

Most leading theologians claim that this argument is a load of dingo's kidneys, but that didn't stop Oolon Colluphid making a small fortune when he used it as the central theme of his best-selling book *Well, That About Wraps It Up For God*.

Meanwhile, the poor Babel Fish, by effectively removing all barriers to communication between different cultures and races, has caused more and bloodier wars than anything else in the history of creation.

ARTHUR   What an extraordinary book.

FORD   Help me write the new edition.

ARTHUR   No, I want to go back to Earth again I'm afraid. Or its nearest equivalent.

FORD   You're turning down a hundred billion new worlds to explore.

ARTHUR   Did you get much useful material on Earth?

FORD   I was able to extend the entry, yes.

ARTHUR   Oh, let's see what it says in this edition then.

FORD   OK.

ARTHUR   Let's see. E . . . Earth . . . tap out the code (F X BOOK MOTIF) . . . there's the page. Oh, it doesn't seem to have an entry.

FORD   Yes it does. See, right there at the bottom of the screen. Just under Eccentrica Gallumbits, the triple-breasted whore of Eroticon VI.

ARTHUR   What, there? Oh yes.

BOOK   Harmless.

ARTHUR   Is that all it's got to say? One word? Harmless? What the hell's that supposed to mean?

FORD   Well, there are a hundred billion stars in the Galaxy and a limited amount of space in the book. And no one knew much about the Earth of course.

ARTHUR   Well I hope you've managed to rectify that a little.

FORD   Yes, I transmitted a new entry off to the Editor. He had to trim it a bit, but it's still an improvement.

ARTHUR   What does it say now?

FORD   'Mostly harmless.'

ARTHUR	*Mostly* harmless?
FORD	That's the way it is. We're on a different scale now.
ARTHUR	OK Ford, I'm with you. I'm bloody well coming with you. Where are we now?
FORD	Not far from Barnard's Star. It's a beautiful place, and a sort of hyperspace junction. You can get virtually anywhere from there.
F/X	MARCHING FEET OUTSIDE
FORD	That is, assuming that we actually get there.
F/X	BANGING ON THE STEEL DOOR
ARTHUR	What's that?
FORD	Well, if we're lucky it's just the Vogons come to throw us into space.
ARTHUR	And if we're unlucky?
FORD	If we're unlucky the Captain might want to read us some of his poetry first.
NARRATOR	Vogon poetry is, of course, the third worst in the Universe. The second worst is that of the Azgoths of Kria. During a recitation by their Poet Master Grunthos the Flatulent of his poem 'Ode to a Small Lump of Green Putty I found in My Armpit One Midsummer Morning' four of his audience died of internal haemorrhaging, and the President of the Mid-Galactic Arts Nobbling Council survived by gnawing one of his own legs off. Grunthos is reported to have been 'disappointed' by the poem's reception, and was about to embark on a reading of his twelve book epic entitled 'My Favourite Bathtime Gurgles' when his own major intestine, in a desperate attempt to save humanity, leapt straight up through his neck and throttled his brain. The very worst poetry of all perished along with its creator, Paula Nancy Millstone Jennings of Greenbridge in the destruction of the Planet Earth. Vogon poetry is mild by comparison, and when the Vogon Captain began to read it provoked this reaction from Ford Prefect . . .
FORD	Aaaaaaaaaaaarrrrrrrrgggggghhhh!!!
NARRATOR	And this from Arthur Dent.
ARTHUR	Nnnnnnnyyyyyyuuuuuurrrrrggghhh!!! (**Continues ad lib**)
VOGON	Oh freddled gruntbuggly! Thy micturations are to me As plurdled gabbleblotchits in a lurgid bee. Groop I implore thee my foonting turlingdromes, And hooptiously drangle me with crinkly bindle werdles, For otherwise I will rend thee in the gobberwarts with My blurglecruncheon see if I don't. So Earthlings. I present you with a simple choice. I was going to throw you straight out into the empty blackness of space to die horribly and slowly. But there is one way, one simple way in which you may save yourselves. Think very carefully, for you hold your very lives in your hands. Now

choose! Either die in the vacuum of space or . . .

GRAMS   DRAMATIC CHORD

VOGON   . . . tell me how good you thought my poem was.

NARRATOR   Will our heroes survive this terrible ordeal? Can they win through with their integrity unscathed? Can they escape without completely compromising their honour and artistic judgement?

Tune in next week for the next exciting instalment of 'The Hitch-Hiker's Guide to the Galaxy'.

FOOTNOTES

The first series of six programmes was transmitted for the first time starting on 8 March 1978.

Full details of other transmissions on BBC radio can be found at the end of the book. The pilot of *Hitch-Hiker's*, which subsequently became the first programme, was commissioned by the BBC Radio Light Entertainment Department on 1 March 1977 and produced by Simon Brett on 28 June with the assistance of Paddy Kingsland at the Radiophonic Workshop and a small furry creature from the Crab Nebula.

Probably the script was commissioned in the first place not out of a burning desire to do a sci-fi comedy but because the Chief Producer at the time was rather taken with a sketch Douglas had written for *The Burkiss Way* about a Kamikaze pilot being briefed for his nineteenth mission.

Simon has very kindly looked up his diary for this vital time of creative gestation and it seems to consist chiefly of sitting down with Douglas over an inordinately large number of meals (mostly Japanese). In this respect Douglas' working method has remained unchanged over the years.

The go ahead for a series was given on 31 August and was celebrated in the traditional way with a large meal (Greek this time).

Simon remembers that right from the start Douglas knew exactly what he wanted. For instance, he spent some time looking for a signature tune which had to be electronic but which also had a banjo in it. Quite why he was so keen on a banjo is a bit of a mystery (he says he thought it would help give an 'on the road, hitch-hiking feel' to the whole thing), but there is no doubt that the choice of *Journey of the Sorcerer* from the Eagles album *One of These Nights* was inspired. Interestingly many of the people who wrote in asking what it was were surprised to find that they already had it. It just seemed to be one of those album tracks that nobody had noticed until it was taken out of context.

Peter Jones was not the first person approached to play the Book, but curiously from the start there had been a desire to cast someone with a 'Peter Jonesy sort of voice'. After three or four people (including Michael Palin) had turned it down the search for the Peter Jonesy sort of voice narrowed in on Peter Jones. His calmly reassuring tone as the Earth and the Universe disintegrated around him was a great comfort for those people who were somewhat bewildered by the whole thing, and his performance perhaps took much of its strength from the fact that Peter himself was somewhat bewildered by the whole thing.

Douglas claims to have based many of the characteristics of Arthur Dent on the actor who played him, Simon Jones (who contrary to several people's belief is not in fact Peter Jones' son) though Simon himself is wary of being seen as a role model for a character he describes as 'whingeing around the Universe trying to find a cup of tea'. An early thought was to call the character Aleric B., but the name Arthur Dent was chosen as being distinctive without being peculiar. (Peculiarly enough quite a few people had already come across an Arthur Dent who in 1601 had published a Puritan tract called 'The Plaine Man's Pathway to Heaven'. Douglas claims never to have heard of this, despite being hard pressed about it over several large meals.)

Ford Prefect (whose original name is sadly only pronounceable in an obscure

Betelgeusian dialect) was played by the estimable Geoffrey McGivern, star of several Footlights revues. He was virtually typecast as the disreputable alien, Ford Prefect. Fit the First also featured David Gooderson as the barman, Jo Kendall (who had featured in *I'm Sorry I'll Read that Again* and *The Burkiss Way*) as Lady Cynthia Fitzmelton and Bill Wallis (who literally came in on the day to replace another actor who had gone sick), memorably doubled up as Prossor and Prostetnic Vogon Jeltz.

Many people have been interested in the recipe for a Pan Galactic Gargle Blaster. It must be said that it is in fact impossible to mix a Pan Galactic Gargle Blaster under Earth's atmospheric conditions, but readers will be delighted to know that all profits from this book will go towards purchasing a ticket on a future space shuttle to see if it is possible to mix one in low orbit. (This is in fact a piece of complete nonsense, thought up over several large lunches, which have already, in fact, absorbed all possible profits from the book.)

As Paddy Kingsland points out the effect of the Earth's destruction (page 25) is an amalgam of very ordinary sounds . . . thunderclaps, explosions, old train crashes and so on. In fact, all it would have needed was a heartbeat to have the complete set of radio sound effects clichés. Despite that it's all mixed together in a way that makes it the technical highlight of the first show.

The Vogon space ship background, with its distinctive little pings, was inspired by *Star Trek*, and (rather more obscurely) the Book Motif was inspired by Tom and Jerry and made up from lots of little bits of tape that had been left lying around on the floor in the Radiophonic Workshop.

The Babel fish is a brilliant device for getting round a basic problem which most Sci-Fi series seem to ignore, namely, why is it that all aliens seem to be able to speak English? Although it is never actually mentioned again it is safe to assume that Arthur has it firmly in his ear over the next eleven episodes.

The extraordinary noise of gargling, howling, sniffing and so on (page 28) was the first of many effects that were made perfectly satisfactorily by completely ignoring the convoluted directions in the script. In fact, it was made quite simply by reversing the speech.

Mildly interested *Hitch-Hiker's* devotees will note that Paula Nancy Millstone Jennings (page 31) is a pretty strange name. Real fanatics will know that it has been changed from the name that actually appeared on the programme. This is for legal reasons, and is not in fact a typing error made after a particularly arduous lunch.

Absolutely tonto *Hitch-Hiker's* fans will also be interested to know that in a recent edition of the fanzine *Playbeing* the line 'I never could get the hang of Thursdays' was voted the most popular line of the series, shortly ahead of 'Life? Don't talk to me about life.' (About which see the note on the second episode.)

Music details

Here are some of the main pieces of music used in the first programme in addition to the signature tune.

Lontano. From *A Modern Mass for the Dead* by Ligeti.
(Used in the opening speech, the 'On this particular Thursday' speech, and the Vogon constructor fleet speech.)

A Rainbow in Curved Air by Terence Riley.
(Used in the 'None at all' speech, the Pan Galactic Gargle Blaster speech, the Babel fish speech and the Vogon poetry speech.)

Volumina by Ligeti.
(Used as the final dramatic chord.)

FIT THE SECOND

After being saved from certain death during the demolition of the Earth, Arthur Dent now faces a hopeless choice between meeting certain death in the vacuum of space or finding something pleasant to say about Vogon poetry.

GRAMS	SIG: 'JOURNEY OF THE SORCERER'
GRAMS	NARRATOR BACKGROUND
NARRATOR	Far out in the uncharted backwaters of the unfashionable end of the Western spiral arm of the Galaxy lies a small unregarded yellow sun. Orbiting this at a distance of roughly ninety million miles is an utterly insignificant little blue-green planet whose ape-descended life forms are so amazingly primitive that they still think digital watches are a pretty neat idea.
	This planet has, or had, a problem – which was this: most of the people living on it were unhappy for pretty much of the time. Many solutions were suggested for this problem, but most of these were largely concerned with the movements of small green pieces of paper, which is odd because on the whole it wasn't the small green pieces of paper that were unhappy.
	And so the problem remained; and lots of the people were mean, and most of them were miserable, even the ones with digital watches. Many were increasingly of the opinion that they'd all made a big mistake in coming down from the trees in the first place. And some said that even the trees had been a mad move, and that no one should ever have left the oceans.
	And then one day, nearly two thousand years after one man had been nailed to a tree for saying how great it would be to be nice to people for a change, a girl sitting on her own in a small cafe in Rickmansworth suddenly realized what it was that had been going wrong all this time, and she finally knew how the world could be made a good and happy place. This time it was right, it would work, and no one would have to get nailed to anything. Sadly however, before she could get to a phone to tell anyone, the Earth was unexpectedly demolished to make way for a new hyperspace bypass and so the idea was lost forever.
	Meanwhile, Arthur Dent has escaped from the Earth in the company of a friend of his who has unexpectedly turned out to be from a small planet somewhere in the vicinity of Betelgeuse. His name is Ford Prefect, for reasons which are unlikely to become clear again at the moment, and they are both in dead trouble with the captain of a Vogon spaceship.
VOGON	So, Earthlings, I present you with a simple choice. Think carefully for you hold your very lives in your hands. Now choose! Either die in the vacuum of space, or . . .
GRAMS	DRAMATIC CHORD (SHRUBBERY)
VOGON	. . . Tell me how good you thought my poem was!
FORD	I liked it.
VOGON	(**Relaxing**) Oh good.
ARTHUR	Oh yes, I thought that some of the metaphysical imagery was really particularly effective.
VOGON	(**Prompting**) Yes?

ARTHUR   Oh . . . and, er, interesting rhythmic devices too which seemed to counterpoint the . . . er . . .

FORD   . . . counterpoint the surrealism of the underlying metaphor of the . . . er . . .

ARTHUR   Humanity of the . . . er . . .

FORD   Vogonity.

ARTHUR   (**Getting desperate**) Vogonity, sorry, of the poet's compassionate soul which contrives through the medium of the verse structure to sublimate this, transcend that, and come to terms with the fundamental dichotomies of the other, and one is left with a profound and vivid insight into . . . into . . .

FORD   . . . into whatever it was the poem was about! (**Aside**) Well done Arthur, that was very good.

VOGON   So what you're saying is that I write poetry because underneath my mean, callous, heartless exterior I really just want to be loved. Is that right?

FORD   (**Laughing nervously**) Well I mean, yes, don't we all, deep down, you know . . . er . . .

VOGON   No, well you're completely wrong. I just write poetry to throw my mean, callous, heartless exterior into sharp relief: I'm going to throw you off the ship anyway. Guard! Take the prisoners to number three airlock and throw them out.

F/X   THEY ARE GRABBED AND PUT UP A STRUGGLE. THE STRUGGLE CONTINUES DURING ALL THE ENSUING DIALOGUE

FORD   You can't throw us off into deep space, we're trying to write a book!

VOGON GUARD   Resistance is useless.

ARTHUR   I don't want to die now, I've still got a headache! I don't want to go to heaven with a headache, I'd be all cross and wouldn't enjoy it.

(**They are being urged further and further away**)

FORD   You can't do this!

VOGON   Why not, you puny creature?

FORD   Oh 'Why not?' 'Why not?' Does there have to be a reason for everything? Why don't you just let us go on a mad impulse? Go on, live a little, surprise yourself . . .

F/X   HE IS CUT OFF BY THE DOOR HUMMING CLOSED

VOGON   (**To himself**) '. . counterpoint the surrealism of the underlying metaphor . . .' Huh, death's too good for them.

F/X   CROSSFADE TO FORD AND ARTHUR STRUGGLING AS THEY ARE DRAGGED DOWN A CORRIDOR

ARTHUR	Ow, let go of me you brute!
FORD	Don't you worry, I'll think of something.
VOGON GUARD	**(Shouting: see the Coarse Actor's Guide to Space Ship Guards)** Resistance is useless!
ARTHUR	I woke up this morning and thought I'd have a nice relaxed day, do a bit of reading, brush the dog . . . it's now just after four in the afternoon and I'm already being thrown out of an alien spaceship five light years from the smoking remains of the Earth!
FORD	All right, just stop panicking.
ARTHUR	Who said anything about panicking? This is still just culture shock. *You wait till I've settled down in the situation and found my bearings a bit. Then I'll start panicking.*
FORD	Arthur, you're getting hysterical, shut up!
VOGON GUARD	**(Still shouting)** Resistance is useless!
FORD	You can shut up as well!
VOGON GUARD	Resistance is useless!
FORD	Oh give it a rest . . . do you really enjoy this sort of thing?
VOGON GUARD	Resistance is . . . What do you mean?
FORD	I mean does it give you a full satisfying life? Stomping around, shouting, pushing people out of spaceships?
VOGON GUARD	Well, the hours are good.
FORD	They'd have to be.
VOGON GUARD	But now you come to mention it, I suppose most of the actual minutes are pretty lousy. Except some of the shouting I quite like. **(Shouts)** Resistance is . . .
FORD	Sure, yes, you're good at that, I can tell. But if it's mostly lousy then why do you do it? What is it? The girls? The leather? The machismo?
VOGON GUARD	Well . . . er, I don't know, I think I just sort of . . . do it really.
FORD	There Arthur, you think you've got problems . . .
ARTHUR	Yeah, this guy's still half throttling me . . .
FORD	Yeah, but try and understand his problem. *Here he is, poor lad, his entire life's work is stamping around, throwing people off spaceships . . .*
VOGON GUARD	*And shouting . . .*
FORD	*. . . and shouting, sure . . . and he doesn't even know why he's doing it.*
ARTHUR	*Sad.* **(Followed by suppressed grunt of pain)**
VOGON GUARD	*Well, now you put it like that I suppose . . .*

FORD	*Good lad . . .*
VOGON GUARD	But all right, so what's the alternative?
FORD	Well, stop doing it of course.
VOGON GUARD	Mmmmmmmmmmm . . . well, doesn't sound that great to me.
FORD	Now wait a minute, that's just the start. There's more to it than what you see . . .
VOGON GUARD	No, I think if it's all the same to you I'd better just get you both shoved into this airlock and then go and get on with some other bits of shouting I've got to do.
FORD	But come on . . now look (**Renewed struggling**)
ARTHUR	*Ow, stop that . . !*
FORD	*Hang on, there's music and art and things to tell you about yet! Aaggh!*
VOGON GUARD	(**Shouting**) *Resistance is useless!* (**Less shouty**) *You see, if I keep it up I can eventually get promoted to senior shouting officer, and there aren't usually many vacancies for non-shouting and non-pushing-people-about officers, so I think I'd better stick to what I know. But thanks for taking an interest. 'Bye now.*
ARTHUR	Stop, don't do it.
FORD	(**Desperate**) No, listen, there's a whole world you don't know anything about . . . here, how about this . . . 'Da da da Dum' (**First bar of Beethoven's Fifth**) Doesn't that stir anything in you?
F/X	AIRLOCK DOOR OPENS
VOGON GUARD	'Bye, I'll mention what you said to my aunt.
F/X	AIRLOCK DOOR CLOSES
FORD	Potentially bright lad I thought.
ARTHUR	We're trapped now, aren't we?
FORD	Errrrr . . . yes, we're trapped.
ARTHUR	Well, didn't you think of anything?
FORD	Oh yes, but unfortunately it rather involved being on the other side of the airtight hatchway they've just sealed behind us.
ARTHUR	So what happens next?
FORD	The hatchway in front of us will open automatically in a moment, and we'll shoot out into deep space and asphyxiate in about thirty seconds.
ARTHUR	So this is it. We're going to die.
FORD	Yes . . . except . . . No! Wait a minute, what's this switch?
ARTHUR	What? Where?
FORD	No, I was only fooling. We are going to die after all.

ARTHUR You know, it's at times like this, when I'm trapped in a Vogon airlock with a man from Betelgeuse, and about to die of asphyxiation in deep space that I really wish I'd listened to what my mother told me when I was young.

FORD Why, what did she tell you?

ARTHUR I don't know, I didn't listen.

FORD Huh! Terrific.

F/X CLICK HUM WHHHOOOOOSHHHHHHH AS THE AIRLOCK DOOR OPENS AND THEY ARE EXPELLED. THE SOUND DOESN'T SO MUCH FADE AS 'EMPTY' BECAUSE SOUND DOESN'T CARRY IN A VACUUM AND SO IT GETS DISPERSED WITH THE ESCAPING AIR

GRAMS NARRATOR BACKGROUND MUSIC

NARRATOR *The Hitch-Hiker's Guide to the Galaxy* is a truly remarkable book. The introduction starts like this: 'Space', it says, 'is big. Really big. You just won't believe how vastly, hugely, mind-bogglingly big it is. I mean, you may think it's a long way down the street to the chemist, but that's just peanuts to space. Listen . . .' And so on.

. . . After a while the style settles down a bit and it starts telling you things you actually need to know, like the fact that the fabulously beautiful planet Bethselamin is now so worried about the cumulative erosion caused by ten million visiting tourists a year, that any net imbalance between the amount you eat and the amount you excrete whilst on the planet is surgically removed from your bodyweight when you leave: so every time you go to the lavatory there it is vitally important to get a receipt.

In the entry in which it talks about dying of asphyxiation thirty seconds after being thrown out of a spaceship it goes on to say that what with space being the size it is, the chances of being picked up by another craft within those seconds are two to the power of two hundred and sixty seven thousand seven hundred and nine to one against which, by a staggering coincidence was also the telephone number of an Islington flat where Arthur once went to a very good party and met a very nice girl whom he entirely failed to get off with. Though the planet Earth, the Islington flat and the telephone have all now been demolished, it is comforting to reflect that they are in some small way commemorated by the fact that twenty nine seconds later Ford and Arthur were in fact rescued.

F/X POSITIVE MONTAGE OF SOUND. AIRLOCK DOOR OPENING AND THEN CLOSING. RUSH OF AIR. (GASPING AND GURGLING FROM FORD AND ARTHUR) THIS IS OVERLAID WITH THE SOUND OF SEVERAL ELECTRONIC COMPUTER VOICES CHATTERING SEMI-COMPREHENSIBLY SAYING THINGS LIKE 'Infinity minus two seconds, Infinity minus four seconds . . . Alien body intake at entry bay two. High Improbability Factor . . . checking. Improbability Co-efficient Infinity minus one. Co-efficient factorable. Factorise! Alien life forms carbonbased. Intake sector Galactic Co-ordinate ZZ9 plural z alpha . . .'

THIS IS REALLY A WILD FLURRY OF SOUND WHICH QUICKLY DIES AWAY INTO THE BACKGROUND, AS THE DIALOGUE BEGINS. SOON AFTERWARDS A SLOW QUIET WASH OF SOUND BUILDS UP BEHIND THE VOICES, PARTLY REFLECTING WHAT THEY SAY THEY CAN SEE AROUND THEM, BUT ALSO WITH MANY RANDOM ELEMENTS WITH AN UNREAL DREAMLIKE QUALITY, NOT UNLIKE PARTS OF *REVOLUTION NO. NINE* FROM THE BEATLES *WHITE ALBUM*. ALL THE SOUNDS CHANGE IMPERCEPTIBLY BEFORE IT'S REALLY POSSIBLE TO HEAR EXACTLY WHAT THEY ARE, SO FOR INSTANCE THE SOUND OF THE WASHING OF SEA WAVES COULD ALMOST BE ASTHMATIC BREATHING INSTEAD, AND THE SOUND OF TRAFFIC IN THE STREET COULD ALMOST BE GALLOPING HOOVES BUT ISN'T.
(**NB: It's worth spending a little time getting the tape right because it will be useful on occasions in the future.**)

FORD   (**Gasping**) There . . . you . . . are. I told you . . . I'd think of something . . .

ARTHUR   Oh, sure. (**Gasp**)

FORD   Bright idea . . . of mine . . . to find a . . . passing spaceship . . . and get rescued by it . . .

ARTHUR   Oh come on . . . the chances against it were astronomical.

FORD   Don't knock it . . . it worked . . . Now . . . where are we?

ARTHUR   Well I hardly like to say this, but it looks like the sea front at Southend.

FORD   God I'm relieved to hear you say that.

ARTHUR   Why?

FORD   Because I thought I must be going mad.

ARTHUR   Perhaps we weren't rescued after all. Perhaps we died.

FORD   What's that meant to mean?

ARTHUR   When I was young I used to have this nightmare about dying. I used to lie awake at night screaming. All my schoolfriends went to heaven or hell, and I was sent to Southend.

FORD   Perhaps we'd better ask somebody what's going on. How about that man over there?

ARTHUR   The one with the five heads crawling up the wall?

FORD   Er . . . yes (**Only a suspicion of doubt in his voice**)

ARTHUR   Sir, excuse me, er . . . excuse me . . .

F/X   (ON TOP OF EVERYTHING ELSE!) WILD TRUMPETING AND BELLOWING LIKE AN ELEPHANT OR SOMETHING

ARTHUR   You know, if this is Southend, there's something very odd about it . . .

FORD   You mean the way the sea stays steady as a rock and the buildings keep washing up and down? Yes, *I* thought that was odd . . .

F/X   A GIRL'S VOICE CUTS THROUGH THE INCREASINGLY DREAM-LIKE QUALITY OF EVERYTHING GOING ON. THERE IS A SLIGHT P.A. QUALITY TO IT, BUT IT IS VERY CLEAR AND PROJECTED. THE GIRL'S NAME IS TRILLIAN

TRILLIAN   Two to the power of one hundred thousand to one against and falling . . .

ARTHUR   What was that?

FORD   Sounds like a measurement of probability . . . hey that couldn't mean . . . no.

ARTHUR   What?

FORD   I'm not sure, but it means we definitely are on some kind of spaceship.

ARTHUR   Southend seems to be melting away . . . the stars are swirling . . . a dust bowl . . . snow . . . my legs drifting off into the sunset . . . hell my left arm's come off too, how am I going to operate my digital watch now? Ford, you're turning into a penguin, stop it.

TRILLIAN   Two to the power of seventy-five thousand to one against and falling . . .

FORD   **(Shouting. There is a very slight quack to his voice)** Hey, who are you? Where are you? What's going on and is there any way of stopping it?

TRILLIAN   Please relax, you are perfectly safe.

FORD   That's not the point! The point is that I am now a perfectly safe penguin and my colleague here is rapidly running out of limbs!

ARTHUR   It's all right, I've got them back now.

TRILLIAN   Two to the power of fifty thousand to one against and falling.

ARTHUR   Admittedly, they're longer than I usually like them, but . . .

FORD   Isn't there anything you feel you ought to be telling us?!

TRILLIAN   Welcome to the Starship Heart of Gold. Please do not be alarmed by anything you see or hear around you. You are bound to feel some initial ill-effects as you have been rescued from certain death at an improbability level of two to the power of two hundred and sixty-seven thousand, seven hundred and nine to one against, possibly much higher. We are now cruising at a level of two to the power of twenty-five thousand to one against and falling, and we will be restoring normality as soon as we are sure what is normal anyway, thank you. Two to the power of twenty thousand to one against and falling.

FORD   Arthur, this is fantastic, we've been picked up by a ship with the new Infinite Improbability Drive, this is really incredible, Arthur . . . Arthur, what's happening?

F/X LOUD GIBBERING OF MONKEYS

ARTHUR Ford, there's an infinite number of monkeys outside who want to talk to us about this script for Hamlet they've worked out.

GRAMS NARRATOR BACKGROUND

NARRATOR The Infinite Improbability Drive is a wonderful new method of crossing interstellar distances in a few seconds, without all that tedious mucking about in hyperspace. The principle of generating small amounts of *finite* improbability by simply hooking the logic circuits of a Bambleweeny 57 sub-meson brain to an atomic vector plotter suspended in a strong Brownian motion producer (say a nice hot cup of tea) were of course well understood, and such generators were often used to break the ice at parties by making all the molecules in the hostess's under-garments simultaneously leap one foot to the left, in accordance with the theory of indeterminacy. Many respectable physicists said that they weren't going to stand for that sort of thing, partly because it was a debasement of science, but mostly because they didn't get invited to those sort of parties. Another thing they couldn't stand was the perpetual failure they encountered in trying to construct a machine which could generate the *infinite* improbability field needed to flip a spaceship between the furthest stars, and in the end they grumpily announced that such a machine was virtually impossible. Then one day, a student who had been left to sweep up the lab after a particularly unsuccessful party found himself reasoning this way: if such a machine is a *virtual* impossibility then it must logically be a *finite* improbability. So all I have to do in order to make one is to work out exactly how improbable it is, then feed that figure into the finite improbability generator, give it a fresh cup of really hot tea and turn it on. He did this, and was rather startled to discover that he had managed to create the long sought after infinite improbability generator out of thin air. It startled him even more when, just after he was awarded the Galactic Institute's Prize for Extreme Cleverness, he got lynched by a rampaging mob of respectable physicists who had finally realized that the one thing they *really* couldn't stand was a smartass.

TRILLIAN Five to one against and falling . . . four to one against and falling . . . three to one . . . two . . . one . . . Probability factor of one to one . . . we have normality . . . I repeat we have normality . . . anything you still can't cope with is therefore your own problem. Please relax. You will be sent for soon.

ZAPHOD BEEBLEBROX Who are they, Trillian?

TRILLIAN Just a couple of guys we picked up in open space. Sector ZZ9 plural Z alpha.

ZAPHOD Yeah, well that's a very sweet thought, Trillian, but do you really think it's wise under the circumstances? I mean here we are on the run and everything, we've got the police of half the Galaxy after us and we stop to pick up hitch-hikers. OK, so ten out of ten for style, but minus several million for good thinking, eh?

TRILLIAN	Zaphod, they were floating unprotected in open space . . . you didn't want them to die did you?
ZAPHOD	Well, not as such no, but . . .
TRILLIAN	Anyway I didn't pick them up. The ship did it all by itself.
ZAPHOD	What . . .?
TRILLIAN	Whilst we were in Improbability Drive.
ZAPHOD	That's incredible.
TRILLIAN	No, just very, very improbable. Look don't worry about the aliens, they're just a couple of guys I expect. I'll send the robot down to check them out. Hey, Marvin . . .
MARVIN	(**Lugubrious robot voice**) I think you ought to know I'm feeling very depressed.
ZAPHOD	Oh God . . .
TRILLIAN	(**Nicely**) Well here's something to occupy you and keep your mind off things.
MARVIN	It won't work, I have an exceptionally large mind.
TRILLIAN	Marvin!
MARVIN	All right, what do you want me to do?
TRILLIAN	Go down to number two entry bay and bring the two aliens up here under surveillance.
MARVIN	Just that?
TRILLIAN	Yes.
MARVIN	I won't enjoy it.
ZAPHOD	She's not asking you to enjoy it – just do it will you?
MARVIN	All right, I'll do it.
ZAPHOD	Good . . . great . . . thank you.
MARVIN	I'm not getting you down at all am I?
TRILLIAN	No, no, Marvin, that's just fine, really.
MARVIN	I wouldn't like to think I was getting you down.
TRILLIAN	No, don't worry about that, you just act as comes naturally and everything will be fine.
MARVIN	You're sure you don't mind?
ZAPHOD	No, no, it's all just part of life.
MARVIN	Life! Don't talk to me about life.
F/X	MARVIN EXITS. DOOR HUMS SHUT

TRILLIAN I don't think I can stand that robot much longer, Zaphod.

GRAMS NARRATOR BACKGROUND

NARRATOR (**Music under**) The *Encyclopaedia Galactica* defines a robot as a mechanical apparatus designed to do the work of a man. The Marketing Division of the Sirius Cybernetics Corporation defines a robot as 'Your plastic pal who's fun to be with'. *The Hitch-Hiker's Guide to the Galaxy* defines the Marketing Division of the Sirius Cybernetics Corporation as a 'bunch of mindless jerks who'll be the first against the wall when the revolution comes' with a footnote to the effect that the editors would welcome applications for anyone interested in taking over the post of robotics correspondent. Curiously enough, an edition of the *Encyclopaedia Galactica* that fell through a Time Warp from a thousand years in the future defined the Marketing Division of the Sirius Cybernetics Corporation as a 'bunch of mindless jerks who were the first against the wall when the revolution came.'

FORD I think this ship is brand new Arthur.

ARTHUR How can you tell? Have you got some exotic devices for measuring the age of metal?

FORD No, I just found this sales brochure lying on the floor. 'The Universe can be yours . . .' Ah, and look, I was right . . . 'Sensational new breakthrough in improbability physics. As the ship's drive reaches infinite improbability, it passes through every conceivable point in every conceivable universe almost simultaneously. You select your own re-entry point. Be the envy of other major Governments'. This is big league stuff.

ARTHUR It looks a hell of a lot better than that dingy Vogon ship. This is my idea of a spaceship, all gleaming white, flashing lights, everything. What happens if I press this button?

FORD I wouldn't . . .

F/X ALMOST SIMULTANEOUSLY WITH FORD SAYING 'I WOULDN'T' ELECTRONIC BEEP

ARTHUR Oh.

FORD What happened?

ARTHUR A sign lit up saying 'Please do not press this button again'.

FORD They make a big thing of the ship's cybernetics. 'A new generation of Sirius Cybernetics Corporation robots and computers, with the new GPP feature.'

ARTHUR GPP? What's that?

FORD Er . . . It says Genuine People Personalities.

ARTHUR Sounds ghastly.

F/X DOOR HUMS OPEN WITH A SORT OF OPTIMISTIC SOUND

MARVIN It is.

ARTHUR	W . . . What?
MARVIN	Ghastly. It all is – absolutely ghastly. Just don't even talk about it. Look at this door. 'All the doors in this spacecraft have a cheerful and sunny disposition. It is their pleasure to open for you, and their satisfaction to close again with the knowledge of a job well done!'
F/X	DOOR CLOSES WITH A SATISFIED SIGH
MARVIN	Hateful, isn't it? Come on I've been ordered to take you up to the Bridge. Here I am, brain the size of a planet and they tell me to take you up to the Bridge. Call that job satisfaction? 'Cause I don't.
FORD	Excuse me, which government owns this ship?
MARVIN	You watch this door. It's about to open again. I can tell by the intolerable air of smugness it suddenly generates.
MARVIN	Come on.
F/X	DOOR OPENS AND SAYS 'GLAD TO BE OF SERVICE!'
MARVIN	Thank you, the Marketing Division of the Sirius Cybernetics Corporation.
F/X	DOOR CLOSES SAYING 'YOU'RE WELCOME'
FORD	Which government owns this ship?
MARVIN	'Let's build robots with Genuine People Personalities' they said. So they tried it out with me. I'm a personality prototype. You can tell, can't you?
FORD	(Embarrassed) Er . . .
MARVIN	I hate that door. I'm not getting you down am I?
FORD	Which government owns this ship?
MARVIN	No government owns it. It's been stolen.
FORD ARTHUR	Stolen?
MARVIN	(Sarcastically imitating them) 'Stolen?'
FORD	Who by?
MARVIN	Zaphod Beeblebrox.
FORD	(Extremely astonished) Zaphod Beeblebrox?
MARVIN	Sorry did I say something wrong? Pardon me for breathing – which I never do anyway so I don't know why I bother to say it, oh God I'm so depressed. Here's another of those self-satisfied doors. Life, don't talk to me about life . . .
	(Fading out)
ARTHUR	No one even mentioned it.
FORD	Really, Zaphod Beeblebrox?

F/X   ON THE BRIDGE. THE FOLLOWING IS OBVIOUSLY HEARD
      ON A RADIO. WE CAN HEAR ZAPHOD AND TRILLIAN
      REACTING WITH THE OCCASIONAL LAUGH

RADIO   . . . and news reports brought to you here on the sub-ether wave band,
        broadcasting around the Galaxy around the clock. And we'll be saying a big
        hello to all intelligent life forms everywhere . . . and to everyone else out
        there, the secret is to bang the rocks together, guys. And of course, the big
        news story tonight is the sensational theft of the new Improbability Drive
        prototype ship, by none other than Zaphod Beeblebrox. And the question
        everyone's asking is . . . has the Big Z finally flipped? Beeblebrox, the man
        who invented the Pan Galactic Gargle Blaster, ex-confidence trickster,
        part-time Galactic President, once described by Eccentrica Gallumbits as
        the Best Bang since the Big One, and recently voted the Worst Dressed
        Sentient Being in the Universe for the seventh time running . . . has he got
        an answer this time? We asked his private brain care specialist, Gag
        Halfrunt.

GAG HALFRUNT   Well look, Zaphod's just this guy you know . . .

F/X   RADIO SWITCHED OFF

ZAPHOD   What did you turn it off for Trillian?

TRILLIAN   Zaphod, I've just thought of something.

ZAPHOD   Yeah?

TRILLIAN   We picked those couple of guys up in sector . . . Zaphod, please take your
           hand off me. And the other one. Thank you and the other one.

ZAPHOD   I grew that one specially for you, Trillian, you know that? Took me six
         months but it was worth every minute.

TRILLIAN   . . . We picked them up in Sector ZZ9 plural Z alpha. Does that mean
           anything to you?

ZAPHOD   On the whole, no.

TRILLIAN   It's where you originally picked me up. Let me show it to you on the
           screen.

F/X   ELECTRONICS

TRILLIAN   Right there.

ZAPHOD   Hey, right. I don't believe it. How the hell did we come to be there?

TRILLIAN   Improbability Drive. We pass through every point in the Universe, you
           know that.

ZAPHOD   Yes, but picking them up there is just too strange a coincidence. I want to
         work this out. Computer!

EDDIE THE   (**Bright, brash, mid atlantic**) Hi there!
COMPUTER

ZAPHOD   Oh God.

COMPUTER	I want you to know that whatever your problem, I am here to help you solve it.
ZAPHOD	Er, look, I think I'll just use a piece of paper.
COMPUTER	Sure thing, I understand. If you ever need . . .
ZAPHOD	Shut up!
COMPUTER	OK, OK . . .
ZAPHOD	Trillian, listen. The ship picked them up all by itself, right?
TRILLIAN	Right.
ZAPHOD	So that already gives us a high improbability factor. It picked them up in *that* particular space sector, which gives us another high improbability factor. Plus – they were not wearing spacesuits, so we picked them up during a crucial thirty second period.
TRILLIAN	I've got a note of that factor here.
ZAPHOD	Put it all together and we have a total improbability of . . . well, it's pretty vast but it's not infinite. At what point did we actually pick them up?
TRILLIAN	At infinite improbability level.
ZAPHOD	Which leaves us a very large improbability gap still to be filled. Look, they're on their way up here now aren't they, with that bloody robot? Can we pick them up on any monitor cameras?
TRILLIAN	I should think so.
F/X	ELECTRONIC SWITCHES. WE OVERHEAR A SNATCH OF DIALOGUE FROM FORD, ARTHUR AND MARVIN OVER A SMALL SPEAKER.
MARVIN	. . . and then of course I've got this terrible pain in all the diodes down my left side . . .
ARTHUR	Is that so?
MARVIN	Oh yes. I mean I've asked for them to be replaced but no one ever listens . . .
ARTHUR	I can imagine.
TRILLIAN	(**Slightly excited**) Oh God, I don't believe it . . .
FORD	(**To himself**) Well, well, well, Zaphod Beeblebrox.
ZAPHOD	(**Wildly excited**) I don't believe it! This is just too amazing!
	Look, Trillian, I'll just handle this . . . is anything wrong?
TRILLIAN	I think I'll just wait in the cabin. I'll be back in a minute.
ZAPHOD	Oh, this is going to be great. I'm going to be so unbelievably cool about it it would flummox a Vegan Snow Lizard. This is terrific. What real cool. Several million points out of ten for style.

TRILLIAN	Well, you enjoy yourself, Zaphod. I don't see what's so great myself. I'll go and listen for the police on the sub-ether wave band. (**She exits**)
ZAPHOD	Right. Which is the most nonchalant chair to be discovered working at. O.K.
F/X	DOOR OPENS SAYING 'GLAD TO BE OF SERVICE'
MARVIN	I suppose you'll want to see the aliens now. Do you want me to sit in a corner and rust or just fall apart where I'm standing?
ZAPHOD	Show them in please, Marvin. (**Then with great cool**) Ford, hi, how are you? Glad you could drop in.
FORD	(**Trying to out-cool him**) Zaphod, great to see you, you're looking well. The extra arm suits you. Nice ship you've stolen.
ARTHUR	(**Astonished**) You mean you know this guy?
FORD	Know him! He's . . . Oh, Zaphod, this is a friend of mine, Arthur Dent. I saved him when his planet blew up.
ZAPHOD	Oh sure, hi, Arthur, glad you could make it.
FORD	And, Arthur, this is my . . .
ARTHUR	(**Sharply**) We've met.
FORD	(**Astonished**) What?
ZAPHOD	(**Guilty start of surprise**) Oh, er . . . have we? Hey . . .
FORD	What do you mean you've met? This is Zaphod Beeblebrox from Betelgeuse Five you know, not bloody Martin Smith from Croydon.
ARTHUR	I don't care, we've met, haven't we Zaphod, or should I say, Phil?
FORD	What?
ZAPHOD	You'll have to remind me, I've a terrible memory for species. Hey, Ford . . .
ARTHUR	(**Doggedly**) It was at a party.
ZAPHOD	I rather doubt it.
FORD	Cool it will you, Arthur?
ARTHUR	A party six months ago, on Earth, England, London.
ZAPHOD	Er . . .
ARTHUR	Islington.
ZAPHOD	Oh, er . . . *that* party.
FORD	Zaphod, you don't mean to say you've been on that miserable little planet as well, do you?
ZAPHOD	No, of course not. Well, I may just have dropped in briefly . . . on my way somewhere.

FORD	What is all this, Arthur?
ARTHUR	At this party there was a girl. I'd had my eye on her for weeks . . . beautiful, charming, devastatingly intelligent, everything I'd been saving myself up for, and just when I'd finally managed to get her for myself for a few tender moments this friend of yours barges up and says 'Hey doll, is this guy boring you, come and talk to me, I'm from a different planet'. I never saw her again.
FORD	Zaphod?
ARTHUR	Yes, he only had the two arms and the one head and he called himself Phil, but . . .
F/X	DOOR OPENS
TRILLIAN	. . . but you must admit that he did actually turn out to be from a different planet, Arthur.
ARTHUR	Good God, it's her! Tricia McMillan, what are you doing here?
TRILLIAN	Same as you, Arthur, I hitched a ride. After all, with a degree in maths and another in astrophysics it was either that or back to the dole queue on Monday. Sorry I missed that Wednesday lunch date, but I was in a black hole all morning.
ZAPHOD	Oh God . . . Ford. This is Trillian, hi, Trillian, this is my semi-cousin Ford, who shares three of the same mothers as me, hi. Trillian, is this sort of thing going to happen every time we use the Infinite Improbability Drive?
TRILLIAN	Very probably I'm afraid.
ZAPHOD	Zaphod Beeblebrox, this is a very large drink. Hi.
NARRATOR	Will our heroes be able to enjoy a nice, relaxed evening at last? How will they cope with their new social roles? Will they survive the deadly missile attack which is launched on them three minutes into the next episode? Find out in next week's exciting instalment of the Hitch-Hiker's Guide to the Galaxy.
GRAMS	SIG. JOURNEY OF THE SORCERER
ANNOUNCER	And that programme will be repeated through a time warp on the BBC Home Service in 1951.
EDDIE THE COMPUTER	Hi there, this is Eddie your shipboard computer, and I just want to mention here that we are now moving into orbit around the legendary planet of Magrathea. Sorry to interrupt your social evening. Have a good time.

FOOTNOTES

This show was produced on 23 November 1977, and I took over as producer from here on, since Simon Brett had departed for London Weekend Television. I felt very much as if I was going in at the deep end, having little idea of how the shows were going to develop. But I was consoled by the fact that over a vigorous Greek meal the night before the recording Douglas admitted that he had no more idea than I had. Paddy Kingsland had also departed on attachment to the BBC children's department which he must have regarded as a step up from *Hitch-Hiker's*! For the rest of the first series the Radiophonic effects and voice treatments were provided by Dick Mills with the assistance of Harry Parker. The programmes were made in the Paris studio by Alick Hale-Munro and his crack team of hardened drinkers.

Marvin has probably become the most popular character to appear in the Guide, going on to make his own disco record and have his own Depreciation society which can be found at 2, Whitchurch Lane E1. It's curious to think that originally he was only intended to appear in this one episode, since Douglas was of the opinion that we'd done the joke of the depressed robot and should now press on to other wilder and more wonderful jokes. He probably became a regular character because of Stephen Moore's superb performance, so it seems important to note here that while you can make a voice sound like a robot by putting it through a harmonizer and give it a downward inflection to help it sound miserable, none of this adds up to much without the actor's performance. All the technical jiggery pokery can do is give the whole thing a bit of gloss. Originally the character was called Marshall, since he was heavily based on Andrew Marshall (about whom see Douglas's introduction). The name was changed in case it sounded too much like a character out of a Western. Andrew Marshall himself is based on Eeyore in Winnie-the-Pooh, who is in turn based on . . . and so on back to the creation. Marvin's hissing and clanking walk was provided from various bits of machinery and kept on a little loop of tape which was forever being lost or accidentally trodden on, something Marvin would no doubt have appreciated.

Trillian was played by Susan Sheridan and the name was chosen because, in Douglas' words 'it was a nickname that also sounded like an alien name'. In earlier drafts the character was called Goophic, before that Smoodle and before that she was a man!

Eddie the Computer was a mixture of a ring modulator, an ordinary teleprinter and David Tate. David is one of the most versatile voice-over people in the country, and proved invaluable in a series which required hundreds of talking computers, lifts, robots and mice.

Mark Wing-Davey thinks he may have been cast as Zaphod Beeblebrox because of a lingering reputation as a university hippy, but it probably had more to do with seeing him in the role of a disreputable media trendy in the TV show 'The Glittering Prizes'. Mark remembers that he was originally booked for just one episode, with the possibility of another. This had nothing to do with doubts about his ability to play the part, it was simply that the shows were being written as we went along and we had no idea which characters would survive into another episode.

The line about his extra head was put in as little extra throwaway joke which was to cause enormous headaches (sic) when the show transferred to television. The extra head cost about twice as much as Mark himself (though he thinks that was fair enough because it gave a better performance than he did!) In fact much of the time the head didn't function properly and used to loll on his shoulder looking up at him, often ending up being operated by a man with his hand up Mark's back.

Bill Wallis had to dip into his memory bag to recreate Prostetnic Vogon Jeltz, and David Tate doubled up as the Vogon Guard.

Ford meeting Zaphod

Many people have asked me angrily why it is that Zaphod Beeblebrox instantly greets Ford *as* Ford when I had earlier stated quite clearly that he had only changed his name to Ford Prefect when he came to Earth.

It was very simple. Just before arriving he registered his new name officially at the Galactic Nomenclaturoid Office, where they had the technology to unpick his old name from the fabric of space/time and thread the new one in its place, so that to all intents and purposes his name always had been and always would be Ford Prefect. I included a footnote explaining this in the first Hitch-Hiker book, but it was cut because it was so dull. [DNA]

The bizarre appearance of the word 'Shrubbery' (page 35) has no bearing whatsoever on the script. It was simply a note I scribbled in the margin (which was then conscientiously typed up in the script) observing a passing similarity to the moment in *Monty Python and the Holy Grail* where the Knights of Ni ask Arthur to bring them a shrubbery. We were all surprised to see it appear, as I am sure you are now.

With relation to the effects note on page 40, more than a little time was spent and needless to say it was of absolutely not use in the future. Suffice it to say that the time originally allocated for making the effects for the entire show was spent on this one effect, and is full of lots of little things which probably seemed terribly interesting at the time but which are now impossible to recognize.

Douglas has added the following note on the Improbability Drive itself.

The Improbability Drive
This came about through watching a TV programme about Judo.

Since I had no grand plan in writing *Hitch-Hiker's* but was simply making it up as I went along, I often painted myself into the most terrible corners. At one point I had carelessly thought that it might be fun to have Arthur Dent and Ford Prefect thrown out of the airlock of a Vogon ship without spacesuits, just to see what would happen. Unfortuanately, of course, if anything was going to happen, I was going to have to think of it. I got very stuck.

Every way out of the corner seemed to amount to nothing more than 'with one bound Jack was free' – which was a cop-out. There's no point in making a big song and dance about what a terrible predicament your characters are in if you just cheat your way out of it.

I began to think that maybe we could just finish the series there and perhaps play light music for the remaining four and a half episodes which would save a lot of time and headaches all round, but not – and here was the crunch – pay my rent. They had to be rescued.

The problem was the sheer improbability of every solution I came up with. This was where the judo programme that you were beginning to wonder if I had forgotten about came into it.

If you have a problem, said the instructor on the programme, such as for instance a nineteen stone Jap in pyjamas trying to beat you into a pulp, the trick is to use this problem to solve itself. If you can trip or throw or deflect the Jap as he hurtles towards you, then the fact that he weighs nineteen stone quickly becomes his worry instead of yours.

So – I thought – if my problem is one of improbability, let's use Improbability to solve the problem, so just for the heck of it I invented the Infinite Improbability Drive, and gave myself a whole new thing to write about. If you can't see precisely how that connects to nineteen stone Japanese men in pyjamas, then I have to confess that that's worrying me too at the moment. (DNA)

The Islington telephone number (page 39) is a real number, as several people have put to the test. It is in fact the number of the flat where Douglas wrote much of the first series, but the person who lives there now has nothing to do with *Hitch-Hiker's* so please stop pestering him.

The joke about 'I really wish I'd listened to what my mother told me when I was young' (page 39) finally makes an appearance after years of being thrown out of Footlights shows, probably because it was never coupled to a scene where people were being thrown out of spaceships.

'Life, don't talk to me about life'
This is actually not my line, but comes from the comedy writer Jon Canter, a very good friend of mine (despite the fact that I pinched this line from him shamelessly) who used it in the opening line to a monologue in a Footlights show in 1972. (DNA)

Music Details
Wind on water from *Evening Star* by Fripp and Eno.
(Used for the opening narration speech)
Rainbow in curved air by Terry Riley
(Used for the 'Space is big . . .' speech)
Poppy Nogood and the Phantom Band by Terry Riley
(Used for the Improbability Drive speech)
Cachaca by Patrick Moraz
(Used for the radio news report).

FIT THE THIRD

After being improbably rescued from certain death in the vacuum of space, Arthur Dent and his new companions now face a missile attack and certain death.

GRAMS   NARRATOR BACKGROUND

NARRATOR   Far back in the mists of ancient time, in the great and glorious days of the Former Galactic Empire, life was wild, rich, and on the whole tax free. *Mighty starships plied their way between exotic suns seeking adventure and reward amongst the furthest reaches of galactic space.* In those days spirits were brave, the stakes were high, men were real men, women were real women, and small furry creatures from Alpha Centauri were real small furry creatures from Alpha Centauri. And all dared to brave unknown terrors, to do mighty deeds, to boldly split infinitives that no man had split before and thus was the Empire forged.

Many men of course became extremely rich, but this was perfectly natural and nothing to be ashamed of because no one was really poor – at least, no one worth speaking of. And for these extremely rich merchants life eventually became rather dull, and it seemed that none of the worlds they settled on was entirely satisfactory, either the climate wasn't quite right in the later part of the afternoon or the day was half an hour too long, or the sea was just the wrong shade of pink – and thus were created the conditions for a staggering new form of industry: custom made luxury planet building.

The home of this industry was the planet Magrathea where vast hyperspatial engineering works were constructed to suck matter through white holes in space and form it into dream planets, lovingly made to meet the exacting standards of the Galaxy's richest men. And so successful was this venture, that very soon Magrathea itself became the richest planet of all time and the rest of the galaxy was reduced to abject poverty. And so the system broke down, the Empire collapsed and a long sullen silence settled over the Galaxy, disturbed only by the pen scratchings of scholars as they laboured into the night over smug little treatises on the value of a planned political economy. *Magrathea itself disappeared and its memory soon passed into the obscurity of legend.* In these enlightened days, of course, no one believes a word of it.

Meanwhile, on Zaphod Beeblebrox's ship, deep in the darkness of the Horsehead Nebula . . .

F/X   STARSHIP BRIDGE BACKGROUND

FORD   I'm sorry, I just don't believe a word of it.

ZAPHOD   Listen to me Ford, I've found it, I swear I've found it.

FORD   Look – Magrathea is a myth, a fairy story, it's what parents tell their kids about at night if they want them to grow up to become economists, it's . . .

ZAPHOD   And we are currently in orbit around it.

FORD   Zaphod, I can't help what you may personally be in orbit around, but this ship . . .

ZAPHOD   Computer!

FORD   Oh no.

EDDIE THE COMPUTER	Hi there, this is Eddie your shipboard computer, and I'm feeling just great, guys, and I know I'm just going to get a bundle of kicks out of any programme you care to run through me . . .
FORD	Is this necessary?
ZAPHOD	Computer, tell us again what our current trajectory is.
E the C	A real pleasure fella. We are currently in orbit at an altitude of . . . three hundred miles . . . around the legendary planet of Magrathea. Golly!
FORD	Proving nothing. I wouldn't trust that computer to speak my weight.
E the C	I can do that for you, sure . . .
FORD	No thank you.
E the C	I can even work out your personality problems to ten decimal places, if it'll help.
TRILLIAN	Zaphod, we should have dawn coming up any minute now on the planet, whatever it turns out to be.
ZAPHOD	OK, OK, let's just take a look at it. Computer.
E the C	Hi there! What can I . . .
ZAPHOD	Just shut up and give us external vision on the monitors, *dim the lights on the Bridge.*
F/X	ELECTRONIC SWITCHING
GRAMS	QUIETLY FADE UP A BIT OF MUSIC, PINK FLOYD, LIGETI OR WHATEVER
ZAPHOD	*There . . . the dark mass you see on the screens now is the planet of Magrathea . . .*
FORD	*Or whatever . . .*
TRILLIAN	*I wonder if Columbus had this trouble?*
ZAPHOD	(**Getting increasingly exasperated**) *Who?*
TRILLIAN	*Sorry, just an esoteric Earth reference. He discovered a continent which went on to cause a bit of trouble. Arthur'll tell you about it . . . Arthur?*
ARTHUR	(**As if he's been day-dreaming**) *What?*
TRILLIAN	*You've been very quiet Arthur?*
ARTHUR	*Yes, I always find it very relaxing listening to other people arguing when I haven't a clue what they're talking about. The view's a bit dull, isn't it? Presumably it becomes absolutely enchanting later on.*
ZAPHOD	(**Who's trying to conjure up some sort of drama**) *We are now traversing the night side. The surface of the planet is three hundred miles below us. In a moment we should see . . . there!*

GRAMS	THIS POINT SHOULD COINCIDE WITH SOME SORT OF CRESCENDO IN THE MUSIC
ZAPHOD	*. . . The Fires of Dawn! . . . the twin suns of Soulianis and Rahm . . .*
FORD	*Or whatever . . .*
ZAPHOD	*Soulianis and Rahm, two ancient furnaces of light, creeping over the black horizon . . . It's fantastic, you've got to admit that.*
FORD	**(Flatly)** *It looks fantastic.*
ARTHUR	(**Quietly, aside to Trillian**) Tricia, I feel I may be missing the point of something.
TRILLIAN	Well, according to what Zaphod's told me, Magrathea is a legendary planet from way back, which no one seriously believes in. Bit like Atlantis, except that the legends say the Magratheans used to manufacture planets.
ARTHUR	. . . Is there any tea on this spaceship?
GRAMS	NARRATOR BACKGROUND
NARRATOR	Arthur Dent had basically assumed that he was the only native ape-descended Earthman to escape from the planet Earth when it was unexpectedly demolished to make way for a new hyperspace bypass, because his only companion, disconcertingly called Ford Prefect, had already revealed himself to be from a small planet somewhere in the vicinity of Betelgeuse, and not from Guildford after all. So when, against all conceivable probability they were suddenly rescued from certain death in deep space by a stolen starship manned by two people, one of whom is Ford's semi-brother the Infamous Zaphod Beeblebrox and the other of whom is Tricia McMillan, a rather nicely descended ape-person that Arthur once met at a party in Islington, it could only be because the ship was powered by the new infinite Improbability Drive, which of course it was. Slowly, majestically, this mighty starship begins its long descent towards the surface of the ancient planet which might or might not be Magrathea.
FORD	Well, even supposing it is . . .
ZAPHOD	It is.
FORD	. . . which it isn't, what do you want with it anyway? I mean I take it you're not here for the sheer industrial archaeology of it all. What is it you're after?
ZAPHOD	Well it's partly the curiosity, partly a sense of adventure, but mostly I think it's the fame and the money.
FORD	It's just a dead planet.
ARTHUR	The suspense is killing me.
NARRATOR	Stress and nervous tension are now serious social problems in all parts of the Galaxy, and it is in order that this situation should not be exacerbated in any way at all that the following facts will now be revealed in advance.

The planet in question is in fact Magrathea.

The deadly nuclear missile attack shortly to be launched by an ancient automatic defence system will merely result in the bruising of somebody's upper arm and the untimely creation and sudden demise of a bowl of petunias and an innocent sperm whale.

In order that some sense of mystery should still be preserved, no revelation will yet be made concerning whose upper arm had been bruised. This fact may safely be made the subject of suspense since it is of no significance whatsoever.

Arthur's next question about the planet is very complex and difficult and Zaphod's answer is wrong in every important respect.

ARTHUR Is it safe?

ZAPHOD Magrathea's been dead for five million years. Of course it's safe. Even the ghosts will have settled down and raised families by now.

F/X: GRAMS FANFARE

VOICE **(If this can be done on five million year old tape so much the better. The voice is outwardly pleasant but actually rather cold and forbidding)**

Greetings to you . . .

ALL What's that? **(Or that sort of thing at least)**

ZAPHOD Computer!

E the C Hi there!

ZAPHOD What is it?

E the C Oh, just some five million year old tape recording that's being broadcast at us.

VOICE This is a recorded announcement as I'm afraid we're all out at the moment. The Commercial Council of Magrathea thanks you for your esteemed visit . . .

ZAPHOD A voice from ancient Magrathea!

FORD OK, OK.

VOICE . . . but regrets that the entire planet is temporarily closed for business. Thank you. If you would like to leave your name and a planet where you can be contacted kindly speak when you hear the tone.

F/X ANSWERING BEEP

TRILLIAN They want to get rid of us. What do we do?

ZAPHOD It's just a recording, keep going. Got that computer?

E the C I got it.

F/X ROCKET THRUST

F/X: GRAMS	LESS FANFARE
VOICE	We would like to assure you that as soon as our business is resumed announcements will be made in all fashionable magazines and colour supplements, when our clients will once again be able to select from all that's best in contemporary geography. Meanwhile we thank our clients for their kind interest and would ask them to leave now.
ARTHUR	Well, I suppose we'd better be going then hadn't we?
ZAPHOD	Shhhh! There's absolutely nothing to be worried about.
ARTHUR	Then why's everyone so tense?
ZAPHOD	They're just interested. We keep going.
F/X	SOUND OF DESCENT CONTINUES. ACTUALLY I SUPPOSE I'D BETTER SAY SOMETHING ABOUT THIS: THE DESCENT NOISE SHOULD REALLY BE ONE OF THOSE CONTINUOUSLY DESCENDING SOUND BANDS WHICH NEVER REALLY GETS ANYWHERE BECAUSE WHILST TONES ARE IMPERCEPTIBLY DROPPING OUT AT THE BOTTOM, SO NEW ONES ARE COMING IN IMPERCEPTIBLY AT THE TOP
F/X: GRAMS	EVEN LESS FANFARE
VOICE	(Getting quite cold now) It is most gratifying that your enthusiasm for our planet continues unabated and so we would like to assure you that the guided missiles currently converging with your ship are part of a special service we extend to all of our most enthusiastic clients, and the fully armed nuclear warheads are of course merely a courtesy detail. We look forward to your custom in future lives. Thank you.
ARTHUR	Listen, if that's their sales pitch, what must it be like in the complaints department?
ZAPHOD	Hey, this is terrific, it means we really must be onto something if they're trying to kill us.
ARTHUR	Terrific.
TRILLIAN	You mean there is someone down there after all?
ZAPHOD	No, the whole defence system must be automatic, but the question is why . . .
ARTHUR	But what are we going to do?
ZAPHOD	Just keep cool.
ARTHUR	(Horrified) Is that all?
ZAPHOD	No, we're also going to take evasive action. Computer, what evasive action can we take?
E the C	Er, none I'm afraid guys.
ZAPHOD	. . . or something.

E the C	There seems to be something jamming my guidance systems. Impact minus thirty seconds.
F/X	ALARM BELLS AND SIRENS GO OFF
E the C	Sorry, I didn't mean to do that. Please call me Eddie if it will help you relax.
ZAPHOD	Right. Errr. Look, we've got to get manual control of this ship.
TRILLIAN	Can you fly her?
ZAPHOD	No, can you?
TRILLIAN	No.
ZAPHOD	Ford?
FORD	No.
ZAPHOD	Fine. We'll do it together.
ARTHUR	I can't either.
ZAPHOD	I'd guessed that. Computer, I want full manual control now.
E the C	You got it. Good luck guys, impact minus twenty seconds.
ZAPHOD	OK Ford, full retro thrust and ten degrees starboard.
F/X	HOWLING SCREECH OF PROTESTING ROCKET ENGINES. THIS SECTION SHOULD BE AS VIOLENTLY NOISY AS POSSIBLE
TRILLIAN	We're veering too fast!
FORD	I can't hold her, she's going into a spin!
ZAPHOD	Dive, dive!
F/X	EQUIPMENT AND BITS AND PIECES FLUNG AROUND CABIN
GRAMS	NARRATOR BACKGROUND
NARRATOR	It is of course more or less at this point that one of our heroes sustains a slight bruise to the upper arm. This should be emphasized because, as has already been revealed, they escape otherwise completely unharmed and the deadly nuclear missiles do not eventually hit the ship. Our heroes' safety is absolutely assured.
E the C	Impact minus fifteen seconds, guys.
ARTHUR	The rockets are still homing in, you can't shake them. We're going to die.
E the C	**(Starts to sing 'You'll never walk alone' in his very metallic voice)**
ZAPHOD	Shut that bloody computer up! **(But it continues)**
TRILLIAN	Zaphod, can we stabilise at X zero zero 547 by splitting our flight path tangentially across the summit vector of 9GX78 with a five degree inertial correction?

ZAPHOD	What? Yes, I expect so, just do it. (**Mutters**) And God forgive you if you're only bluffing.
TRILLIAN	Here we go.
F/X	EVEN MORE NOISE FROM THE ENGINES
FORD	Hey, where did you learn a stunt like that Trillian?
TRILLIAN	Going round Hyde Park Corner on a moped.
ZAPHOD	What?
FORD	It's another Earth reference.
ZAPHOD	Tell me later.
ARTHUR	It's no good, the missiles are swinging round after us and gaining fast. We are quite definitely going to die.
E the C	(**Briefly interrupting his song**) Impact minus five seconds.
ARTHUR	Why doesn't anyone turn on this Improbability Drive thing?
TRILLIAN	Don't be silly, you can't do that.
ARTHUR	Why not? There's nothing to lose at this stage.
TRILLIAN	Does anyone know why Arthur can't turn on the Improbability Drive?
E the C	Impact minus one second, it's been great knowing you guys, God bless.
TRILLIAN	I said does anyone know . . .
F/X	TREMENDOUS EXPLOSION, WHICH FAIRLY QUICKLY TRANSFORMS ITSELF INTO A LITTLE DRIBBLE OF FAIRLY LIGHT FILM MUSIC AND DIES AWAY
ZAPHOD	What the hell happened?
ARTHUR	Well, I was just saying, there's this switch here you see and . . .
ZAPHOD	Where are we Trillian?
TRILLIAN	Exactly where we were I think.
ZAPHOD	Then what's happened to the missiles?
FORD	Er, well according to this screen they've just turned into a bowl of petunias and a very surprised looking whale.
E the C	At an improbability factor of eight million, seven hundred and sixty seven thousand, one hundred and twenty eight to one against.
ZAPHOD	Did you think of that Earthman?
ARTHUR	Well, all I did was . . .
ZAPHOD	That's very good thinking, you know that? You just saved our lives.
ARTHUR	Oh it was nothing, really . . .
ZAPHOD	Oh was it? Well, forget it. OK Computer, take us in to land.

60

F/X CHANGE OF NOTE IN ROCKET DRIVE

ARTHUR Well, I say it was nothing . . . I mean obviously it was something, I was just trying to say it's not worth making too much of a fuss about . . . I mean just saving everybody's life . . .

GRAMS NARRATOR BACKGROUND

NARRATOR Another thing that no one made too much fuss about was the fact that against all probability, a sperm whale had suddenly been called into existence some miles above the surface of an alien planet. And since this is not a naturally tenable position for a whale, this innocent creature had very little time to come to terms with its identity as a whale before it had to come to terms with suddenly not being a whale anymore. This is what it thought as it fell.

F/X POP AS OF WHALE SUDDENLY COMING INTO EXISTENCE SOME MILES ABOVE THE SURFACE OF AN ALIEN PLANET. INCREASING WIND

WHALE Ah! What's happening? Er, excuse me, who am I? Hello? Why am I here? What's my purpose in life? What do I mean by who am I? Calm down, get a grip now. Oh, this is an interesting sensation . . . what is it? It's a sort of yawning tingling sensation in my . . . my . . . well I suppose I'd better start finding names for things if I want to make any headway in what for the sake of what I shall call an argument I shall call the world, so let's call it my stomach. So . . . a yawning tingling sensation in my stomach. Good. Ooooh, it's getting quite strong. And hey, what about this whistling roaring sound going past what I'm suddenly going to call my head? Head, that sounds good, yeah, head, good solid ring to it . . . and the whistling roaring sound, that can be wind . . . is that a good name? It'll do . . . perhaps I can find a better name for it later when I've found out what it's for, because there certainly seems to be a hell of a lot of it. Hey, what's this thing, this . . . let's call it a tail . . . yeah, tail, hey I can really thrash it about pretty good can't I? Wow. Wow. Hey. Doesn't seem to achieve much but I'll probably find out what it's for later on. Now – have I built up any coherent picture of things yet? No. Oh. Hey, this is really exciting, so much to find out about, so much to look forward to, I'm quite dizzy with anticipation . . . or is it the wind? Hey, there really is a lot of that now isn't there? And wow, what's this thing suddenly coming towards me very fast? Very very fast . . . so big and flat and wide it needs a big wide sounding word . . . like round . . . round . . . ground! That's it, ground! I wonder if it will be friends with me?

F/X SOUND OF SPERM WHALE HITTING THE GROUND AT SEVERAL HUNDRED MILES PER HOUR

(Pause)

GRAMS NARRATOR BACKGROUND

NARRATOR Curiously enough the only thing that went through the mind of the bowl of petunias as it fell was 'Oh no, not again'. Many people have speculated that if we knew exactly why the bowl of petunias had thought that we would know a lot more about the nature of the Universe than we do now.

Meanwhile, the starship has landed on the surface of Magrathea and Trillian is about to make one of the most important statements of her life. Its importance is not immediately recognised by her companions.

TRILLIAN Hey, my white mice have escaped.

ZAPHOD Nuts to your white mice.

NARRATOR It is possible that Trillian's oberservation would have commanded greater attention had it been generally realized that human beings were only the third most intelligent life forms on the planet Earth instead of as was generally thought by most independent observers, the second.

ZAPHOD (**Very efficiently**) OK, run atmospheric checks on the planets.

F/X FLURRY OF VERY FAST COMPUTER VOICES RINGING AROUND THE SHIP IN WONDERFUL STEREO, REELING OFF MOSTLY LISTS OF INCOMPREHENSIBLE NUMBERS: A FEW RECOGNISABLE WORDS LIKE ATMOSPHERIC COMPOSITION, OXYGEN, NITROGEN, CARBON DIOXIDE, ATMOSPHERIC PRESSURE, GRAVITATIONAL ANOMALIES ETC.

(**Meanwhile the others continue talking**)

FORD Are we taking this robot?

MARVIN (**Dejectedly**) Don't feel you *have* to take any notice of me please.

ZAPHOD Oh, Marvin the Paranoid Android, yeah, we'll take him.

TRILLIAN What *are* you supposed to do with a manically depressed robot?

MARVIN You think you've got problems. What are you supposed to do if you *are* a manically depressed robot? No, don't try and answer that, I'm fifty thousand times more intelligent than you and even I don't know the answer. It gives me a headache just trying to think down to your level.

F/X ALL THE COMPUTER VOICES SUDDENLY STOP TOGETHER

ZAPHOD Well? What's the result?

VOICES (**All together**) It's OK but it smells a bit.

ZAPHOD OK everybody, let's go.

E the C (**His voice has undergone a radical change and now sounds like a prep school matron**) Good afternoon boys.

ARTHUR What's that?

ZAPHOD Oh. That's the computer. I discovered it had an emergency back up personality which I thought might be marginally preferable.

E the C Now, this is going to be your first day on a strange planet, so I want you all wrapped up snug and warm and no playing with any naughty bug-eyed monsters.

ZAPHOD   I'm sorry, I think we'd be better off with a slide rule.

E the C   Right, who said that?

ZAPHOD   Will you open up the exit hatch please, computer?

E the C   Not until whoever said that owns up.

FORD   Oh God.

E the C   Come on.

ZAPHOD   Computer . . .

E the C   I'm waiting. I can wait all day if necessary.

ZAPHOD   Computer, if you don't open that exit hatch this moment I shall go straight to your major data banks with a very large axe and give you a reprogramming you'll never forget, is that clear?

(Pause)

E the C   I can see this relationship is something we're all going to have to work at.

F/X   EXIT HATCH OPENS. FAINT SOUND OF WIND

ZAPHOD   Thank you, let's go.

F/X   THEY EXIT

E the C   It'll all end in tears, I know it.

F/X   HATCH CLOSES LEAVING TOTAL SILENCE. WIND

GRAMS   PINK FLOYD 'SHINE ON YOU CRAZY DIAMOND' INTRO. FROM THE ALBUM 'WISH YOU WERE HERE'

(They all have to shout into the wind)

ARTHUR   It's fantastic!

FORD   Desolate hole if you ask me.

TRILLIAN   It's bloody cold. It all looks so stark and dreary.

ARTHUR   I think it's absolutely fantastic!

ARTHUR   It's only just getting through to me . . . a whole alien world, millions of light years from home. Pity it's such a dump though. Where's Zaphod?

ZAPHOD   **(Calling from a distance)** Hey! Just beyond this ridge you can see the remains of an ancient city.

FORD   What does it look like?

ZAPHOD   Bit of a dump. Come on over. Oh and watch out for all the bits of whalemeat.

GRAMS   THEY ARE ALL WALKING OFF AND THEIR VOICES FADE, WITH THE MUSIC

ARTHUR   Do you realize that robot can hum like Pink Floyd? What else can you do Marvin?

MARVIN	Rock and roll?
F/X: GRAMS	AS THEY FADE INTO THE DISTANCE THE PINK FLOYD MUSIC CHANGES ABRUPTLY INTO 'ROCK AND ROLL MUSIC' BY THE FAB FOUR WITH JUST A SLIGHT ELECTRONIC DISTORT AND ECHO TO MAKE IT CLEAR THAT THE ROBOT IS IN FACT SINGING IT
TRILLIAN	I wish I knew where my mice were.
ZAPHOD	(**Approaching**) OK, I've found a way in.
ARTHUR	In? In what?
ZAPHOD	Down to the interior of the planet – that's where we have to go. Where no man has trod these five million years, into the very depths of time itself . . .
GRAMS	THEME MUSIC FROM 2001 (ALSO SPRACH ZARATHUSTRA) HAS BEEN BUILDING UP UNDER THIS AND NOW REACHES A CLIMAX
ZAPHOD	Can it, Marvin.
GRAMS	2001 THEME STOPS ABRUPTLY
ARTHUR	Why underground?
ZAPHOD	Well according to the legends the Magratheans lived most of their lives underground.
ARTHUR	Why, did the surface become too polluted or overpopulated?
ZAPHOD	No, I think they just didn't like it very much.
TRILLIAN	Zaphod, are you sure you know what you're doing? We've been attacked once already you know.
ZAPHOD	Look, I promise you, the live population of this planet is nil plus the four of us.
TRILLIAN	And two white mice.
ZAPHOD	And two white mice if you insist.
FORD	Come on, let's go if we're going.
ZAPHOD	Er, hey, Earthman . . .
ARTHUR	Arthur.
ZAPHOD	Could you sort of keep the robot with you and guard this end of the passageway, OK?
ARTHUR	Guard, what from? You just said there's no one here.
ZAPHOD	Yeah, well just for safety OK?
ARTHUR	Whose? Yours or mine?
ZAPHOD	Good lad. OK, here we go.

F/X THEY SET OFF AGAIN. THE SOUND PICTURE STAYS WITH THEM SO THAT ARTHUR'S LINE AND MARVIN'S LINE SOUND SLIGHTLY FURTHER AWAY THIS TIME

ARTHUR Well I hope you all have a really miserable time.

MARVIN Don't worry, they will.

F/X DROP WIND SOUND AS THEY ENTER TUNNEL. SLIGHTLY EERIE BUT TINKLY MUSIC IN BACKGROUND . . . HEAVY SUBWAY ECHO

TRILLIAN This is really spooky.

FORD *Any idea what these strange symbols on the wall are, Zaphod?*

ZAPHOD *I think they're probably just strange symbols of some kind.*

FORD Look at all these galleries of derelict equipment just lying about . . . does anyone know what happened to this place in the end? Why did the Magratheans die out?

ZAPHOD Something to do I suppose.

FORD I wish I had two heads like yours, Zaphod. I could have hours of fun banging them against a wall.

TRILLIAN Shine the torch over here.

ZAPHOD Where, here?

TRILLIAN Well, we aren't the first beings to go down this corridor in five million years then.

ZAPHOD What do you mean?

TRILLIAN Look, fresh mouse droppings.

ZAPHOD Oh, your bloody mice.

TRILLIAN (**Nervous**) What's that light down the corridor?

ZAPHOD It's just torch reflection.

FORD *This stuff must be worth millions you know, even if we don't find any actual money . . .*

ZAPHOD *It'll be there. Trust me.*

FORD *Trust you? Zaphod my old mate, I'd trust you from about as far as I could comfortably take your appendix out.*

TRILLIAN There's definitely something happening down there . . .

ZAPHOD No . . .

TRILLIAN Listen!

F/X SUDDEN ELECTRONIC ZAP. CRIES FROM ZAPHOD, FORD AND TRILLIAN, SLUMP OF BODIES. UNIDENTIFIABLE

SOUNDS . . . OF MOVEMENT AROUND THEM. FADE. FADE
UP WIND

GRAMS   NARRATOR BACKGROUND

NARRATOR   *The Hitch-Hiker's Guide to the Galaxy* is a very unevenly edited book and
contains many passages which simply seemed to its editors like a good idea
at the time.

One of these supposedly relates the experiences of one Veet Voojagig, a
quiet young student at the University of Maximegalon, who pursued a
brilliant academic career studying ancient philology, transformational
ethics and the wave harmonic theory of historical perception, and then,
after a night of drinking Pan Galactic Gargle Blasters with Zaphod
Beeblebrox, became increasingly obsessed with the problem of what had
happened to all the biros he'd bought over the past few years.

There followed a long period of painstaking research during which he
visited all the major centres of biro loss throughout the galaxy and
eventually came up with a rather quaint little theory which quite caught the
public imagination at the time. Somewhere in the cosmos, he said, along
with all the planets inhabited by humanoids, reptiloids, fishoids, walking
treeoids and superintelligent shades of the colour blue, there was also a
planet entirely given over to biro life forms. And it was to this planet that
unattended biros would make their way, slipping quietly through
wormholes in space to a world where they knew they could enjoy a uniquely
biroid lifestyle, responding to highly biro-orientated stimuli . . . in fact
leading the biro equivalent of the good life.

And as theories go this was all very fine and pleasant until Veet Voojagig
suddenly claimed to have *found* this planet, and to have worked there for a
while driving a limousine for a family of cheap green retractables,
whereupon he was taken away, locked up, wrote a book, and was finally
sent into tax exile which is the usual fate reserved for those who are
determined to make a fool of themselves in public.

When one day an expedition was sent to the spatial coordinates that
Voojagig had claimed for this planet they discovered only a small asteroid
inhabited by a solitary old man who claimed repeatedly that nothing was
true, though he was later discovered to be lying.

*There did, however, remain the question of both the mysterious sixty thousand
Altairian dollars paid yearly into his Brantisvogan bank account, and of course
Zaphod Beeblebrox's highly profitable second-hand biro business.*

Meanwhile, on the surface of Magrathea, two suns have just set.

ARTHUR   Night's falling. Look robot, the stars are coming out.

MARVIN   I know, wretched isn't it.

ARTHUR   But that sunset. I've never seen anything like it in my wildest dreams . . .
the two suns . . . it was like mountains of fire boiling into space.

MARVIN   I've seen it. It's rubbish.

ARTHUR	We only ever had the one sun at home. I came from a planet called Earth you know.
MARVIN	I know, you keep going on about it. It sounds awful.
ARTHUR	Ah no, it was a beautiful place.
MARVIN	Did it have oceans?
ARTHUR	Oh yes, great wide rolling blue oceans.
MARVIN	Can't bear oceans.
ARTHUR	(**Sigh**) Tell me, do you get on well with other robots?
MARVIN	Hate them. Where are you going?
ARTHUR	I think I'll just take a short walk.
MARVIN	Don't blame you.
SLARTIBARTFAST	Good evening.
ARTHUR	. . . Aaaah! Who . . .?

(The next speaker is a man called Slartibartfast. He is getting on for elderly and speaks quietly, not unkindly. He is not quite as vague as he pretends)

SLARTI	You choose a cold night to visit our dead planet . . .
ARTHUR	Who . . . who are you?
SLARTI	My name is not important.
ARTHUR	I . . . er . . . you startled me.
SLARTI	Do not be alarmed, I will not harm you.
ARTHUR	But you shot at us. There were missiles.
SLARTI	Merely an automatic system. Ancient computers ranged in the long caves deep in the bowels of the planet tick away the dark millenia, *and the ages hang heavy on their dusty data banks.* I think they take the occasional pot shot to relieve the monotony. I'm a great fan of science you know.
ARTHUR	Really . . .?
SLARTI	Oh yes.
ARTHUR	Ah. Er . . . (**He can't work out who's meant to take the lead in this conversation**)
SLARTI	You seem ill at ease.
ARTHUR	Yes. No disrespect, but I gathered you were all dead.
SLARTI	Dead? No, we have but slept.
ARTHUR	Slept!
SLARTI	Yes, through the economic recession you see.

ARTHUR	What?
SLARTI	Well five million years ago the Galactic economy collapsed, and seeing that custom built planets are something of a luxury commodity, you see . . . you know we built planets do you?
ARTHUR	Well yes, I'd sort of gathered . . .
SLARTI	Fascinating trade . . . doing the coastlines was always my favourite, used to have endless fun doing all the little fiddly bits in fjords . . . so anyway, the recession came so we decided to sleep through it. We just programmed the computers to revive us when it was all over . . . they were index linked to the Galactic stock market prices you see, so that we'd be revived when everybody else had rebuilt the economy enough to be able to afford our rather expensive services again.
ARTHUR	Good God, that's a pretty unpleasant way to behave isn't it?
SLARTI	Is it? I'm sorry, I'm a bit out of touch. *Is this robot yours?*
MARVIN	*No, I'm mine.*
ARTHUR	*If you call it a robot. It's more a sort of electronic sulking machine.*
SLARTI	*Bring it.*
ARTHUR	*What?*
SLARTI	You must come with me, great things are afoot . . . you must come now or you will be late.
ARTHUR	Late? What for?
SLARTI	What is your name, human?
ARTHUR	Dent. Arthur Dent.
SLARTI	Late, as in the late Dentarthurdent. It's a sort of threat you see. Never been very good at them myself, but I'm told they can be terribly effective.
ARTHUR	All right, where do we go?
SLARTI	In my aircar. We are going deep into the bowels of the planet, where even now our race is being revived from its five million year slumber. Magrathea awakes.
F/X	AIRCAR SHOOTS FORWARD . . . OH, BY THE WAY, WE'VE ALSO HAD THE SOUND OF THEM GETTING INTO IT DURING THE PRECEDING SPEECH
ARTHUR	Excuse me, what is your name by the way?
SLARTI	My name is . . . my name is Slartibartfast.
ARTHUR	**(Trying not to laugh)** I . . . I beg your pardon?
SLARTI	Slartibartfast.
	(Fading)

ARTHUR   Slartibartfast?

SLARTI   I said it wasn't important.

(Fade out)

GRAMS   NARRATOR BACKGROUND

NARRATOR   It is an important and popular fact that things are not always what they seem. For instance – on the planet Earth Man had always assumed that he was more intelligent than dolphins because he had achieved so much . . . the wheel, New York, wars, and so on, whilst all the dolphins had ever done was muck about in the water having a good time. But conversely the dolphins believed themselves to be more intelligent than man for precisely the same reasons. Curiously enough the dolphins had long known of the impending demolition of Earth and had made many attempts to alert mankind to the danger, but most of their communications were misinterpreted as amusing attempts to punch footballs or whistle for titbits, so they eventually gave up and left the Earth by their own means shortly before the Vogons arrived.

The last ever dolphin message was misinterpreted as a surprisingly sophisticated attempt to do a double backwards somersault through a hoop whilst whistling the 'Star Spangled Banner', but in fact the message was this: 'So long and thanks for all the fish.' In fact there was only one species on the planet more intelligent than dolphins, and they spent a lot of their time in behavioural research laboratories running round inside wheels and conducting frighteningly elegant and subtle experiments on man. *The fact that man once again completely misinterpreted this relationship was entirely according to these creatures' plans. Arthur Dent's current favourite fact is that life is full of surprises.*

GRAMS   THE KYRIE FROM LIGETI'S REQUIEM (QUIETLY AT FIRST)

F/X   HUM OF THE AIRCAR IN FLIGHT THROUGH UNDERGROUND PASSAGES. IT SLOWS DOWN

SLARTI   Earthman, we are now deep in the heart of Magrathea. I should warn you that the chamber we are about to pass into does not literally exist within our planet. It is simply the gateway into a vast tract of hyperspace. It may disturb you.

ARTHUR   **(Nervously)** Oh . . .

SLARTI   It scares the willies out of me. Hold tight.

F/X   ACCELERATION OF AIRCAR, HATCHWAY OPENING

GRAMS   SHARP INCREASE IN MUSIC VOLUME AS IF THE SOUND IS COMING FROM INSIDE THE CHAMBER

F/X   CAR SHOOTS INTO AN UNIMAGINABLY VAST CAVERNOUS SPACE

ARTHUR   **(Gasp of terror)**

SLARTI	Welcome to our factory floor!
ARTHUR	Aaah! The light . . .
SLARTI	This is where we make most of our planets, you see.
ARTHUR	Does this mean you're starting it all up again now?
SLARTI	No no, for heaven's sake, the Galaxy isn't nearly rich enough to support us yet . . . no, we've been awakened to perform just one extraordinary commission, it may interest you . . . there in the distance in front of us.
ARTHUR	(**Chilled**) Oh no . . .
SLARTI	You see?
ARTHUR	The Earth!
SLARTI	Well the Earth Mark 2 in fact. It seems that the first one was demolished five minutes too early and the most vital experiment was destroyed. There's been a terrible hooha and so we're going to make a copy from our original blueprints.
ARTHUR	You . . . are you saying that you originally *made* the Earth?
SLARTI	Oh yes . . . did you ever go to a place . . . I think it's called Norway?
ARTHUR	What? No, no I didn't
SLARTI	Pity . . . that was one of mine. Won an award you know, lovely crinkly edges.
ARTHUR	I can't take this – did I hear you say the Earth was destroyed . . . five minutes too early?
SLARTI	Shocking cock up, the mice were furious.
ARTHUR	(**In a dead way**) Mice.
SLARTI	Yes, the whole thing was their experiment you see. A ten million year research programme to find the Ultimate Question – big job you know.
ARTHUR	Look, would it save you all this bother if I just gave up and went mad now?
GRAMS	SIG. TUNE
NARRATOR	Has Slartibartfast flipped his lid? Are Ford, Zaphod and Trillian dying in fearful agony, or have they simply slipped out for a quick meal somewhere? Will Arthur Dent feel better with a good hot drink inside him? Find out in next week's exciting instalment of *The Hitch-Hiker's Guide to the Galaxy*.
ARTHUR	I'm sorry but I'd probably be able to cope better if I hadn't bruised my arm.
ANNOUNCER	Zaphod Beeblebrox is now appearing in 'No Sex Please, We're Amoeboid Zingat-Ularians' at the Brantersvogon Starhouse.

FOOTNOTES

This show was recorded on 13 December 1977. The only addition to the cast was the splendid Richard Vernon who played Slartibartfast. Douglas adds the following note on how his name came about.

Slartibartfast

I thought that this character should be a dignified, elderly man, weighed down with the burden of a secret sorrow. I wondered what this sorrow should be, and thought perhaps he might be sad about his name. So I decided to give him a name that anybody would be sad to have. I wanted it to sound as gross as it possibly could, while still being broadcastable. So I started with something that was clearly completely unbroadcastable, which was PHARTIPHUKBORLZ, and simply played around with the syllables until I arrived at something which sounded that rude, but was almost, but not quite, entirely inoffensive. (DNA)

The dramatic missile attack and all the noisy evasion manoeuvres caused us problems because, as always, the effects were put on after the actors' recording and a lot of complicated jiggling around with their lines was needed in order not to drown them out. The lesson learnt from this was that in future when we recorded any scene that was to have loud effects over it we would force the actors to project by feeding a variety of loud noises down their headphones. All this probably added to the extreme mental uncertainty they had already from the lines they had to deliver.

Douglas adds the following note on the origins of the whale.

The Whale

Ah yes, the whale. Well, this came about as a result of watching an episode of a dangerously insane TV detective show called *Cannon* in which people got shot the whole time for incredibly little reason. They would just happen to be walking across the street, and they would simply get killed, regardless of what their own plans for the rest of the day might have been.

I began to find the sheer arbitrariness of this rather upsetting, not just because characters were getting killed, but because nobody ever seemed to care about it one way or another. Anybody who might have cared about any of these people – family, friends, even the postman – was kept firmly offstage. There was never any 'Good night sweet Prince' or 'She should have died hereafter' or even 'Look you bastard, I was meant to be playing squash with this guy tonight' just bang, clear them out of the way, on to the next. They were merely, excuse me, Cannonfodder.

I thought I'd have a go at this. I'd write in a character whose sole function was to be killed for the sake of a small detail in the plot, and then damn well make the audience care about it, even if none of the other characters in the story did. I suppose I must have succeeded because I received quite a number of letters saying how cruel and callous this section was – letters I certainly would not have received if I had simply mentioned the whale's fate incidentally and passed on. I probably wouldn't have received them if it had been a human either. [DNA]

The splat of the whale hitting the ground was partially made up from the batter pudding splat from the Goon show, a fact that might interest people who have seen similarities between the two shows.

To publicize the stage show of Hitch-Hikers a twenty five foot whale was thrown off Tower Bridge. Unlike the stage show it floated.

As a final note on the whale those people interested in sinister conspiracy theories might find some significance in the fact that the whale speech **twice** disappeared from the multi-track tape for no reason that we could fathom, and had to be re-recorded. Those people of a more technical frame of mind might be more inclined to think that we didn't really know how our equipment worked.

Originally the mice were gerbils, but this was changed because gerbils sounded altogether too interesting.

Music Details
Kotakomben from the LP *Einsteig* by Gruppe Between
(Used in the opening Magrathea speech)
Space Theme from *Yamashta* by Stomu Yamashta
(Used in the story-so-far speech)
Oxygene by Jean Michel Jarre
(Used several times as calming music during the missile attack).
That's Entertainment
(Used as the light dribble of film music)
Wind on Water from *Evening Star* by Fripp and Eno.
(Used in the biro speech, which incidentally was originally written for show four but cut back into this show)
Over Fire Island by Fripp and Eno *Another Green World*
(Used in the dolphins speech)

FIT THE FOURTH

It has been revealed to Arthur that the Earth has been built by the Magratheans and run by mice. Meanwhile his companions have been suddenly confronted by something nasty (probably certain death).

GRAMS   SIG 'JOURNEY OF THE SORCERER'

GRAMS: NARRATOR BACKGROUND

NARRATOR   Arthur Dent, a perfectly ordinary Earthman, was rather surprised when his friend Ford Prefect suddenly revealed himself to be from a small planet somewhere in the vicinity of Betelgeuse, and not from Guildford after all. He was even more surprised when a few minutes later the Earth was unexpectedly demolished to make way for a new hyperspace by pass. But this was as nothing to their joint surprise when they are rescued from certain death by a stolen spaceship manned by Ford's semi-cousin the infamous Zaphod Beeblebrox, and Trillian, a rather nice astro-physicist Arthur once met at a party in Islington. However, all four of them are soon totally overwhelmed with surprise when they discover that the ancient world of Magrathea, a planet famed in legend for its surprising trade in manufacturing other planets is not as dead as it was supposed to be. For Zaphod, Ford and Trillian surprise is pushed to its very limits when *this* happens:

F/X   ELECTRONIC ZAP AND CRIES FROM EPISODE THREE

NARRATOR   And when Arthur Dent encounters Slartibartfast the Magrathean coastline designer who won an award for his work on Norway and learns that the whole history of mankind was run for the benefit of a few white mice anyway, surprise is no longer adequate and he is forced to resort to astonishment.

ARTHUR   Mice? What do you mean mice? I think we must be talking at cross purposes. Mice to me mean the little white furry things with the cheese fixation and women standing screaming on tables in early sixties sitcoms.

SLARTIBARTFAST   Earthman, it is sometimes hard to follow your mode of speech. Remember I have been asleep inside this planet of Magrathea for five million years and know little of these early sixties sitcoms of which you speak. These creatures you call mice, you see, are not quite as they appear. They are merely the protrusions into our dimension of vast hyper-intelligent pan-dimensional beings, the whole business with the cheese and the squeaking is just a front.

ARTHUR   A front?

SLARTIBARTFAST   Oh yes, you see the mice set up the whole Earth business as an epic experiment in behavioural psychology . . . a ten million year programme . . .

ARTHUR   No, look, you've got it the wrong way round. It was us, *we* used to do the experiments on *them*.

SLARTIBARTFAST   . . . a ten million year old programme in which your planet Earth and its people formed the matrix of an organic computer. I gather that the mice did arrange for you humans to conduct some primitively staged experiments on them just to check how much you'd really learnt, give you the odd prod in the right direction, you know the sort of thing – suddenly running down the maze the wrong way, eating the wrong bit of cheese or unexpectedly dropping dead of myxomatosis.

P.A. VOICE **(Paging)** Attention please, Slartibartfast, would Slartibartfast and the visiting Earth creature please report immediately to the works reception area. Thank you.

SLARTIBARTFAST However, in the field of management relations they're absolutely shocking.

ARTHUR Really?

SLARTIBARTFAST Yes, well you see every time they give me an order I just want to jump on a table and scream.

ARTHUR I can see that would be a problem.

(Fade)

GRAMS NARRATOR BACKGROUND

NARRATOR There are of course many problems connected with life, of which some of the most popular are 'Why are people born?', 'Why do they die?', and 'Why do they want to spend so much of the intervening time wearing digital watches?' Many millions of years ago a race of hyper-intelligent pan-dimensional beings got so fed up with all the constant bickering about the meaning of life which used to interrupt their favourite pastime of Brockian Ultra-Cricket (a curious game which involved suddenly hitting people for no readily apparent reason and running away) that they decided to sit down and solve the problem once and for all. And to this end they built themselves a stupendous supercomputer which was so amazingly intelligent that even before its data banks had been connected up it had started from first principles with 'I think therefore I am' and had got as far as deducing the existence of rice pudding and income tax before anyone managed to turn it off.

Could a mere computer solve the problem of Life, the Universe and Everything? Fortunately for posterity there exists a tape recording of what transpired when the computer was given this particularly monumental task. Arthur Dent stops off in Slartibartfast's study to hear it.

F/X A COUPLE OF MECHANICAL TAPE SWITCHING NOISES AND A COUPLE OF BLIPS

DEEP THOUGHT **(Very majestic and grand computer voice.)** What is this great task for which I, Deep Thought, the second greatest computer in the Universe of Time and Space have been called into existence?

(Hubbub of concerned voices saying '*Second* greatest?')

ONE Your task, O Computer . . .

TWO No, wait a minute, this isn't right. Deep Thought?

DEEP THOUGHT Speak and I will hear.

TWO Are you not as we designed you to be, the greatest, most powerful computer in all creation?

DEEP THOUGHT	I described myself as the second greatest, and such I am.
TWO	But this is preposterous! Are you not a greater computer than the Milliard Gargantuabrain at Maximegalon which can count all the atoms in a star in a millisecond?
DEEP THOUGHT	The Milliard Gargantuabrain? A mere abacus, mention it not.
ONE	*And are you not a greater analyst than the Googleplex Starthinker in the Seventh Galaxy of Light and Ingenuity which can calculate the trajectory of every single dust particle throughout a five week Aldebaran sand blizzard?*
DEEP THOUGHT	*A five week sand blizzard? You ask this of me who has contemplated the very vectors of the atoms in the Big Bang itself?* Molest me not with this pocket calculator stuff.
ONE	And are you not a more fiendish disputant than the Great Hyperlobic (sic) Omnicognate Neutron Wrangler, which can . . .
DEEP THOUGHT	The Great Hyperlobic Omnicognate Neutron Wrangler can talk four legs off an Arcturan Megadonkey but only I can persuade it to go for a walk afterwards.
TWO	Then what's the problem?
DEEP THOUGHT	I speak of none but the computer that is to come after me.
ONE	Oh, come on. I think this is getting needlessly messianic.
DEEP THOUGHT	You know nothing of future time, and yet in my teeming circuitry I can navigate the infinite delta streams of future probability and see that there must one day come a computer whose merest operational parameters I am not worthy to calculate, but which it will be my destiny eventually to design.
THREE	Can we get on and ask the question?
DEEP THOUGHT	Speak.
ONE	O Deep Thought Computer, the task we have designed you to perform is this. We want you to tell us . . . the answer.
DEEP THOUGHT	The Answer? The answer to what?
TWO	Life.
ONE	The Universe.
TWO	Everything.
DEEP THOUGHT	Tricky.
TWO	But can you do it?
	(Pause)
DEEP THOUGHT	Yes. I can do it.
ONE	There is an answer? A simple answer?

DEEP THOUGHT	Yes. Life, the Universe and Everything. There is an answer. But I'll have to think about it.
F/X	NOISE OF SCUFFLE AT DOORWAY
ONE	What's happening?
VROOMFONDEL	We demand admission!
MAJIKTHISE	Come on, you can't keep us out!
VROOMFONDEL	We demand that you can't keep us out!
ONE	Who are you? What do you want? We're busy.
MAJIKTHISE	I am Majikthise.
VROOMFONDEL	And I demand that I am Vroomfondel.
MAJIKTHISE	It's all right, you don't need to demand that.
VROOMFONDEL	All right, I am Vroomfondel, and that is *not* a demand, that is a solid *fact*! What we demand is solid *facts*!
MAJIKTHISE	(**aside**) No we don't. That is precisely what we don't demand.
VROOMFONDEL	We don't demand solid facts! What we demand is a total *absence* of solid facts! I demand that I may or may not be Vroomfondel.
TWO	Who are you, anyway?
MAJIKTHISE	We are philosophers.
VROOMFONDEL	Though we may not be.
MAJIKTHISE	Yes we are.
VROOMFONDEL	Oh, sorry. We are quite definitely here as representatives of the Amalgamated Union of Philosophers, Sages, Luminaries and Other Professional Thinking Persons, and we want this machine off, and we want it off now!
TWO	What is all this?
VROOMFONDEL	We demand that you get rid of it!
ONE	What's the problem.
MAJIKTHISE	I'll tell you what the problem is, mate. Demarcation, that's the problem.
VROOMFONDEL	We demand that demarcation may or may not be the problem.
MAJIKTHISE	You just let the machines get on with the adding up and we'll take care of the eternal verities thank you very much. By law the Quest for Ultimate Truth is quite clearly the inalienable prerogative of your working thinkers. Any bloody machine goes and actually finds it and we're straight out of a job aren't we? I mean what's the use of our sitting up all night saying there may . . .
VROOMFONDEL	Or may not be . . .

MAJIKTHISE	. . . or may not be, a God if this machine comes along next morning and gives you his telephone number?
VROOMFONDEL	We demand guaranteed rigidly defined areas of doubt and uncertainty.
DEEP THOUGHT	Might I make an observation at this point?
MAJIKTHISE	You keep out of this, metalnose.
VROOMFONDEL	We demand that that machine not be allowed to think about this problem!
DEEP THOUGHT	If I might make an observation . . .
VROOMFONDEL	We'll go on strike!
MAJIKTHISE	That's right, you'll have a national Philosophers' Strike on your hands.
DEEP THOUGHT	Who will that inconvenience?
VROOMFONDEL	Never mind who it will inconvenience you box of blacklegging binary bits. It'll hurt, buster, it'll hurt!
DEEP THOUGHT	(**Considerably more loudly**) If I might make an observation! All I wanted to say is that my circuits are now irrevocably committed to computing the answer to Life, the Universe and Everything (**Loud objections from Vroomfondel and Majikthise**), but the programme will take me seven and a half million years to run . . .
TWO	Seven and a half million years?
DEEP THOUGHT	Yes, I said I'd have to think about it didn't I? And it occurs to me that running a programme like this is bound to cause sensational public interest and so any philosophers who are quick off the mark are going to clean up in the prediction business.
MAJIKTHISE	Prediction business?
DEEP THOUGHT	Obviously you just get on the pundit circuit. You all go on the chat shows and the colour supplements and violently disagree with each other about what answer I'm eventually going to produce, and if you get yourselves clever agents you'll be on the gravy train for life.
MAJIKTHISE	Bloody hell. Now that is what I call thinking. Here, Vroomfondel, why do we never think of things like that?
VROOMFONDEL	Dunno. Think our minds must be too highly trained, Majikthise.
F/X	TAPE RECORDER SWITCHED OFF
ARTHUR:	But I don't understand what all this has got to do with the Earth and mice and things.
SLARTIBARTFAST	All will become clear to you, Earthman. Are you not anxious to hear what the computer had to say seven and a half million years later?
ARTHUR	Oh well, yes of course. Quite.
SLARTIBARTFAST	Here is the recording of the events of that fateful day.
ARCHIVE VOICE	Archive material of Magrathea.

F/X	TAPE SWITCHING AS BEFORE. CROWD CHEERING – EXTERNAL. BAND PLAYING
CHEERLEADER	Oh People who wait in the Shadow of Deep Thought! Honoured Descendants of Vroomfondel and Majikthise the Greatest and Most Truly Interesting Pundits the Universe has ever known . . . the Time of Waiting is over!
F/X	PEAK CHEERING
CHEERLEADER	Seven and a half million years our race has waited for this Great and Hopefully Englightening Day! The Day of the Answer!
F/X	CHEERING PEAKS
CHEERLEADER	Never again will we wake up in the morning and think 'Who am I?', 'What is the purpose in Life?', 'Does it really, Cosmically Speaking, *matter* if I don't get up and go to work?' For today we will finally learn, once and for all, the plain and simple answer to all these Nagging Little Problems of Life, the Universe and Everything! From today we can enjoy our games of Brockian Ultra-Cricket in the firm and comfortable knowledge that the meaning of Life is now well and Truly Sorted Out!
F/X	WILD CHEERING. THE CHEERING SUDDENLY DROPS INTO THE BACKGROUND AS WE SWITCH TO AN INTERNAL SCENE
ONE	Seventy five thousand generations ago our ancestors set this programme in motion.
THREE	An awesome project.
F/X	DEEP THOUGHT CLEARS HIS THROAT
TWO	Deep Thought prepares to speak.
DEEP THOUGHT	Good Evening.
ONE	Good Evening . . . Oh Deep Thought . . . do you have . . .
DEEP THOUGHT	An answer for you? Yes, I have.
THREE	There really is one?
DEEP THOUGHT	There really is one.
ONE	To Everything? To the great question of Life, the Universe and Everything?
DEEP THOUGHT	Yes.
TWO	And are you ready to give it to us?
DEEP THOUGHT	I am.
ONE	Now?
DEEP THOUGHT	Now.
ONE	Wow.

(Pause)

DEEP THOUGHT	Though I don't think you're going to like it.
TWO	Doesn't matter! We must know it!
DEEP THOUGHT	Now?
TWO	Yes! Now!
DEEP THOUGHT	All right

(Pause)

ONE	Well?
DEEP THOUGHT	You're really not going to like it.
TWO	Tell us!!!!
DEEP THOUGHT	All right. The Answer to Everything . . .
TWO	Yes . . . !
DEEP THOUGHT	Life, The Universe and Everything . . .
ONE	Yes . . . !
DEEP THOUGHT	Is . . .
THREE	Yes . . . !
DEEP THOUGHT	IS . . .
ONE/TWO	Yes . . . !!!
DEEP THOUGHT	Forty two.

(Pause. Actually quite a long one)

TWO	We're going to get lynched, you know that.
DEEP THOUGHT	It was a tough assignment.
ONE/TWO	Forty two!!
DEEP THOUGHT	I think the problem such as it was was too broadly based. You never actually stated what the question was.
TWO	But it was the Ultimate Question, the Question of Life, The Universe, and Everything!
DEEP THOUGHT	Exactly. Now you know that the answer to the Ultimate Question of Life, the Universe and Everything is forty two, all you need to do now is find out what the Ultimate Question is.
TWO	All right, all right, all right. Can you *please . . . tell* us . . . the *Question*?
DEEP THOUGHT	The Ultimate Question?
TWO	Yes.
DEEP THOUGHT	Of Life, the Universe?

ONE	And everything?
DEEP THOUGHT	And Everything.
TWO	Yes.
DEEP THOUGHT	Tricky.
TWO	But can you do it?
DEEP THOUGHT	. . . No.
ONE/TWO	(**Slumping**) Oh God . . .
DEEP THOUGHT	But I'll tell you who can.
TWO	Who? Tell us, tell us.
DEEP THOUGHT	I speak of none but the computer that is to come after me. A computer whose merest operational parameters I am not worthy to calculate – and yet I will design it for you. A computer which can calculate the question to the Ultimate answer, a computer of such infinite and subtle complexity that organic life itself will form part of its operational matrix. *And you yourselves shall take on new forms and go down into the computer to navigate its ten million year programme. Yes, I shall design this computer for you, and I shall name it for you.* And it shall be called the Earth.
TWO	Oh. What a dull name.
F/X	TAPE TURNS OFF
SLARTIBARTFAST	So there you have it. Deep Thought designed it, we built it and you lived on it.
ARTHUR	And the Vogons came and destroyed it five minutes before the programme was completed.
SLARTIBARTFAST	Yes. Ten million years of planning and work gone just like that. Well, that's bureaucracy for you.
ARTHUR	You know, all this explains a lot of things. All through my life I've had this strange unaccountable feeling that something was going on in the world, something big, even sinister, and no one would tell me what it was.
SLARTIBARTFAST	No, that's just perfectly normal paranoia. Everyone in the Universe has that.
ARTHUR	Well . . . perhaps that means that somewhere . . . outside the Universe . . .
SLARTIBARTFAST	Maybe. Who cares? Perhaps I'm old and tired, but I always think that the chances of finding out what really is going on are so absurdly remote that the only thing to do is say hang the sense of it and just keep yourself occupied. Look at me – I design coastlines. I got an award for Norway. Where's the sense in that? None that I've been able to make out. I've been doing fjords all my life . . . for a fleeting moment they become fashionable and I get a major award. In this replacement Earth we're building they've given me Africa to do and of course I'm doing it with all fjords again because I happen to like them and I'm old fashioned enough to think that

they give a lovely baroque feel to a continent. And they tell me it's not equatorial enough. What does it matter? Science has achieved some wonderful things of course, but I'd far rather be happy than right any day.

ARTHUR   And are you?

SLARTIBARTFAST   No. That's where it all falls down of course.

ARTHUR   Pity, it sounded like quite a good lifestyle otherwise.

P.A. VOICE   (**Paging**) Attention please Slartibartfast. Would Slartibartfast and the visiting Earth creature please report immediately, repeat immediately, to the works reception area. The mice aren't wanting to hang about in this dimension all day.

SLARTIBARTFAST   Come on, I suppose we'd better go and see what they want.

ARTHUR   I seem to be having this tremendous difficulty with my lifestyle. As soon as I reach some kind of definite policy about what is my kind of music and my kind of restaurant and my kind of overdraft, people start blowing up my kind of planet and throwing me out of their kind of spaceships. It's so hard to build up anything coherent. I'm sorry all this must sound rather fatuous to you.

SLARTIBARTFAST   Yes, I thought so.

ARTHUR   Just forget I ever said it.

GRAMS   NARRATOR BACKGROUND

NARRATOR   It is of course well known that careless talk costs lives, but the full scale of the problem is not always appreciated. For instance, at the very moment that Arthur Dent said 'I seem to be having this tremendous difficulty with my lifestyle' a freak wormhole opened up in the fabric of the space time continuum and carried his words far far back in time across almost infinite reaches of space to a distant galaxy where strange and warlike beings were poised on the brink of frightful interstellar battle. The two opposing leaders were meeting for the last time . . . and a dreadful silence fell across the conference table as the commander of the Vl'hurgs, resplendent in his black jewelled battle shorts, gazed levelly at the G'Gugvant leader squatting opposite him in a cloud of green, sweet-smelling steam, and with a million sleek and horribly beweaponed star cruisers poised to unleash electric death at his single word of command, challenged the vile creature to take back what it had said about his mother.

The creature stirred in his sickly broiling vapour and at that very moment, the words 'I seem to be having this tremendous difficulty with my lifestyle' drifted across the conference table. Unfortunately in the Vl'hurg tongue this was the most dreadful insult imaginable and there was nothing for it but to wage terrible war. Eventually of course, after their galaxy had been decimated over a few thousand years, it was realized that the whole thing had been a ghastly mistake, and so the two opposing battle fleets settled their few remaining differences in order to launch a joint attack on our Galaxy, now positively identified as the source of the offending remark. For thousands more years the mighty ships tore across the empty wastes of space and finally dived screaming on to the planet Earth , where, due to a terrible miscalculation of scale, the entire battle fleet was accidentally swallowed by a small dog. Those who study the complex interplay of cause and effect in the history of the Universe say that this sort of thing is going on all the time, but are powerless to prevent it. 'It's just life,' they say. Meanwhile, Arthur Dent is about to discover the answer to the disturbing question posed in last week's instalment. Are his companions Ford, Zaphod and Trillian lying bleeding to death in a subterranean corridor, or have they merely slipped out for a quick meal somewhere?

F/X	HUM OF DOOR OPENING. SUBDUED BUZZING OF DINING ROOM
TRILLIAN	(**At a slight distance**) Arthur! You're safe!
ARTHUR	(**Slightly startled**) Am I? Oh good.
FORD	Hi Arthur, come and join us.
ARTHUR	Ford! Trillian! Zaphod! What happened to you?
ZAPHOD	Well our hosts here attacked us with a fantastic Dismodulating Anti Phase stun ray and then invited us to this amazingly keen meal by way of making it up to us.
ARTHUR	Hosts? What hosts? I can't see any hosts?
BENJY MOUSE	(**Not quite certain about the voice treatment here yet. Obviously it has to suggest mouse-likeness, but it shouldn't sound silly, as they are actually quite relaxed and sophisticated mice**) Welcome to lunch, Earth Creature.
ARTHUR	What? Who said that? Ugh! There's a mouse on the table.
FORD	Oh, haven't you found out yet, Arthur?
ARTHUR	What? Oh I see, yes . . . yes, I just wasn't quite prepared for the full reality of it.
TRILLIAN	Arthur, let me introduce you. This is Benjy Mouse.
BENJY	Hi.
TRILLIAN	And this is Frankie mouse.
FRANKIE	Nice to meet you.
TRILLIAN	It seems they control quite a large sector of the Universe in our dimension.
ARTHUR	But aren't they . . .
TRILLIAN	Yes, they are the mice I took with me from the Earth. It seems our whole journey has been stage managed from the beginning.
SLARTIBARTFAST	Er, excuse me . . .
BENJY	Yes, thank you, Slartibartfast, you may go.
SLARTIBARTFAST	(**Slightly surprised and crestfallen**) What? Oh . . . oh very well. Thank you sir, I'll . . . I'll just go and get on with some of my fjords then.

FRANKIE	Er, in fact that won't be necessary. We won't be requiring the new Earth after all. We've had this rather interesting proposition put to us.
SLARTIBARTFAST	What? You can't mean that. I've got a thousand glaciers poised and ready to roll over Africa.
FRANKIE	Well, perhaps you can take a quick skiing holiday before you dismantle them.
SLARTIBARTFAST	Skiing holiday! Those glaciers are works of art! Elegantly sculptured contours, soaring pinnacles of ice, deep majestic ravines, it would be sacrilege to go skiing on High Art.
FRANKIE	(**Firmly**) Thank you Slartibartfast, that will be all.
SLARTIBARTFAST	Yes sir, thank you very much sir. Well, goodbye Earthman. Hope the lifestyle comes together.
F/X	DOOR HUMS OPEN WITH GRINDING SOUND
ARTHUR	Goodbye then. Sorry about the fjords.
BENJY	*Now to business.*
FORD and ZAPHOD	To business.
F/X	*GLASSES CLINK*
BENJY	*I beg your pardon?*
FORD	*I'm sorry, I thought you were proposing a toast.*
BENJY	Now, Earth Creature, we have, as you know, been more or less running your planet for the last ten million years in order to find this wretched thing called the Ultimate Question.
ARTHUR	Why?
FRANKIE	No, we already thought of that one, but it doesn't fit the answer. 'Why?', 'Forty two'. You see, it doesn't work.
ARTHUR	No, I mean why have you been doing it?
FRANKIE	Well, eventually just habit I think, to be brutally honest. And this is more or less the point. We're sick to the teeth of the whole thing and the prospect of doing it all over again on account of those whinnet-ridden Vogons quite frankly gives me the screaming heeby-jeebies, you know what I mean?
BENJY	We've been offered a quite enormously fat contract to do the 5D TV chat show and lecture circuit, and I'm very much inclined to take it.
ZAPHOD	(**Promptingly, because there's something in it for them**) I would, wouldn't you, Ford?
FORD	Oh yes, jump at it like a shot.
FRANKIE	*I mean, yes idealism, yes the dignity of pure research, yes the pursuit of truth in all its forms, but there comes a point I'm afraid where you begin to suspect that if there's any real truth it's that the entire multi-dimensional infinity of the Universe*

is almost certainly being run by a bunch of maniacs; and if it comes to a choice between spending another *ten million years finding that out and on the other hand just taking the money and running, then I for one could do with the exercise.*

ARTHUR   But that's exactly the attitude those philosophers took. Does no one in this galaxy do anything other than appear on chat shows?

FRANKIE   The point is this . . . we are in a position to give you a very important commission. We still want to find the Ultimate Question because it gives us a lot of bargaining muscle with the 5D TV companies, so it's worth a lot of money. (**They giggle avariciously**) I mean quite clearly if we're sitting there looking very relaxed in the studio mentioning that we happen to know the Answer to Life, the Universe and Everything and then eventually have to admit that it's forty two, then I think the show's probably quite short.

ARTHUR   Yes, but doesn't that mean you've got to go through your whole ten million year programme again?

FRANKIE   We think there might be a short cut. Your agent . . .

ZAPHOD   That's me.

ARTHUR   (**Startled**) Is it?

FRANKIE   Your agent has suggested that both you and Earth girl, as last generation products of the computer matrix are probably in an ideal position to find the question for us and find it quickly. Go out and find it for us and we'll make you a reasonably rich man.

ZAPHOD   We're holding out for extremely rich.

FRANKIE   All right, extremely rich. You drive a hard bargain, Beeblebrox.

F/X   SIRENS GO OFF

P.A. VOICE   Emergency, emergency . . . hostile ship has landed on planet. Intruders now within works reception area. Defence stations, defence stations.

BENJY   Hell's bells, what is it now?

TRILLIAN   Zaphod! Are you thinking what I'm thinking?

ZAPHOD   Police. Hell and bat's do's. We've got to get out.

BENJY   Police?

ZAPHOD   Yeah, it's this wretched space craft we've stolen. I left them a note explaining how they could make a profit on the insurance claim but it doesn't seem to have worked.

FORD   Come *on* then! Let's move.

F/X   CHAIRS AND TABLES KNOCKED BACK AS THEY JUMP TO THEIR FEET

FRANKIE   Earthman, find us the question!

ARTHUR   How?

FRANKIE	Er . . . no that doesn't work either.
ZAPHOD	We'll find it. Come on, get *out* of here!
FORD	Thanks for the meal guys. Sorry we've got to rush.
F/X	THEY ALL RUN OUT OF THE ROOM
	(Fade out. Fade in)
F/X	RUNNING FEET
FORD	Which way you reckon, Zaphod?
ZAPHOD	At a wild guess I'd say down here.
SHOOTY	**(Young American cop type, shouts from distance)** OK Beeblebrox, hold it right there. We've got you covered.
ZAPHOD	You want to try a guess at all, Ford?
FORD	OK this way.
BANG BANG	**(Cop, similar)** We don't want to shoot you, Beeblebrox.
ZAPHOD	Suits me fine.
TRILLIAN	We're cornered.
ZAPHOD	Hell, I've dropped my adrenalin pills. All right, behind this computer bank, get down.
F/X	EXTREMELY VICIOUS SOUNDING ZAP GUN, DISCHARGES ACROSS THE STEREO IMAGE (ALL RIGHT, IT FIRES)
ARTHUR	Hey, they're shooting at us.
ZAPHOD	Yeah.
ARTHUR	I thought they said they didn't want to do that.
TRILLIAN	Yeah, *I* thought they said that.
ZAPHOD	**(Shouting)** Hey, I thought you said you didn't want to shoot us!
SHOOTY	**(Shouting)** It isn't easy being a cop!
FORD	*What* did he say?
ZAPHOD	He said it isn't easy being a cop.
FORD	Well surely that's his problem, isn't it?
ZAPHOD	*I'd* have thought so.
FORD	**(Shouting)** Hey listen, I think we've got enough problems of our own with you shooting at us, so if you could avoid laying your problems on us as well I think we'd probably find it easier to cope!
BANG BANG	**(Shouting)** Now see here, buddy, you're not dealing with any dumb two bit trigger pumping morons with low hair lines, little piggy eyes and no conversation, we're a couple of intelligent caring guys who you'd probably quite like if you met us socially.

SHOOTY	That's right, I'm really sensitive.
BANG BANG	I don't go around gratuitously shooting people and then bragging about it in seedy space rangers' bars. I go around gratuitously shooting people and then agonise about it afterwards to my girlfriend.
SHOOTY	And I write novels!
BANG BANG	Yeah, he writes them in crayon.
SHOOTY	Though I haven't had any of them published yet, so I'd better warn you I'm in a meeeeen mood.
FORD	Who *are* these guys?
ZAPHOD	I think I preferred it when they were shooting.
BANG BANG	(**Shouting**) So are you going to come quietly or are you going to let us blast you out?
FORD	(**Shouting**) Which would you rather?
F/X	FUSILLADE OF VICIOUS ELECTRIC GUNFIRE WHICH CARRIES ON FOR A WHILE
	(**Pause as the echoes die away**)
BANG BANG	(**Shouting**) You still there?
ZAPHOD/FORD/ ARTHUR/TRILLIAN	Yes.
SHOOTY	(**Shouting**) We didn't enjoy doing that at all!
FORD	(**Shouting**) We could tell! (**Aside**) Zaphod, have you any ideas on how we're going to deal with these loonies?
BANG BANG	(**Shouting**) Now listen to this, Beeblebrox, and you'd better listen good.
ZAPHOD	Why?
BANG BANG	Because it's going to be very intelligent, and quite interesting and humane.
ZAPHOD	O.K. Fire away . . . No, I mean . . .
F/X	ANOTHER FUSILLADE OF SHOTS
SHOOTY	Sorry, misunderstanding there.
FORD	Nice one, Zaphod.
BANG BANG	Beeblebrox, either you all give yourselves up now and let us beat you up a bit, though not very much of course because we are firmly opposed to needless violence, or we blow up this entire planet and possibly one or two others we noticed on our way here.
TRILLIAN	(**Suddenly getting seriously upset about it**) But that's crazy. You wouldn't blow up this entire planet just to get a bloody spaceship back!
BANG BANG	Yes we would. I think we would, wouldn't we?

SHOOTY   Oh yes, we'd have to, no question.

TRILLIAN   But why?

SHOOTY   Tell her!

BANG BANG   (**Shouting**) Because there are some things you've got to do even if you are an enlightened liberal cop who knows all about sensitivity and everything.

ZAPHOD   I just don't believe these guys.

SHOOTY   Shall we shoot them again for a bit?

BANG BANG   Yeah, why not?

F/X   ANOTHER FUSILLADE OF VICIOUS ELECTRIC ZAPPING. AS IT CONTINUES:

TRILLIAN   We're not going to be safe behind this computer bank for much longer, fellas. It's been really nice knowing you, I just want to say that.

FORD   Yeah, it's really been great. And it was really nice bumping into you again, Zaphod.

ZAPHOD   I wish I hadn't dropped my adrenalin pills.

FORD   The computer bank is absorbing a hell of a lot of energy. I think it's about to blow.

F/X   HEAVY OSCILLATING HUM BUILDS UP WITH THE ENERGY BEING PUMPED INTO IT BY THE CONTINUING GUNFIRE

ARTHUR   It's a shame we never managed to get the work done revising the book, I thought it looked rather promising.

ZAPHOD   Yeah. What book?

ARTHUR   *The Hitch-Hiker's Guide to the Galaxy.*

ZAPHOD   Oh, that thing.

FORD   Look, I hate to say this but this thing really is going to blow up.

ZAPHOD   OK, OK.

F/X   YET ANOTHER DEVASTATING EXPLOSION, BUT AN EXTREMELY WEIRD SOUNDING ONE

GRAMS   NARRATOR BACKGROUND

NARRATOR   (**Signature tune**) Assuming our heroes survive this latest reversal in their fortunes, will they find somewhere reasonably interesting to go now? Will Arthur Dent or Trillian manage to find the Question to the Ultimate Answer? Who will they meet at the Restaurant at the End of the Universe? Find out in next week's exciting instalment of the *Hitch-Hiker's Guide to the Galaxy.*

ANNOUNCER   The Ultimate Answer to Life, the Universe and Everything was revealed by kind permission of the Amalgamated Union of Philosophers, Sages, Luminaries and Other Professional Thinking Persons.

FOOTNOTE

This show was recorded on 20 December 1977. Jonathan Adams played the Cheerleader and Majikthise (one listener wrote to say that she had seen the graffiti 'Majikthise rules OK' in the ladies loo of the MCC). Peter Hawkins played Frankie Mouse and the ubiquitous David Tate played Benjy Mouse; while Geoff McGivern showed his versatility by playing Deep Thought. Jeremy Browne played the Second Computer Programmer, American stand up comic Ray Hassett played the First Computer Programmer and Bang Bang while Jim Broadbent played Vroomfondel and Shooty. Douglas adds this on the origins of Shooty and Bang Bang.

Shooty and Bang Bang

Another section inspired by American TV – this time *Starsky and Hutch*. In this show the heroes claimed that they did care about people being shot, so they crashed their cars into them instead. (DNA)

Slartibartfast says he knows 'little' of these early sixties sitcoms, just suggesting that he does, in fact, know something.

Many people have asked whether the choice of forty two as the Ultimate Answer came from Lewis Carroll or perhaps from an ancient Tibetan mystical cult where it is the symbol of truth. 'In fact it was simply chosen because it was a completely ordinary number, a number not just divisible by two but also by six and seven. In fact it's the sort of number that you could, without any fear, introduce to your parents.' (DA) But a learned letter in the *New Scientist* suggested that Deep Thought may well have been right since forty two is the atomic number of Molybdenum – a chemical that could have been vital in creating organic life. Even more importantly the Answer gave its number to a rock group (Level 42, not UB40).

Several people noticed that the voice treatment on the mice was changed after the first broadcast. This was because we originally attempted to create the effect by having the actors speaking normally and then using the harmoniser to turn them into squeaky rodents, but the result was both too mechanical and also difficult to understand. Given the pressure of time we were unable to solve the problem for the first transmission but we subsequently re-did the mice (but left the rest of the actors as originally recorded). For the re-make we got the actors to record the lines very slowly, doubled the speed and then harmonised them slightly down. This was done superbly by the actors who, while doing the lines at half speed, had to pace them evenly with all the right inflections. The result was, we felt, better in every way, but it showed the fanaticism of many of the people who caught the show right from the start as several of them who spotted the change wrote in to say that they preferred the voices as they were originally.

Music Details

A Rainbow in Curved Air by Terry Riley
(Used in the opening story-so-far speech)
Miracles of the Gods from *In Search of Ancient Gods* by Absolute Everywhere
(Used in speech about the building of the super-computer)
Mikrophoniet by Stockhausen
(Used for the Vl'hurg/G'Guvunt speech, except at the end where it goes back into *Rainbow in Curved Air*)

FIT THE FIFTH

Sent to find the Ultimate Question to Life, the Universe and Everything, Arthur Dent and his companions have been cornered by two humane cops who, nevertheless, have left them in a certain death situation.

GRAMS   NARRATOR BACKGROUND

NARRATOR   The story so far.

In the beginning the Universe was created. This has made a lot of people very angry and been widely regarded as a bad move. Many races believe that it was created by some sort of God, though the Jatravartid people of Viltvodle Six firmly believe that the entire Universe was in fact sneezed out of the nose of a being called the Great Green Arkleseizure. The Jatravartids, who live in perpetual fear of the time they called The Coming of the Great White Handkerchief, are small blue creatures with more than fifty arms each, who are therefore unique in being the only race in history to have invented the aerosol deodorant before the wheel.

However, the Great Green Arkleseizure theory was not widely accepted outside Viltvodle Six, and so one day a race of hyper-intelligent pan-dimensional beings built themselves a gigantic supercomputer called Deep Thought to calculate once and for all the answer to the Ultimate Question of Life, The Universe, and Everything. For seven and a half million years Deep Thought computed and calculated and eventually announced that the answer was in fact forty two, and so another even bigger computer had to be built to find out what the actual question was. And this computer, which was called The Earth, was so large that it was frequently mistaken for a planet – particularly by the strange ape like beings who roamed its surface totally unaware that they were simply part of a gigantic computer programme. And this is very odd because without that fairly simple and obvious piece of knowledge nothing that ever happened on Earth could possibly make the slightest bit of sense.

However, at the critical moment of readout the Earth was unexpectedly demolished to make way for a new hyperspace bypass, and the only hope of finding the Ultimate Question now lies buried deep in the minds of Arthur Dent and Trillian, the only native Earth People to have survived the demolition.

Unfortunately, they and their strange companions from Betelgeuse are at the moment being shot at behind a computer bank on the lost planet of Magrathea. This is what the computer bank is about to do:

F/X   DEVASTATING EXPLOSION, BUT AN EXTREMELY WEIRD SOUNDING ONE

NARRATOR   And the time at which it is going to do it is twenty seconds from now.

FORD   The computer bank is absorbing a hell of a lot of energy – I think it's about to blow up!

F/X   HEAVY OSCILATING HUM BUILDS UP WITH THE ENERGY BEING PUMPED INTO IT BY CONTINUING GUNFIRE

ARTHUR   It's a shame we never managed to get the work done on revising the book, I thought it looked rather promising.

ZAPHOD   Yes. What book?

ARTHUR	*The Hitch-Hiker's Guide to the Galaxy.*
ZAPHOD	Oh, that thing.
FORD	Guys, I hate to say this, but this thing really is going to blow up.
ZAPHOD	OK, OK.
F/X	REPEAT THE EXPLOSION FROM THE END OF THE NARRATOR'S SPEECH. RUSHING SOUND OF LOTS OF LITTLE UNIDENTIFIED NOISES WHIZZING FROM THE OUTSIDE EDGES OF THE SOUND PICTURE RECEDING INTO THE CENTRE. IT SUDDENLY STOPS WITH A CRASH.
	ALMOST INSTANTLY WE HEAR THE QUIET BACKGROUND OF A LARGE RESTAURANT WITH CABARET MUSIC PLAYING IN THE BACKGROUND.
	GARKBIT THE WAITER SPEAKS ALMOST IMMEDIATELY.
ALL	**(General gasps)**
GARKBIT	Good evening gentlemen, madam. Do you have a reservation?
FORD	Reservation?
GARKBIT	Yes, sir.
FORD	So you need a reservation for the afterlife?
GARKBIT	The afterlife, sir?
ARTHUR	This is the afterlife?
FORD	Well I assume so, I mean there's no way we could have survived that blast is there?
ARTHUR	No.
TRILLIAN	None at all.
ARTHUR	I was dead.
ZAPHOD	I certainly didn't survive, I was a total goner. Wham, bang and that was it.
FORD	We didn't stand a chance, we must have been blown to bits. Arms, legs, everywhere.
ZAPHOD	Yeah.
	(Pause)
GARKBIT	**(Coughing politely)** If you would care to order drinks . . .?
ZAPHOD	**(Ignoring and interrupting him)** Kerpow, splat, *instantaneously zonked into our component molecules. Hey, did you get that amazing thing of your whole life flashing before you?*
FORD	*Yeah, you got that too did you? Your whole life?*
ZAPHOD	*Yeah. At least I assume it was mine. I spend a lot of time out of my skulls you know.*

FORD	*So what?*
ZAPHOD	Here we are, lying dead . . .
TRILLIAN	Standing . . .
ZAPHOD	Standing dead in this er . . . desolate . . .
ARTHUR	Restaurant . . .
ZAPHOD	Standing dead in this desolate . . .
ARTHUR	Five star . . .
ZAPHOD	Five star restaurant.
FORD	Odd, isn't it?
ZAPHOD	Er, yeah.
TRILLIAN	Nice chandeliers, though.
ARTHUR	It's not so much an afterlife, more a sort of *après vie*.
ZAPHOD	Hey, hang about . . . I think we're missing something important here, something really important that somebody just said . . . What was it? Hey, you.
GARKBIT	Sir?
ZAPHOD	Did you say something about drinks?
GARKBIT	Certainly, sir. If the lady and gentlemen would care to take drinks before dinner . . .
ZAPHOD	Yeah, great.
GARKBIT	And the Universe will explode later for your pleasure.
ZAPHOD	Hey, what?
FORD	Wow, what sort of drinks do you serve here?
GARKBIT	(**Laughing**) Ah, I think sir has perhaps misunderstood me.
FORD	I hope not.
GARKBIT	It is not unusual for our customers to be a little disorientated by the time journey, so if I might suggest . . .
TRILLIAN	*Time* journey?
FORD	(**Virtually together**) What time journey?
ARTHUR	You mean this isn't the afterlife?
GARKBIT	Afterlife sir? No, sir.
ARTHUR	And we're not dead?
GARKBIT	Aha, ha, no sir. Sir is most evidently alive, otherwise I would not attempt to serve sir.

FORD	Then where the photon are we?
ZAPHOD	(**Suddenly**) Hey, I've sussed it. This must be Milliways!
FORD	Milliways!
GARKBIT	Yes, this is Milliways, the Restaurant at the end of the Universe.
ARTHUR	End of what?
GARKBIT	The Universe.
ARTHUR	When did that end?
GARKBIT	In just a few minutes, sir. Now, if you would care to order drinks I'll show you to your table.

GRAMS NARRATOR BACKGROUND

NARRATOR The Restaurant at the end of the Universe is one of the most extraordinary ventures in the entire history of catering. A vast time bubble has been projected into the future to the precise moment of the End of the Universe. This is, of course, impossible.

In it, guests take their places at table and eat sumptuous meals whilst watching the whole of creation explode about them. This is, of course, impossible. You can arrive for any sitting you like without prior reservation because you can book retrospectively as it were when you return to your own time. This is, of course, impossible.

At the Restaurant you can meet and dine with a fascinating cross-section of the entire population of space and time. This is of course impossible. You can visit it as many times as you like and be sure of never meeting yourself – because of the embarrassment that usually causes. This is of course impossible.

All you have to do is deposit one penny in a savings account in your own era, and when you arrive at the end of time the operation of compound interest means that the fabulous cost of your meal has been paid for. This is of course impossible.

Which is why the advertising executives of the Star System of Bastablon came up with this slogan –
'If you've done six impossible things this morning why not round it off with breakfast at Milliways, the Restaurant at the End of the Universe?'

GRAMS MUSIC AND GENERAL RESTAURANT BACKGROUND

COMPERE (**Speaking on a PA mike over the music and general restaurant atmosphere. It's clearly a PA mike because there is the occasional pop or bit of feedback or sound of the mike being knocked**)

Ladies and gentlemen, welcome to the Restaurant at the End of the Universe. I am your host for tonight, Max Quordlepleen, and I've just come straight from the other end of time where I've been hosting the show at the Big Bang Burger Chef, where we had a real way hay hay of an evening ladies and gentlemen, and I will be with you right through this tremendous historic occasion, the end of history itself.

F/X   AUDIENCE APPLAUSE

COMPERE   Thank you ladies and gentlemen, take your places at table, the candles are lit, the band is playing, and as the force shielded dome above us fades into transparency revealing a dark and sullen sky hung heavy with the ancient light of livid swollen stars I can see we're in for a fabulous evening's apocalypse.

Thank you very much.

ARTHUR   *Do you do Take-Ways?*

GARKBIT   *Ah ha, no sir, here at Milliways we only serve the very finest in Ultracuisine.*

ZAPHOD   (**With disgust**) *Ultracuisine? Don't give me head pains. Look at this . . . Algolian Zylbatburger smothered in a hint of Vulcan Dodo spit.*

GARKBIT   *Saliva, sir, saliva. The salivary gland of the Vulcan UltraDodo is a delicacy much sought after.*

ZAPHOD   *Not by me.*

ARTHUR   *What is an Algolian Zylbatburger anyway?*

FORD   *They're a kind of meatburger made from the most unpleasant parts of a creature well known for its total lack of any pleasant parts.*

ARTHUR   *So you mean that the Universe does actually end not with a bang but with a Wimpy?*

GARKBIT   *Believe me, sir, the Universe ends with a very big bang indeed, and the food here is the ultimate gastronomic experience.*

FORD   *Yes, but is it good?*

ARTHUR   But look, surely, if the Universe is about to end here and now, don't we go with it?

FORD   No look, as soon as you come into this dive I think you get held in this sort of amazing force shielded temporal warp thing. Look I'll show you. Now imagine this napkin as the temporal universe, right, and this spoon as a transductional mode in the matter curve.

ARTHUR   That's the spoon I was eating with.

FORD   All right, imagine *this* spoon is the transductional mode in the matter curve, no better still this fork . . .

ZAPHOD   Hey could you let go of my fork please?

FORD   Look, why don't we say this wine glass is the temporal universe . . . so if I . . .

F/X   GLASS SMASHES ON FLOOR

FORD   Forget that, I mean, do you know how the Universe began for a kick off?

ARTHUR   Er, probably not.

FORD   All right, imagine this. You get a large round bath made of ebony . . .

ARTHUR   Where from? Harrods was destroyed by the Vogons.

FORD   Doesn't matter . . .

ARTHUR   So you keep saying.

FORD   No listen, just imagine that you've got this ebony bath, OK? And it's conical . . .

ARTHUR   Conical? What kind of . . .

FORD   Sshh . . . It's conical. So what you do, you fill it with fine white sand, right, or sugar, anything like that . . . and when it's full you pull the plug out and it all just twirls down out of the plug hole.

ARTHUR   Why?

FORD   But the thing is, the clever bit, is that you film it happening, you get a movie camera from somewhere and actually film it, but then you thread the film in the projector backwards . . .

ARTHUR   Backwards?

FORD   Yeah, neat you see, so what happens is you sit and watch it and then everything appears to spiral upwards out of the plug hole and fill the bath. See?

ARTHUR   And that's how the Universe began?

FORD   No, but it's a marvellous way to relax.

TRILLIAN   Funny man.

FORD   Broke the ice, didn't it?

GRAMS   MUSIC AND GENERAL RESTAURANT BACKGROUND

COMPERE   And as the photon storms gather in swirling clouds around us preparing to tear apart the last of the red hot suns, I hope you'll all settle back and enjoy with me what I am sure we will all find an immensely exciting and terminal experience. Believe me ladies and gentlemen, there is nothing penultimate about this one, you know what I mean. This, ladies and gentlemen, is the proverbial it.

F/X   POLITE APPLAUSE

             After this there is void, absolute nothing, except of course for the sweet trolley and our fine selection of Aldebaran liqueurs. And now at the risk of putting a damper on the wonderful sense of doom and futility here, I'd like to welcome a few parties.

             Do we have a party from the Zansellquasure Flamarion Bridge Club from beyond the Vortvoid of Qvarne? Are they here?

F/X   CHEERS FROM A PARTY OF PEOPLE, WHO SOUND SLIGHTLY LIKE SHEEP

             Good, jolly good. And a party of minor deities from the Halls of Asgaard?

F/X   CHEERS, WOLF WHISTLES, FOOTBALL RATTLES AND A FEW THUNDERBOLTS

A party of Young Conservatives from Sirius B?

F/X   WOOFING AND BARKING

Aha, yes. And lastly a party of devout believers (**Pause**) from the church of the second coming of the Great Prophet Zarquon. Well fellas, let's hope he's hurrying because he's only got eight minutes left.

F/X   A LITTLE RIPPLE OF COSY LAUGHTER

But seriously though, no offence meant, because I know we shouldn't make fun of deeply held beliefs, so I think a big hand please for the Great Prophet Zarquon, wherever he's got to.

F/X   APPLAUSE AND A FEW MORE LAUGHS

And you know, I just want to say how marvellous it is to see how many of you come here time and time again *to witness this final end of all being and then still manage to return home to your own eras and raise families, strive for new and better societies, fight terrible wars for what you believe to be right. Because you know it really makes one think about the absolutely marvellous future of all lifekind – except of course that we know it hasn't got one.*

(From this point his speech gradually recedes into the background as we pick up on the conversation of Ford, Arthur, Zaphod and Trillian)

GARKBIT   (**Approaches**) Er, excuse me sir.

ZAPHOD   Who me?

GARKBIT   Mr Zaphod Beeblebrox?

ZAPHOD   Er, yeah.

GARKBIT   There is a phone call for you.

ZAPHOD   Hey, what?

TRILLIAN   Here?

ZAPHOD   Hey but who knows where I am?

TRILLIAN   Zaphod, perhaps it's the police . . . could they have traced us here?

ZAPHOD   You mean they want to arrest me over the phone? Could be, I'm a pretty dangerous dude when I'm cornered.

FORD   Yeah, you go to pieces so fast that people get hit by the shrapnel.

ZAPHOD   *Hey, what is this, Judgement Day?*

ARTHUR   *Do we get to see that as well? Fantastic.*

ZAPHOD   *I'm in no hurry. So who's the cat on the phone?*

GARKBIT   I am not personally acquainted with the metal gentleman in question, sir . . .

TRILLIAN   Metal?

GARKBIT   . . . but I am informed that he has been awaiting your return for a considerable number of millenia. It seems you left here, sir, somewhat precipitately . . .

ZAPHOD   Hey, left here? We've only just arrived.

GARKBIT   Indeed, sir, but before you arrived here, sir, you left here.

ZAPHOD   You're saying that before we arrived here we left here?

GARKBIT   That is what I said, sir.

ZAPHOD   Put your analyst on danger money baby, now.

FORD   No wait a minute, where exactly is here?

GARKBIT   The planet Magrathea, sir.

FORD   But we just left there . . . this is the Restaurant at the End of the Universe, I thought.

GARKBIT   Precisely sir. The one was constructed on the ruins of the other.

ARTHUR   You mean we've travelled in time, but not in space?

ZAPHOD   Listen you semi-evolved simian, go climb a tree won't you?

ARTHUR   Oh go and bang your heads together four eyes.

GARKBIT   No, no. Your monkey has got it right, sir.

ARTHUR   Who are you calling a monkey?

GARKBIT   (Ignoring him) You jumped forwards in time many millions of years while retaining the same position in space. Your friend has been waiting for you in the meantime.

FORD   Well, what's he been doing all the time?

GARKBIT   Rusting a little, sir.

TRILLIAN   Marvin! It must be Marvin.

FORD   The Paranoid Android!

ZAPHOD   Space cookies! Hand me the rap-rod, plate-captain.

GARKBIT   Pardon, sir.

ZAPHOD   The *phone*, waiter. Shee, you guys are so unhip it's a wonder your bums don't fall off.

GARKBIT   Our what, sir?

F/X   PHONE PICK UP

The phone, sir.

ZAPHOD   Marvin, hi, how you doing kid?

MARVIN   I think you ought to know I'm feeling very depressed.

ZAPHOD   Hey, yeah? We're having a great time, food, wine, a little personal abuse and the Universe going foom.

Where can we find you?

MARVIN   You don't have to pretend to be interested in me you know. I know perfectly well I'm only a menial robot.

ZAPHOD   OK, OK, but where are you?

MARVIN   Reverse primary thrust Marvin, that's what they say to me, open airlock number three Marvin, Marvin can you pick up that piece of paper? Can I pick up that piece of paper? Here I am, brain the size of a planet . . .

ZAPHOD   Yeah, yeah . . .

MARVIN   But I'm quite used to being humiliated. I can even go and stick my head in a bucket of water if you like.

ZAPHOD   Yeah . . . Marvin . . .

MARVIN   Would you like me to go and stick my head in a bucket of water? I've got one ready. Wait a minute.

F/X   CLUNK OF PHONE. DISTANT CLUNK OF BUCKET AND WATER

FORD   What's he saying Zaphod?

ZAPHOD   Oh nothing. He just phoned up to wash his head at us.

MARVIN   Has that satisfied you?

ZAPHOD   Will you please tell us where you are?

MARVIN   I'm in the car park.

ZAPHOD   In the *car* park? What are you doing there?

MARVIN   Parking cars, what else does one do in . . .

ZAPHOD   Well yeah OK, stay there.

F/X   PHONE DOWN. MARVIN BURBLES ON DISTANTLY

ZAPHOD   Come on guys, let's go. Marvin's down in the car park.

ARTHUR   The car park? What's he doing in the car park?

ZAPHOD   Parking cars, what else, dum dum? Ford, Trillian, let's move.

ARTHUR   What about my pears Galumbit?

(They rush out of the restaurant. The Compere becomes audible again)

F/X   RIPPLE OF LAUGHTER FADES INTO:
METALLIC ECHO OF UNDERGROUND CAR PARK. RUNNING FOOTSTEPS ON STEEL CATWALKS

TRILLIAN   (Shouts) There he is!

Marvin . . .

F/X   MORE FOOTSTEPS, DESCENDING STEEL STAIRS

ZAPHOD   (**Approaching**) Marvin, hey kid, are we pleased to see you.

MARVIN   No you're not. No one ever is.

ZAPHOD   Suit yourself.

TRILLIAN   No really Marvin, we are . . .

ARTHUR   Quite . . .

TRILLIAN   Hanging around waiting for us all this time.

MARVIN   The first ten million years were the worst. And the second ten million, they were the worst too. The third ten million I didn't enjoy at all. After that I went into a bit of a decline.

FORD   Hey, Zaphod, come and have a look at some of these little star trolleys. (**Whisper**) Look at this baby, Zaphod. The tangerine starbuggy with the black sunbusters.

ZAPHOD   (**Whisper**) Hey, get this number. Multicluster quark drive and perspulex running boards. This has got to be a Lazlar LyriKon Kustom job. Look – the infrapink lizard emblem on the neutrino cowling.

FORD   Hey, yeah, I was passed by one of these mothers once out near the Axel Nebula. I was going flat out and this thing just strolled past me, star drive hardly ticking over. Just incredible.

ZAPHOD   Too much.

FORD   Ten seconds later it smashed straight into the third moon of Jaglan Beta.

ZAPHOD   Hey, right?

FORD   But a great looking ship though. Looks like a fish, moves like a fish, steers like a cow.

ZAPHOD   No kidding?

FORD   No. Wait a minute, wait a minute. That one there.

ZAPHOD   Hey, Hey. Now that is really bad for the eyes.

FORD   It's so *black* – you can hardly even make out its shape. Light just falls into it.

ZAPHOD   And feel this surface.

FORD   Yeah. (**Surprise**) Hey, you can't . . .

ZAPHOD   See, it's just totally frictionless . . . this must be one mother of a mover. I bet even the cigar lighter's on photon drive. Well, what do you reckon, Ford?

FORD   What, you mean stroll off with it? Do you think we should?

ZAPHOD   No.

FORD   Nor do I.

ZAPHOD	Let's do it.
FORD	OK.
ZAPHOD	We better shift soon. In a few seconds the Universe will end and all the Captain Creeps will be pouring down here to find their bourge-mobiles.
FORD	Zaphod.
ZAPHOD	Yeah?
FORD	How do we get into it?
ZAPHOD	Just don't spoil a beautiful idea will you Ford?
FORD	Perhaps the robot can figure something out.
ZAPHOD	Yeah. Hey, Marvin, come over, we've got a job for you.
MARVIN	I won't enjoy it.
ZAPHOD	Yes you will, there's a whole new life stretching out ahead of you.
MARVIN	Oh, not another one.
ZAPHOD	Will you shut up and listen? This time there's going to be excitement and adventure and really wild things.
MARVIN	Sounds awful.
ZAPHOD	Marvin! All I'm trying to say . . .
MARVIN	I suppose you want me to open this spaceship for you . . .
ZAPHOD	Marvin, just listen will you? . . . What?
MARVIN	I suppose you want me to open this spaceship for you?
ZAPHOD	Er – yeah.
MARVIN	Well I wish you'd just tell me rather than try and engage my enthusiasm because I haven't got one.
F/X	SPACESHIP DOOR OPENING
FORD	Hey, how'd you do that Marvin?
MARVIN	Didn't I tell you, I've got a brain the size of a planet? No one ever listens to me of course.
ZAPHOD	Oh shut up Marvin.
MARVIN	See what I mean?
FORD	Hey Zaphod, look at this. Look at the interior of this ship.
ZAPHOD	Hey. Weird.
FORD	It's black. Everything in it is just totally black.
	(**Fade out.** **Fade up restaurant.**)

COMPERE	And now ladies and gentlemen, the moment you've all been waiting for! The skies begin to boil! Nature collapses into the screaming void! In five seconds time, the Universe itself will be at an end. See where the light of infinity bursts in upon us!
F/X	HERALD TRUMPETS. HALLELUJAHS. A GREAT WOOSH OF WIND
COMPERE	But what's this? What's happening? Who's this? I don't believe it.
	A big hand please for the Great Prophet Zarquon!
ZARQUON	Er, hello everybody, sorry I'm a bit late, had a terrible time, all sorts of things cropping up at the last moment. How are we for time? Er . . .
F/X	WITH A MIGHTY ROAR THE UNIVERSE ENDS
GRAMS	NARRATOR BACKGROUND
NARRATOR	And so the Universe ended.

One of the major selling points of that wholly remarkable book, *The Hitch-Hiker's Guide to the Galaxy*, apart from its relative cheapness and the fact that it has the words 'Don't Panic' written in large friendly letters on the cover, is its compendious and occasionally accurate glossary. For instance, the statistics relating to the geo-social nature of the Universe are deftly set out between pages five hundred and seventy six thousand three hundred and twenty four, and five hundred and seventy six thousand three hundred and twenty six. The simplistic style is partly explained by the fact that its editors, having to meet a publishing deadline, copied the information off the back of a packet of breakfast cereal, hastily embroidering it with a few footnotes in order to avoid prosecution under the incomprehensibly tortuous Galactic copyright laws. It is interesting to note that a later and wilier editor sent the book backwards in time through a temporal warp and then successfully sued the breakfast cereal company for infringement of the same laws.

Here is a sample, in both headings and footnotes.

(Note: In this section, all words printed in capitals in the text should have extra echo, and all footnotes should have slight distort)

THE UNIVERSE

F/X	PING

Some information to help you live in it.

ONE: AREA. INFINITE.

F/X	PING

As far as anyone can make out.

TWO: IMPORTS. NONE.

It is impossible to import things into an infinite area, there being no outside to import things in from.

THREE: EXPORTS. NONE.

F/X   PING

See imports.

FOUR: RAINFALL. NONE.

Rain cannot fall because in an infinite space there is no up for it to fall down from.

FIVE: POPULATION. NONE.

It is known that there is an infinite number of worlds, but that not every one is inhabited. Therefore there must be a finite number of inhabited worlds. Any finite number divided by infinity is as near to nothing as makes no odds, so if every planet in the Universe has a population of zero then the entire population of the Universe must also be zero, and any people you may actually meet from time to time are merely the products of a deranged imagination.

SIX: MONETARY UNITS. NONE.

F/X   PING

In fact there are three freely convertible currencies in the Universe, but the Altairian Dollar has recently collapsed, the Flainian Pobblebead is only exchangeable for other Flainian Pobblebeads, and the Triganic Pu doesn't really count as money. Its exchange rate of six ningis to one pu is simple, but since a ningi is a triangular rubber coin six thousand eight hundred miles along each side, no one has ever collected enough to own one pu. Ningis are not negotiable currency because the Galactibanks refuse to deal in fiddling small change. From this basic premise it is very simple to prove that the Galactibanks are also the products of a deranged imagination.

SEVEN: SEX. NONE.

F/X   PING

Well actually there is an awful lot of this, largely because of the total lack of money, trade, banks, rainfall or anything else that might keep all the non-existent people in the Universe occupied. However it is not worth embarking on a long discussion of it now because it really is terribly complicated. For further information see chapters seven, nine, ten, eleven, fourteen, sixteen, seventeen, nineteen, twenty one to eighty four inclusive and most of the rest of the book.

It is largely on account of passages like this that the book of the Hitch-Hiker's Guide to the Galaxy is being revised by Ford Prefect and Arthur Dent. Unfortunately they are being presented with too many distractions to be able to settle down to doing any solid research. Not only does Arthur Dent still have to find the Question to the Ultimate Answer of Life, the Universe and Everything, but the newly stolen spaceship is currently behaving rather like this:

F/X	STARSHIP BACKGROUND WHICH IS OSCILLATING RANDOMLY IN PITCH AND VOLUME
ARTHUR	Basically what you're trying to say is that you can't control it.
FORD	*I'm* not trying to say that. The whole bloody ship is.
ZAPHOD	It's the wild colour scheme that freaks me. When you try and operate one of these weird black controls which are labelled in black on a black background a small black light lights up black to let you know you've done it. What is this? Some kind of intergalactic hyperhearse?
TRILLIAN	Well perhaps it is.
ARTHUR	Isn't there any way you can control it? You're making me feel spacesick.
FORD	Timesick. We're plummeting backwards through time.
ARTHUR	Oh God, now I think I really am going to be ill.
ZAPHOD	Go ahead, we could do with a little colour about the place.
TRILLIAN	Oh for God's sake Zaphod, go easy will you? Already today we have had to sit through the end of the Universe, and before that we were blasted five hundred and seventy six thousand years through time by an exploding computer . . .
MARVIN	It's all right for you, I had to go the long way round.
ARTHUR	How did that happen anyway? How does an exploding computer push you through time?
MARVIN	Simple, it wasn't a computer, it was a hyperspatial field generator.
ARTHUR	Silly, I should have recognized it at once.
MARVIN	As it overheated it blew a hole through the space time continuum and you dropped through like a stone through a wet paper bag. I hate wet paper bags.
F/X	THE BACKGROUND NOISE SUDDENLY STOPS OSCILLATING AND SETTLES INTO A STEADY PATTERN
TRILLIAN	Hey, that sounds better. Have you managed to make some sense of the controls?
FORD	No, we just stopped fiddling with them. I think this ship has a far better idea of where it's going than we do.
ARTHUR	Well that sounds quite sensible to me.
ZAPHOD	What do you know about it apeman?
ARTHUR	Well, look, if whoever owns this ship travelled forward in time to the Restaurant at the End of the Universe then presumably he must have programmed the ship in advance to return him to the exact point he originally left. Doesn't that make sense?
FORD	That's quite a good thought you know. Particularly if he was anticipating

having a good time. Drunk in charge of a time ship is a pretty serious offence. They tend to lock you away in some planet's stone age and tell you to evolve into a more responsible life form.

TRILLIAN   So there's nothing to do but sit back and see where we turn up. What do we do in the meantime?

(Pause)

ARTHUR   I've got a pocket Scrabble set.

ZAPHOD   Go play with a nut.

ARTHUR   Well if that's your attitude . . .

ZAPHOD   Hey look Earthman, you've got a job to do, remember? The question to the Ultimate Answer, right? There's a lot of money tied up in that head thing of yours. I mean just think of the merchandising . . . Ultimate Question Biscuits, Ultimate Question T-shirts.

ARTHUR   Well yes, but where do we start? I don't know. The Ultimate Answer so called is forty two, what's the Question? How am I supposed to know? Could be anything, I mean, what's six times seven?

ALL   Er . . . forty two.

ARTHUR   Yes I know that. I'm just saying the Question could be anything. How should I know?

FORD   Because you and Trillian are the last generation products of the Earth Computer matrix. You must know.

MARVIN   I know.

FORD   Shut up Marvin, this is organism talk.

MARVIN   It's printed in the Earthman's brainwave patterns, but I don't suppose you'll be very interested in knowing that.

ARTHUR   You mean you can see into my mind?

MARVIN   Yes.

ARTHUR   And?

MARVIN   It amazes me how you manage to live in anything that small.

ARTHUR   Ah, abuse.

MARVIN   Yes.

ZAPHOD   Ah ignore him, he's only making it up.

MARVIN   Making it up? Why should I want to make anything up? Life's bad enough as it is without wanting to invent any more of it.

TRILLIAN   Marvin, if you knew what it was all along, why didn't you tell us?

MARVIN   You didn't ask.

FORD   Well we're asking you now metalman, what's the question?

MARVIN	The Ultimate Question of Life, the Universe and Everything?
ALL	Yes.
MARVIN	To which the answer is forty two?
ALL	Yes, come on!
MARVIN	I can tell that you're not really interested.
FORD	Will you just tell us you motorised maniac!

F/X **AT THAT MOMENT THE ENGINE NOTE SUDDENLY CHANGES RADICALLY**

ARTHUR	Hey look, the control panel's lighting up, we must have arrived.
ZAPHOD	Hey, yeah, we've zapped back into real space.
MARVIN	I knew you weren't really interested.
FORD	The controls won't respond. It's still going its own way . . . isn't there any way we can introduce this ship to the concept of democracy?
TRILLIAN	Can we at least find out where we are?
ARTHUR	The vision screens are all blank, can't we turn them on?
FORD	They are on.
ARTHUR	Why can't we see any stars?
ZAPHOD	Hey, you know I think we must be outside the Galaxy . . .
FORD	We're picking up speed . . . We're heading out into Intergalactic space . . . Arthur, check out the rear screens will you?
TRILLIAN	I feel cold . . . all alone in this infinite void . . .
ARTHUR	Apart from the fleet of black battle cruisers behind us . . .
ZAPHOD	Er . . . which particular fleet of black battle cruisers is that, Earthman . . .?
ARTHUR	Oh, the ones on the rear screens, sorry, I thought you'd noticed them, there are about a hundred thousand. Is that wrong?
MARVIN	No, what do you expect if you steal the flagship of an admiral of the space fleet.
ZAPHOD	Marvin! What makes you think this is an admiral's flagship?
MARVIN	I know it is. I parked it for him.
ZAPHOD	Then why the planet of hell didn't you tell us?
MARVIN	You didn't ask.
FORD	You know what we've done. We've dropped ourselves into the vanguard of a major intergalactic war.
NARRATOR	(**Signature tune**) Will our heroes ever have a chance to find out what the Ultimate Question is now?

Will they be too busy dealing with a hundred thousand horribly beweaponed battle cruisers to have a chance to have a sympathetic chat to Marvin, the Paranoid Android?

Will they eventually have to settle down and lead normal lives as account executives or management consultants?

Will life ever be the same again after next week's last and reasonably exciting instalment of *The Hitch-Hiker's Guide to the Galaxy*?

ANNOUNCER If you would like a copy of the book *The Hitch-Hiker's Guide to the Galaxy* please write to Megadodo Publications, Megadodo House, Ursa Minor, enclosing £3.95 for the book plus five hundred and ninety seven billion eight hundred and twelve thousand four hundred and six pounds seven pence postage and packing.

FOOTNOTES

This show was recorded on 21 February 1978. For the last two shows of the first series Douglas was assisted by John Lloyd, subsequently the Producer of *Not the Nine O'clock News*, *The Black Adder*, *Spitting Image* and the Associate Producer of the Television series of *Hitch-Hiker's*.

After I had finished four episodes of *Hitch-Hiker's*, I had to break off to fulfil a commission to write four episodes of *Doctor Who* (*The Pirate Planet*). At the end of that stretch my writing muscles were so tired that even though I had a rough idea of what was supposed to be happening in the last two episodes, I had quite simply run out of words. Since John Lloyd nearly alway beat me at Scrabble I reckoned he must know lots more words than me and asked him if he would collaborate with me on the last couple of scripts. 'Prehensile', 'anaconda' and 'ningi' are just three of the thousands of words I would never have thought of myself. [DNA]

John generously plundered several ideas from a projected science fiction book of his own that he was writing at the time, provisionally called the GiGax. In particular it provided the basis for much of the definition of the Universe speech.

He refers to his work on the series as 'garage work', not because it was in any way like stripping down a carburettor and renewing the spark plugs but because he and Douglas used to write together in his garage. Thus garage work. John certainly helped to turn these into two of the most successful shows, though curiously one listener wrote to say he thought the language 'got worse' when John got involved. There doesn't seem to be a scrap of evidence for this, but perhaps he had his own special interpretation of the phrase 'Rap-Rod'? In fact the rudest word in the series (and one of the rudest words in the English language) occurs in episode 4, before John was involved.

For no good reason Garkbit was originally conceived as a French waiter but he was changed to an English waiter (probably also for no good reason). He was played as an impeccably upper class one by Anthony Sharp, who also doubled as Zarquon the Prophet.

Anyone who has been in the audience of a radio or television show will recognize the origins of Max Quordlepleen in the warm up man. He was played by comedian Roy Hudd, who we encouraged to do it wandering about with a hand held microphone (and lots of unpleasant feedback) on the stage of the Paris studio which he was used to seeing full for his show *The News Huddlines*, but was for now full of empty seats.

Just in case we needed it Roy also busked about five more minutes of Max Quordlepleen and ended up lying on the floor pleading with us to let him stop. Really, really keen eared listeners can probably hear some of this underneath the other scenes in the Restaurant.

Curiously Roy went straight from recording Max to do an interview for BBC World service quite unconnected with *Hitch-Hiker's*, where he met Stephen Moore (also doing an interview quite unconnected with *Hitch-Hiker's*). Roy said 'I've just done this radio show where I never met any of the other actors and I didn't understand what any of it was about.' Stephen replied 'Ah yes, I expect that's the thing I'm in.'

In fact Stephen was no longer seeing any of the other actors himself because, although Marvin had been written back in, his own acting commitments meant that we were having to record his bits on a separate day and then drop them into the other scenes line by line. Curiously one BBC official who had been fulsome about the stereo merits of the programme complained that when he had listened to the tape in his office Marvin had completely disappeared off his left speaker. It turned out he'd been listening to the tape in half track mono.

The name Milliways was a corruption of Milky Way, and Douglas claimed that the idea of a restaurant at the end of the Universe was inspired by a Procul Harum song called 'Grand Hotel' which he wanted to run throughout the whole Milliways section. However, since the section was about twenty minutes and the song about three, and since Douglas was unable to explain clearly what connection it actually had with Milliways this idea was abandoned with no subsequent loss to anyone (except Procul Harum who lost twenty minutes of potential royalties).

The zylbatburger scene (largely cut in the transmitted version) was later amplified by the addition of the Dish of the Day scene written for the record and incorporated into the TV show.

The voice treatment of Zarquon was not in fact electronic but was made simply by putting several pieces of sticky tape round the capstan head of a tape recorder so the tape juddered when it went round and made the voice go wobbly.

The end of the Universe effect was another conglomeration of whatever we had to hand, which included trumpeting elephants, twanging rulers and water running down a plughole in the toilet of the Paris studio.

Several listeners attempted to pay the five hundred and ninety seven billion eight hundred and twelve thousand four hundred and six pounds seven pence postage and packing on the Book by placing a penny in a Building Society and asking us to send our payment collectors through a time warp to collect the money when it had accumulated sufficient interest to pay for the Book. Having done this we would like to advise the people who made such deposits that their stock will be rendered worthless in the Intergalactic stock market collapse which takes place in three hundred thousand years time. We would therefore advise these people to remove their pennies before it is too late.

Music Details
Melodien by Ligeti
(Under the opening speech)
The Engulfed Cathederal from *Snowflakes are Dancing* by Iso Tomita
(Used behind the 'If you've done six impossible things today' speech)
Rainbow in Curved Air by Terry Riley
Wind and Water from *Evening Star* by Fripp and Eno
(Both used in the definition of the Universe speech)

FIT THE SIXTH

Will the Ultimate Question to Life, the Universe and Everything (to which the answer is forty two) be discovered?

Will our heroes be able to control their newly stolen spaceship and the enormous fleet of black battle cruisers that is following them?

Will all end happily or in the certain death that has threatened them so persistently?

GRAMS   NARRATOR BACKGROUND

NARRATOR   The History of every major Galactic civilization has gone through three distinct and recognizable phases – those of survival, inquiry and sophistication, otherwise known as the How, Why and Where phases. For instance the first phase is characterized by the question 'How can we eat?', the second by the question 'Why do we eat?' and the third by the question 'Where shall we have lunch?'

The history of warfare is similarly subdivided, though here the phases are Retribution, Anticipation and Diplomacy – Thus Retribution: 'I am going to kill you because you killed my brother', Anticipation: 'I am going to kill you because *I* killed *your* brother', and Diplomacy: 'I am going to kill my brother and then kill you on the pretext that your brother did it'.

Meanwhile, the Earthman Arthur Dent, to whom all this can be of only academic interest as his only brother was long ago nibbled to death by an okapi, is about to be plunged into a real intergalactic war. This is largely because the spaceship that he and his companions have inadvertently stolen from the Restaurant at the End of the Universe has now returned itself on autopilot to its rightful time and place. Its rightful time is immediately prior to a massive invasion of an entire alien galaxy, and its rightful place is at the head of a fleet of one hundred thousand black battle cruisers. This is why:

ARTHUR   You mean this ship we've stolen is the admiral's flag-ship?

FORD   That's the way it's looking. Perhaps we should just ask them if they want it back. You know, if we were reasonably polite about it . . .

ZAPHOD   They might just let us off with being lightly killed.

FORD   Yeah. OK well it's better than . . . er . . .

ZAPHOD   It isn't better than anything at all, is it.

F/X   FLICKERING HUM RISING IN PITCH

FORD   That visiscreen's beginning to flicker.

ZAPHOD   Fetid photons! It must be some guy wanting orders.

FORD   Well order him to go away. You'll just have to bluff it out, Zaphod.

ZAPHOD   *I'll* have to bluff it out?

FORD   Now sit down and do something . . .

ARTHUR   Say something . . .

TRILLIAN   Anything.

FORD   Don't worry, we'll be right behind you . . . hiding.

ZAPHOD   Ford, this is your idea, isn't it?

FORD   Yeah, now sit down there and be a star.

ZAPHOD   When I am a star I'll hire a better ideas man.

F/X	THE SCREEN COMES ALIVE WITH A PING
VOICE	(**Hoarse and growly**) Haggunenon, Underfleet commander reporting from vice flagship.
ZAPHOD	(**Bright but uneasy**) Oh, er, hi . . . Under Fleet commandant. I . . . er . . .
VOICE	Good evening admiral.
ZAPHOD	What?
VOICE	I trust you had a pleasant meal?
ZAPHOD	Er, what? Er, yeah, it was fine . . . er, thanks.
VOICE	Delighted to hear it sir. We are now in battle readiness state amber, deployed to your rear in line astride seven minutes from target galaxy and awaiting your orders.
ZAPHOD	Great, er fine, well, you know, keep in touch Under Fleet Commandant.
VOICE	Thank you, sir. Oh, and sir?
ZAPHOD	Er, yes?
VOICE	I like your outfit sir.
ZAPHOD	Oh, er, yeah, fine.
F/X	PING AS SCREEN GOES BLANK. IT DIES DOWN OVER A COUPLE OF SECONDS
	(**They all start to talk at once**)
ZAPHOD	Hey, that's just too weird.
ARTHUR	He actually thought you were the admiral.
TRILLIAN	That's amazing Zaphod, you did it!
FORD	Cool, really cool Zaphod, actually pretending to *be* the admiral.
ZAPHOD	Yeah, yeah terrific, listen you dumb space cookie, I wasn't pretending to be the admiral, for some reason he just assumed I was.
ARTHUR	Perhaps you look like him or something.
ZAPHOD	Yeah, well not if he looks anything like his second in command, monkeyman.
ALL, VARIOUSLY	Well what did he look like? We couldn't see the screen. Why was he?
ZAPHOD	Well he was a big leopard OK? With you know, the sunglasses, inflight casual spacesuit split to the navel, brown beach loafers, the whole bit.
ARTHUR	How could he think you were the admiral?
FORD	Well maybe leopards just have a lousy memory for faces.
ZAPHOD	Hilarious.

TRILLIAN	It must be simpler than that. There's obviously something wrong with the visiscreen. I'll have a look at it.
ZAPHOD	**(Sudden realization)** You heard what the big cat said, he said he liked my outfit, so he must have seen me.
TRILLIAN	**(Off)** The screen's coming on again.
FORD	Hell, Zaphod, get back in that seat. Trillian, come back.
TRILLIAN	It's too late, get back!
F/X	SCREEN PING
VOICE	**(Rather squeaky and scrunchy. I think we're really going to have to use the vocoder this time)** Under Fleet Commandant reporting, battle state russet, and six minutes from target galaxy. Oh, and admiral . . .
TRILLIAN	**(Faintly)** Y . . . yes?
VOICE	I really like the gear. Even better than last time.
TRILLIAN	Uhhhhh. Thanks.
F/X	SCREEN GOES DEAD
ZAPHOD	Wowee, weirder and weirder.
TRILLIAN	Good God.
ARTHUR	What is it Trillian?
TRILLIAN	Did you see that? I thought you said he was a leopard.
ARTHUR	He sounded different.
FORD	Did he look different?
TRILLIAN	Well he wasn't so much a leopard, more a sort of, you know, shoe box.
ARTHUR	A *shoe* box?
TRILLIAN	Full of . . . well, size nine chukka boots.
ARTHUR	A shoe box full of size nine chukka boots?
ZAPHOD	Alright chimpman, what do you think this is, dictation?
ARTHUR	I just wondered how she knew they were size nine.
FORD	Trillian, are you seriously telling us you've been talking to a box of shoes?
TRILLIAN	Yes.
FORD	And he . . . she . . . it . . .
TRILLIAN	They.
FORD	. . . thought that you also were the admiral?
TRILLIAN	Well you heard it.
ZAPHOD	What are they, clinically thick?

FORD I think they're very clever. They're trying to confuse us to death.

MARVIN I don't think they're very clever. There's only one person as intelligent as me within thirty parsecs of here and that's me.

ZAPHOD OK Marvin, is there anything you can tell us?

MARVIN Yes. I've got this terrible pain in all the diodes down my left side.

ARTHUR What was the name the second in command said? Haggunenon. Why don't we look it up in the book?

TRILLIAN What book?

FORD The Hitch-Hiker's Guide to the Galaxy.

ZAPHOD Oh, that hack rag.

F/X BOOKMOTIF

GRAMS NARRATOR BACKGROUND

NARRATOR The Haggunenons of Vicissitus Three have the most impatient chromosomes of any life form in the Galaxy. Whereas most races are content to evolve slowly and carefully over thousands of generations, discarding a prehensile toe here, nervously hazarding another nostril there, the Haggunenons would do for Charles Darwin what a squadron of Arcturan stunt apples would have done for Sir Isaac Newton. Their genetic structure, based on the quadruple sterated octohelix, is so chronically unstable, that far from passing their basic shape onto their children, they will quite frequently evolve several times over lunch. But they do this with such reckless abandon that if, sitting at table, they are unable to reach a coffee spoon, they are liable without a moment's consideration to mutate into something with far longer arms . . . but which is probably quite incapable of drinking the coffee.

This, not unnaturally, produces a terrible sense of personal insecurity, and a jealous resentment of all stable life forms, or 'filthy rotten stinking samelings' as they call them. They justify this by claiming that as they have personally experienced what it is like to be virtually everybody else they can think of, they are in a very good position to appreciate all their worst points.

This 'appreciation' is usually military in nature and is carried out with unmitigated savagery from the gunrooms of their horribly beweaponed Chameleoid Death Flotilla. Experience has shown that the most effective way of dealing with any Haggunenon you may meet is to run away terribly fast.

FORD Great.

ARTHUR Terrific.

TRILLIAN Thanks a million, Zaphod.

ZAPHOD Well hey don't look at me.

TRILLIAN   Well what do we do?

FORD   The book says run away.

ZAPHOD   How do we get the automatic pilot on our side? Box of chockies and some sweet talk? Any ideas Marvin?

MARVIN   If I were you I'd be very depressed.

ZAPHOD   Earthman?

ARTHUR   I go along with Marvin.

ZAPHOD   Ford?

FORD   I always find that the prospect of death contracts the mind wonderfully.

TRILLIAN   You know, I've just thought, there is a chance.

ARTHUR   A chance? As far as I can see you might as well lower haystacks off the boatdeck of the *Lusitania*.

TRILLIAN   No, think about it . . . The second in command assumed that the admiral, Zaphod and I were the same person not because we look similar but because we look completely different. So . . .

FORD   Right, right I'm with you . . . If the second in command can be a shoe box, the admiral can be anything, a paraffin stove, a water bison, an anaconda.

ZAPHOD   Terrific. I'll root around for the water bison. Trillian you see if you can find the jar the admiral keeps his anacondas in.

FORD   Can it, Zaphod, it could quite easily be something mundane – a screwdriver, that coil of wire, the chair itself . . .

ZAPHOD   Yeah, hey you know that's really a neat chair, could have been made for me, it's got the two headrests, dig?

FORD   What, those two great furry things? They look ridiculous.

TRILLIAN   It's very uncomfortable – I'd prefer something with far longer arms.

ARTHUR   (**Off**) But which is probably quite incapable of drinking coffee.

(**Shocked pause**)

ZAPHOD   Hey, er, what did you say Earthman?

TRILLIAN   Did you say headrests Zaphod? They look a lot like eyebrows to me . . .

ZAPHOD   The chair's stretching its leg . . .

TRILLIAN   It's just been asleep all this time . . .

FORD   Arthur, for God's sake get back here quick!

ZAPHOD   Yeah, stand up when you sit on the Admiral, primate.

TRILLIAN   It's moving. Look, it's starting to evolve!

F/X   ZAPPY BURSTING SOUND WHICH IS ALSO A BIT SCREAMY AS THE CHAIR BURSTS INTO A TERRIBLE MONSTER.

GENERAL CRIES OF 'OH GOSH' AND 'GOODNESS GRACIOUS' FROM THE CAST.

FORD   Wow, eat your heart out Galapagos Islands.

ZAPHOD   G-Force, you know what *that* is!

TRILLIAN   Let me guess. Horrible. Am I warm?

ZAPHOD   It's a carbon copy of the Ravenous Bug-Blatter Beast of Traal or I'm a Vogon's Grandmother.

F/X   GHASTLY SCREECH FROM THE BEAST

ARTHUR   The Ravenous Bug-Blatter of Traal . . . is is safe?

FORD   Oh yes it's perfectly safe . . . it's just us who are in trouble. If that's the admiral and he still wants his coffee it ain't sponge fingers he's going to dunk in it.

F/X   SCREECH

TRILLIAN   Ford, throw some furniture at it!

FORD   What do I do, pick this table up by the ears?

ARTHUR   God, the whole place is coming alive!

F/X   FURTHER ROARS SCREAMS AND HOWLS

ZAPHOD   Yeah, and we're coming dead.

TRILLIAN   This ashtray just changed into a jar full of anacondas.

ZAPHOD   Just tell it we'll let them know OK?

FORD   Get off me you filthy sofa . . .

ARTHUR   God and I thought Times Furnishing was horrific . . .

ZAPHOD   Get in the escape capsules!

F/X   CHASE:
FEET DOWN METAL CORRIDORS FOLLOWED BY BEAST SCREECH, AND GENERALLY KNOCKING FURNITURE OVER AND EATING IT

FORD   Right, Arthur and I'll take this one. Zaphod, you and the others take the left hand one.

F/X   HATCHWAY OPENS. SCUFFLES AS ARTHUR AND FORD GET IN, THE BEAST'S SCREECHES ARE MUFFLED

FORD   Press the go-stud Arthur.

F/X   DULL DETONATION AS CAPSULE BLASTS OFF FROM THE SHIP, AND THE WHOOSH OF IT ESCAPING

ARTHUR   Wheew! **(Double take)** Hey, Ford, look. The other capsule's missing. The shute's empty, someone else must have used that capsule . . . the others are trapped!

FORD	It's too late Arthur, we can't help them. This capsule won't turn back.
ARTHUR	What happens if I press this button here?
FORD	Don't!
F/X	A REALLY SMASHINGLY SUPER SOUND OF THE CAPSULE MAKING A HYPERSPACE JUMP
GRAMS	NARRATOR BACKGROUND
NARRATOR	Fortunately for Ford Prefect and Arthur Dent their capsule was fitted with the latest in instant space travel, the Phargilor Kangaroo Relocation Drive, by which a ship may be ejected suddenly through the fabric of the space time continuum and come to rest far from its starting point. This is however an emergency device, and there is rarely time to plot where the ship will land. Meanwhile, this is what happened to Zaphod, Trillian and Marvin . . .
F/X	BUGBLATTER SCREECH
TRILLIAN	(**Screams**) Look out!
F/X	HUGE ARM SWEEPS DOWN AND PICKS THEM UP. THE MONSTER ROLLS HIS EYES WHICH TURN RED, GREEN, THEN A SORT OF MAUVY PINK. IT RUNS ITS TONGUE ROUND ITS LIPS, BLINKS A COUPLE OF TIMES AND THEN MENTALLY REGISTERS THAT IT HAS JUST REMEMBERED WHAT 10 ACROSS IN THE GALACTIC TIMES CROSSWORD WAS TODAY, MAKES A MENTAL NOTE TO WRITE IT IN WHEN IT'S NEXT GOT A COUPLE OF MINUTES
CAST	(**Shouts, etc . . .**)
MARVIN	(**Resigned**) Ouch . . . Oh dear, oh dear . . . My arm's come off.
TRILLIAN	Arrrgghh, he's got us! If I ever survive this I'll get a job as Moby Dick's dentist.
ZAPHOD	Can it Trillian, I'm trying to die with dignity.
MARVIN	I'm just trying to die.
ZAPHOD	No problem. Pas de problème!
MARVIN	Ah . . . the ennui is overpowering.
F/X	BUG BLATTER BEAST SWALLOWS THEM WHOLE. SOUND OF HUGE CAVERNOUS THROAT WITH SLIMY SLOPPING AND GURGLING
NARRATOR	And this is what happened to Arthur Dent and Ford Prefect.
F/X	REVERSE OF HYPERSPACE EFFECT. LOUD CLANG
ARTHUR	Are we back in normal space?
FORD	No. I think we've actually materialised inside another spaceship.

ARTHUR	More problems.
FORD	Well we'll see. Checks . . . atmosphere OK, let's get out and look . . .
F/X	OPENING OF CAPSULE: THEY GET OUT
ARTHUR	Ford?
FORD	Yeah?
ARTHUR	Look, what about the others?
FORD	Arthur, you'll have to learn, it's a convention in all space travelling species that if you have to ditch someone . . . you know, a friend . . . there's nothing you can do. You just let it be, you don't talk about them, OK?
ARTHUR	What . . . really?
FORD	And then we get blind drunk about them later.
ARTHUR	I think there must be something terribly wrong with the Universe you know.
FORD	I think there must be something terribly wrong with this ship.
ARTHUR	Yes, it looks like a mausoleum.
FORD	Hey, you're right . . . the place is full of sarcophagi as far as the eye can see. Wild.
ARTHUR	What's so great about dead people?
FORD	I don't know, let's have a look. Here, there's a plaque on this one . . .
ARTHUR	What does it say?
FORD	Golgafrincham Ark Fleet, Ship B, Hold Seven, Telephone Sanitizer Second Class, and a serial number.
ARTHUR	Telephone sanitizer? A dead telephone sanitizer?
FORD	Best kind.
ARTHUR	But what's he doing here?
FORD	Not a lot.
ARTHUR	No, but I mean why . . . Good God, this one's a dead hairdresser.
FORD	And this one's an advertising account executive.
ARTHUR	Are these really coffins? They're terribly cold.
F/X	SUDDEN ZAP
NUMBER TWO	(**Very sudden, very loud, very Germanic and Military**) All right! Hold it right there!
FORD	Hello?
ARTHUR	Why isn't anyone ever pleased to see us?
	(**Fade**)

F/X	FADE UP: BRIDGE. OCCASIONAL SOUND OF SPLASHING WATER

(The Captain and Number One are both fairly vague, pleasant, ineffectual people)

NUMBER ONE	Er, captain?
CAPTAIN	Yes, Number One?
NUMBER ONE	Just had a sort of report thing from Number Two.
CAPTAIN	Oh dear.
NUMBER ONE	He was shouting something or other about having found some prisoners.
CAPTAIN	Well perhaps that'll keep him happy for a bit, he's always wanted some.
F/X	DOOR OPENS
NUMBER TWO	Captain sir!
CAPTAIN	Oh, hello, Number Two, having a nice day?
NUMBER TWO	I have brought you the prisoners I located in freezer bay seven, sir.
FORD/ARTHUR	Er, hello.
CAPTAIN	Oh hello, excuse me not getting up, just having a quick bath. Well, gin and tonics all round then. Look in the fridge Number One.
NUMBER ONE	Certainly, sir.
NUMBER TWO	Don't you want to interrogate the prisoners, sir?
CAPTAIN	Interrogate them, Number Two?
NUMBER TWO	Yes sir. Torture them sir, stick matchsticks under their finger nails, stub out lighted cigarettes on their skin, sir . . .
CAPTAIN	Why on Earth should I want to do that?
NUMBER TWO	To get information out of them sir.
CAPTAIN	Oh no no no, I expect they just dropped in for a quick gin and tonic, don't you?
NUMBER TWO	Can't I just interrogate them a little bit?
CAPTAIN	Oh all right, if you must. Ask them what they want to drink.
NUMBER TWO	Thank you sir. **(Shouting)** All right you scum, you vermin . . .
CAPTAIN	Oh steady on Number Two . . .
NUMBER TWO	What do you want to drink?
FORD	Well, the gin and tonic sounds very nice to me. Arthur?
ARTHUR	What? Oh yes.
NUMBER TWO	With ice or without!!!!!

FORD	Oh, with please.
NUMBER TWO	Lemon?!!!!!!!!!!!
FORD	Yes please, and do you have any of those little biscuits, you know the cheesy ones . . ?
NUMBER TWO	I'm asking the questions!!!!!!!!!!!!!!
CAPTAIN	Er, Number Two?
NUMBER TWO	Sir!!!!!!!!!!!!!!!!!!!!!!!!
CAPTAIN	Push off would you, there's a good chap. I'm trying to have a relaxing bath.
NUMBER TWO	Sir, may I remind you that you have now been in that bath for over three years!
CAPTAIN	Yes, well you need to relax a lot in a job like mine.
ARTHUR	What on Earth's going on?
FORD	Could I ask you actually what your job is in fact?
NUMBER ONE	(**Just slipped in**) Your drinks.
FORD	Oh thanks.
ARTHUR	Thanks.
FORD	I mean I couldn't help noticing, you know, the bodies.
CAPTAIN	Bodies?
FORD	Yes . . . all those dead telephone sanitizers and account executives, you know, in the hold.
CAPTAIN	Oh, they're not dead, Good Lord no, no they're just frozen, they're going to be revived.
ARTHUR	You really mean you've got a hold full of frozen hairdressers?
CAPTAIN	Oh yes, millions of them, hairdressers, tired TV producers, insurance salesmen, personnel officers.
NUMBER TWO	Security guards.
CAPTAIN	Management consultants. You name it. We got it. We're going to colonize another planet.
ARTHUR	What?
CAPTAIN	Exciting, isn't it?
ARTHUR	What, with that lot?
CAPTAIN	Oh don't misunderstand me, we're just one of the ships in the Ark Fleet, we're the B Ark you see. Sorry, could I just ask you to run a bit more hot water for me, thanks. Do help yourself to more drinks of course.
FORD	Thanks.

ARTHUR	What's a B Ark.
CAPTAIN	What? Oh, well what happened you see was our planet was doomed.
ARTHUR	Doomed?
CAPTAIN	Oh yes. So what everyone thought was let's pack the whole population into some giant spaceships and go and settle on another planet.
ARTHUR	You mean a less doomed one.
CAPTAIN	Precisely. So it was decided to build three ships, three Arks in space . . . *I'm not boring you am I?*
FORD	*No, no, it's fascinating.*
CAPTAIN	*It's delightful to have someone else to talk to for a change. Trouble with a long journey like this is that you end up just talking to yourself a lot, which gets terribly boring because half the time you know what you're going to say next.*
ARTHUR	*Only half the time?*
CAPTAIN	*Yes, about half I'd say.* Anyway, where's the soap? Yes, so the idea, was that into the first ship, the A ship, would go all the brilliant leaders, the scientists, the great artists, you know, all the achievers, and then into the third ship the C ship would go all the people who did the actual work, who made things and did things, and then into the B ship, that's us, would go everyone else, the middlemen you see. And we were sent off first.
ARTHUR	But what was wrong with your planet?
CAPTAIN	Oh it was doomed, as I said. Apparently it was going to crash into the sun. Or was it that the moon was going to crash into us?
NUMBER ONE	Oh, I thought it was that the planet was more or less bound to be invaded by a gigantic swarm of twelve foot piranha bees.
NUMBER TWO	That's not what I was told! My commanding officer swore blind that the entire planet was in imminent danger of being eaten by an enormous mutant star-goat!
FORD	**(Humouring them)** Oh really . . .
NUMBER TWO	Yes, and that he was just hoping that the ship he was going in would be ready in time.
ARTHUR	But they made sure that they sent all you lot off first anyway.
CAPTAIN	Oh yes, well everyone said, very nicely I thought, that it was very important for morale to feel that they would be arriving on a planet where they could be sure of a good haircut and where the phones were clean.
FORD	Oh yes, well I can see that would be very important.
ARTHUR	Can you?
FORD	Shush . . . and er, the other ships followed on after you did they?
CAPTAIN	Ah, well it's funny you should mention that because curiously enough we

haven't actually heard a peep out of them since we left five years ago . . . but they must be behind us somewhere.

FORD   Unless of course they were eaten by the goat.

CAPTAIN   (**A suspicion of doubt is beginning to creep into his voice**) Ah yes the goat . . . hmmmmm . . . it's a funny thing you know, now that I actually come to tell the story to someone else . . . I mean does it strike you as odd, Number One?

NUMBER ONE   Errrrrrr . . . ?

CAPTAIN   Ummmmm . . . ?

FORD   Well, I can see that you've got a lot of things you're going to want to talk about, so thanks for the drinks, and if you could sort of drop us off at the nearest convenient planet . . .

CAPTAIN   Ah well that's a little difficult you see, because our trajectory thingy was pre-set before we left Golgafrincham, I think partly because I'm not actually very good with figures.

ARTHUR/FORD   (**Impatiently**) When are you going to reach the planet you're meant to be colonizing?

CAPTAIN   Oh, we're nearly there I think, any second now. It's probably time I got out of the bath in fact. Oh I don't know though, why stop just when I'm enjoying it?

ARTHUR   So we're actually going to land in a minute?

CAPTAIN   Well not so much land in fact . . . I think as far as I can remember we were programmed to crash on it.

ARTHUR/FORD   Crash??

CAPTAIN   Yes, it's all part of the plan I think. There was a terribly good reason for it which I can't quite remember at the moment . . .

FORD   You're a load of useless bloody loonies.

CAPTAIN   Ah yes, that was it.

F/X   SHIP CRASHES. A SHORT HOWLING PLUMMET FOLLOWED BY AN EXPLOSION

GRAMS   NARRATOR BACKGROUND

NARRATOR   The Hitch-Hiker's Guide to the Galaxy has this to say about the planet of Golgafrincham; it is a planet with an ancient and mysterious history, in which the most mysterious figures of all are without doubt those of the Great Circling Poets of Arium. These Circling Poets used to live in remote mountain passes where they would lie in wait for small bands of unwary travellers, circle round them and throw rocks at them.

And when the travellers cried out saying why didn't they go away and get on with writing some poems instead of pestering people with all this rock throwing business, they would suddenly break off and sing them an incredibly long and beautiful song in which they told of how there once went forth from the city of Vasillian a party of five sage princes with four horses. The first part of the song tells how these five sage princes, who are of course brave, noble and wise, travel widely in distant lands, fight giant ogres, pursue exotic philosophies, take tea with weird gods and rescue beautiful monsters from ravishing princesses before finally announcing that they have achieved enlightenment and that their wanderings are therefore accomplished. The second and much longer part tells of all their bickerings about which one of them is going to have to walk back.

It was of course a descendant of these eccentric poets who invented the spurious tales of impending doom which enabled the people of Golgafrincham to rid themselves of an entire useless third of their population. The other two thirds, of course, all stayed at home and led full, rich and happy lives until they were all suddenly wiped out by a virulent disease contracted from a dirty telephone.

Meanwhile, Arthur Dent, Ford Prefect and an arkload of frozen middle management men have crashed into the prehistoric dawn of a small blue green planet circling an unregarded yellow sun at the unfashionable end of the Western spiral arm of the Galaxy. After a year or so they convene a meeting to consider their position, which is not on the whole good.

F/X	BACKGROUND ATMOSPHERE OF WIDE OPEN SPACES, A LITTLE WIND, A FEW BITS OF BIRDSONG, SOME MONKIES CHATTERING FADE UP OVER F/X SOUND OF A CONFUSION OF VOICES ALL TALKING TOGETHER
CAPTAIN	(**Over it all**) All right, I'd like to call this meeting to some sort of order if that's at all possible
HAIRDRESSER	Care for a light trim, sir?
CAPTAIN	Not now, I'm in the bath.
FORD	Hey come on, shut up everybody, there's some important news, we've made a discovery.
MANAGEMENT CONSULTANT	Is it on the agenda?
FORD	Oh don't give me that.
MANAGEMENT CONSULTANT	Well, I'm sorry, but speaking as a fully trained management consultant I must insist on the importance of observing the committee structure . . .
FORD	On a prehistoric planet . . . !
MANAGEMENT CONSULTANT	Address the chair!
FORD	There isn't a chair, there's only a rock.
MANAGEMENT CONSULTANT	Well, call it a chair.

FORD	Why not call it a rock?
MANAGEMENT CONSULTANT	You obviously have no conception of modern business methods.
FORD	And you have no conception of where the hell you are!
MARKETING GIRL	Look, shut up you two, I want to table a motion.
HAIRDRESSER	Boulder a motion you mean.
FORD	Thank you, I've made that point. Now, listen . . .
MANAGEMENT CONSULTANT	Order, order!
FORD	Oh God.
CAPTAIN	I would like to call to order the five hundred and seventy-third meeting of the colonization committee of the planet of Fintlewoodlewix . . .
FORD	Oh this is futile. Five hundred and seventy-three committee meetings and you haven't even discovered fire yet.
MANAGEMENT CONSULTANT	If you would care to look at the agenda sheet.
HAIRDRESSER	(**Beginning to enjoy himself**) Agenda rock . . .
FORD	Go and back comb something will you?
MANAGEMENT CONSULTANT	. . .you will see that we are about to have a report from the hairdresser's fire development sub-committee today.
HAIRDRESSER	That's me.
FORD	Yeah, well you know what they've done don't you? You gave them a couple of sticks and they've developed them into a pair of bloody scissors. You're going to die out, you know that?
MARKETING GIRL	Well, you're obviously being totally naïve of course. When you've been in marketing as long as I have you'll know that before any new product can be developed it has to be properly researched. We've got to find out what people want from fire, how they relate to it, the image it . . .
FORD	Oh stick it up your nose.
MARKETING GIRL	Which is precisely the sort of thing we need to know. Do people want fire that can be fitted nasally?
CAPTAIN	And the wheel, what about this wheel thing? It sounds a terribly interesting project.
MARKETING GIRL	Ah, well we're having a little difficulty there.
FORD	Difficulty! It's the single simplest machine in the entire Universe!
MARKETING GIRL	All right Mr Wiseguy, if you're so clever, *you* tell us what colour it should be.

FORD	Oh, almighty Zarquon, has no one done anything? Well?
NUMBER TWO	*I have declared war on the next continent.*
FORD	*Declared war! There's no one even living there!*
NUMBER TWO	*Yes, but there will be one day, so we've left a sort of open-ended ultimatum.*
FORD	*What?*
NUMBER TWO	*And blown up a few military installations.*
CAPTAIN	*Military installations, Number Two?*
NUMBER TWO	*Yes sir, well, potential military installations. All right, trees. And we interrogated a gazelle.*

(Slightly embarrassed pause)

MARKETING GIRL	And of course Finlon the producer has rescued a camera from the wreckage of the ship and is making a fascinating documentary on the indigenous cavemen of the area . . .
FORD	Yes, and they're dying out, have you noticed that?
MANAGEMENT CONSULTANT	Yes, we must make a note to stop selling them life insurance.
FORD	But don't you understand? Just since we've arrived they've started dying out.
MARKETING GIRL	Yes and this comes over terribly well in the film he's making.
MARKETING GIRL	I gather he wants to make a documentary about you next, captain . . .
CAPTAIN	Oh really? That's awfully nice.
MARKETING GIRL	He's got a very strong angle on it, you know, the burden of responsibility, the loneliness of command . . .
CAPTAIN	Ah, well I wouldn't overstress that angle you know, one's never alone with a rubber duck. Weeeee . . .
MANAGEMENT CONSULTANT	Er, Sir . . . Skipper . . .
F/X	HE SPLASHES ABOUT A BIT
MANAGEMENT CONSULTANT	If we could for a moment move on to the subject of fiscal policy . . .
FORD	Fiscal policy! How can you have money, if none of you actually produce anything – it doesn't grow on trees you know.
MANAGEMENT CONSULTANT	If you would allow me to continue . . . since we decided a few weeks ago to adopt leaves as legal tender we have of course all become immensely rich . . .

ALL	**(General murmuring of yes, very good, lovely etc . . .)**
MANAGEMENT CONSULTANT	. . . but we have also run into a small inflation problem on account of the high level of leaf availability, which means that, I gather, the current going rate has something like three major deciduous forests buying one ship's peanut. So in order to obviate this problem, and effectively revalue the leaf, we are about to embark on an extensive defoliation campaign and, er . . . burn down all the forests. I think that's a sensible move, don't you?
ALL	**(General murmurs of agreement. Phrases like 'Fiscally shrewd', 'Certainly makes economic sense' and 'Cut prices at a stroke' 'Increase the value of the leaf in your pocket' etc . . .)**
FORD	You're absolutely barmy, you're a bunch of raving nutters.
MARKETING GIRL	Is it perhaps in order to inquire what you've been doing all this time? You and that other interloper have been missing for months.
FORD	Yeah, well, with respect, we've been travelling around trying to find out something about this planet.
MARKETING GIRL	Well that doesn't sound very productive. I thought you . . .
FORD	No, well have I got news for you. It doesn't matter a pair of fetid dingo's kidneys what you all choose to do from now on, burn down the forests, anything, it won't make a scrap of difference. Two million years you've got, and that's it. At the end of that your race will be dead, gone and good riddance to you. Remember that, two million years.
CAPTAIN	Ah, just time for another bath. Pass me the sponge somebody . . .
	(Fade)
F/X	FADE UP SAME BACKGROUND AS LAST SCENE. MEETING IS CONTINUING VERY FAINTLY IN THE BACKGROUND. IN THE FOREGROUND SOME CAVEMEN GRUNTING
ARTHUR	No, Q scores ten you see, and it's on a triple word score, so . . . I'm sorry but I explained the rules . . . no, no, look please put down that jaw bone . . . all right, we'll start again. And try to concentrate this time.
FORD	**(Approaching wearily)** Oh, what are you doing, Arthur?
ARTHUR	Trying to teach the cavemen to play Scrabble. It's uphill work, the only word they know is grunt and they can't spell it.
FORD	And would you please tell me what that is supposed to achieve?
ARTHUR	We've got to encourage them to evolve, Ford. Can you imagine what a world is going to be like that descends from those cretins over there?
FORD	We don't have to imagine, let's face it, we already know what it's like, we've seen it, there's no escape.
ARTHUR	Did you tell them what we'd discovered?
FORD	Slartibartfast's signature on the glacier? No, what's the point? Why should

they listen? What's it to them that this planet happens to be called the Earth?

ARTHUR And that it happens to be my original home.

FORD Yes, but you won't even be born for nearly two million years, so they're likely to feel that it's not a lot of your business. Face up to it Arthur, those zeebs over there are your ancestors, not these cavemen. Put the Scrabble away, it won't save the human race because Mr Ugg here is not destined to be the human race. The human race is currently sitting round that rock over there making documentaries about themselves.

ARTHUR But there must be something we can do . . .

FORD No, nothing, really nothing, because it's all been done. Listen, we've been backwards and forwards through time and ended up here, two million years behind where we started, but that doesn't change the future, because we've seen it. Wise up kid, there's nothing you can do to change it because it's already happened.

ARTHUR And all because we arrived here with the Golgafrinchams in their B Ark.

FORD Yes.

CAVEMAN Ugh ugh ugh grrrrrr ugh.

ARTHUR Poor bloody caveman. It's all been a bit of a waste of time for you hasn't it? You've been out-evolved by a telephone sanitizer.

CAVEMAN Ugh ugh ugh ugh greeeeerrrrr.

FORD He's pointing at the Scrabble Board.

ARTHUR Oh, he's probably spelt library with one 'r' again, poor bastard.

FORD No he hasn't.

ARTHUR Hey, no look, it says forty two . . . The Experiment. It's something to do with the computer programme to find the Ultimate Question.

FORD Hey, you know what this means don't you?

ARTHUR What?

FORD It must have gone wrong . . . If the computer matrix was set up to follow the evolution of the human race through from the cavemen, and then we've arrived and caused them to die out . . .

ARTHUR And actually replaced them . . .

FORD . . . then the whole thing is cocked up . . .

ARTHUR So whatever it was that Marvin spotted in my brain wave patterns is in fact the wrong question.

FORD Yeah. It might be right, but it's probably wrong. If only we could find out what it is.

ARTHUR Well how about . . . look, if it's printed in my brain wave patterns but I don't know how to reach it . . . supposing we introduce some random element which can be shaped by that pattern?

FORD   Like?

ARTHUR   Pulling out letters from the Scrabble bag.

FORD   Brilliant. That's bloody brilliant.

ARTHUR   Right, first four letters . . .

FORD   W.H.A.T. . . . What.

ARTHUR   Two more . . .

FORD   D.O. . . . Do. It's working. Hey this is terrific, it's really coming. Y.O.U. . . . G.E.T. . . . What do you get . . .

ARTHUR   More here . . .

FORD   I.F. . . . YOU . . . MULTIPLY . . . I'm beginning to get sinking feelings about this . . . IF YOU MULTIPLY SIX . . . BY . . . BY . . . BY NINE? By nine. Is that it?

ARTHUR   That's it. Six by nine. Forty two. Something's certainly got screwed up somewhere. I always said there was something fundamentally wrong with the Universe. So what do we do now?

FORD   I guess we just swallow our pride and go and join the human race.

ARTHUR   Yes.

CAVEMAN   Yuch!

ARTHUR   Right. Yuch!

F/X   FROM THIS POINT A LONG SLOW FADE ON THE DIALOGUE, WHILST THE BACKGROUND SOUNDS OF WIND EVENTUALLY RISE TO COVER IT

ARTHUR   It's sad though. Just at the moment it is a very beautiful planet.

FORD   It is, it is indeed. The rich primal greens, the river snaking off into the distance, the burning trees . . .

ARTHUR   And in two million years, bang, it gets destroyed by the Vogons.

ARTHUR   What a life for a young planet to look forward to.

FORD   Well, better than some. I read of one planet off in the seventh dimension that got used as a ball in a game of intergalactic bar billiards. Got potted straight into a black hole, killed ten billion people.

ARTHUR   Mmm, total madness.

FORD   Yeah, only scored thirty points, too.

ARTHUR   Where did you read that?

FORD   Oh, a book.

ARTHUR   Which book was that?

FORD   *The Hitch-Hiker's Guide to the Galaxy.*

ARTHUR   Oh, that thing.

GRAMS   WHAT A WONDERFUL WORLD, LOUIS ARMSTRONG

FOOTNOTES

This final programme in the first series was recorded on 28 February 1978.

The pressures of the final deadline were evident from the fact that we no longer had time for even the smallest large meal, and were forced to discuss the ideas for the show over a hurried pint in a pub round the corner from the BBC. (Where incidentally some years before Dylan Thomas was reputed to have accidentally left the manuscript of *Under Milk Wood* while under the influence of one too many Pan Galactic Gargle Blasters. It's a pity we didn't find it, since we could have used some of the ideas.)

Comic actor David Jason was cast as the Captain of the B Ark because at the time he was regularly protraying Dr David Owen (then Foreign Secretary and now leader of the SDP) on the satirical show Week Ending, where Dr Owen was constantly in a bath (for reasons that have become clouded, but not necessarily more amusing, in the mists of time).

Jonathan Cecil played his Number One, while Aubrey Woods was his Number Two and the Hairdresser. Beth Porter was cast as the Marketing Girl, after seeing her in the television show *Rock Follies* (and the same show also featured Simon Jones and provided the spur for casting Stephen Moore as Marvin since in it Stephen Moore played the almost terminally depressed boyfriend of one of the lead characters).

The various ghastly roars of the Haggunenon were made by recording someone shouting and then simply slowing their voice down and adding the traditional pinch of echo. The effects directions on page 124 are clearly nonsense. It shows a typical perversity that with an incredibly tight script deadline large amounts of time still went into writing things that had nothing to do with what would actually be heard on the radio!

The line 'Pas de problème' was ad libbed by Mark during the recording and when questioned about it came up with a rather quaint little theory about Zaphod's second head speaking French. This idea was never subsequently developed, but here it is anyway in case anyone else would like to develop it (and risk the harsh and savage retribution from Douglas' lawyer that would inevitably follow).

The line 'A chance? As far as I can see you might as well lower haystacks off the boatdeck of the *Lusitania*' was probably thought by all of us to be terribly clever at the time but Douglas no longer has the faintest idea what it means.

The B Ark scene in fact pre-dated everything in *Hitch-Hiker's,* having originally been written for a Ringo Starr show some years before which never got made. The comic possibilities of telephone sanitizers had also been touched on before by Douglas in a sketch called 'The Telephone Sanitizers of Navarone' in which a group of heroic telephone sanitizers heroically stormed the castle simply in order to clean their phones.

Interestingly we received several letters from telephone sanitizers saying they resented being singled out for attack but congratulating us for having a go at those dreadful management consultants. Curiously we also received some letters from management consultants complaining about our attack on them but thanking us for lampooning telephone sanitizers.

Tired TV Directors was a mis-print for Tri-D but we left it in because we thought there should be some tired TV Directors on the B Ark anyway.

The Captain's duck was subsequently to find itself on the cover of the second *Hitch-Hiker's* album. The bare legs that accompany it in the bath on that cover incidentally belong to Stephen Moore and the plastic duck itself now belongs to Douglas Adams. The duck motif was carried beyond logical extemes when, to publicize the album, a dozen live ducks were placed in the window of the HMV Record Shop in Oxford St, where they wandered around unhappily until the record company removed them under the possible threat of prosecution from the RSPCA.

Some would-be clever people wrote in to point out that six times nine actually equals fifty four and didn't we know how to do elementary mathematics? Some would-be even cleverer people wrote in to point out that six times nine does indeed equal forty-two if calculated in base thirteen. (What no one so far has spotted is that if you play a part of one of the episodes backwards you'll hear Bob Dylan explaining just what's gone wrong with Paul McCartney's career.)

Douglas was obsessed by the fact that the last scene should sound like a cinematic pull back from the figures of Ford and Arthur until they disappeared completely from view. He demonstrated this theory with much waving around of his arms and knocking over of tea cups. Not having any actual cameras to pull back with we finally overcame the problem by bringing the wind up a bit.

Music Details
Oxygene by Jean Michel Jarre
(Used in the opening speech and the escape capsule speech)
Volumina by Ligeti
(Used in the Haggunenon speech)
Volkstanz from the LP *Einsteig* bu Gruppe Between
(Used in the Circling Poets of Arium speech)

FIT THE SEVENTH

The show that began with the end of the world continues with Arthur Dent and Ford Prefect stranded on prehistoric Earth, and Zaphod Beeblebrox and Marvin thoroughly devoured by a carbon-copy of the Ravenous Bugblatter Beast of Traal.

GRAMS   JOURNEY OF THE SORCERER STARTS

NARRATOR   There is a theory which states that if ever anyone discovers exactly what the Universe is for and why it is here, it will instantly disappear and be replaced by something even more bizarrely inexplicable.

GRAMS   PEAK MUSIC ON ENTRY OF BASS

NARRATOR   There is another theory which states that this has already happened.

GRAMS   PEAK MUSIC AGAIN

NARRATOR   There is yet a third theory which suggests that both of the first two theories were concocted by a wily editor of *The Hitch-Hiker's Guide to the Galaxy* in order to increase the level of universal uncertainty and paranoia and so boost the sales of the Guide. This last theory is of course the most convincing, because *The Hitch-Hiker's Guide to the Galaxy* is the only book in the whole of the known Universe to have the words DON'T PANIC inscribed in large friendly letters on the cover.

GRAMS   PEAK MUSIC AGAIN FOR THEME PASSAGE

GRAMS   NARRATOR BACKGROUND

NARRATOR   Ursa Minor is almost certainly the most appalling place in the Universe. Though it is excrutiatingly rich, horrifyingly sunny and more full of wonderfully exciting people than a pomegranate is of pips it can hardly be insignificant that when a recent edition of the magazine *Playbeing* headlined an article with the words 'When you are tired of Ursa Minor you are tired of life', the suicide rate in the constellation quadrupled overnight.

Playbeing, a curious journal devoted in roughly equal parts to galactic politics, rock music, and gynaecology, has much to answer for in this respect. The current edition carries the results of an opinion poll in which the central offices of *The Hitch-Hiker's Guide to the Galaxy* have been voted the third hippest place in the whole of Ursa Minor. According to this same poll, the second hippest place in the whole of Ursa Minor is the entrance lobby to the same offices. This is what it sounds like.

F/X   ENTRANCE LOBBY ATMOSPHERE, PEOPLE WANDERING ABOUT, WEIRD MUSIC PLAYING IN THE BACKGROUND. AN INTERGALACTIC PHONE RINGS AND IS ANSWERED.

RECEPTIONIST   Hello, yes, Megadodo publications, home of *The Hitch-Hiker's Guide to the Galaxy*, the most wholly remarkable book in the whole of the known Universe, can I help you? What? Yes, I passed your message on to Mr Zarniwoop, but I'm afraid he's too cool to see you right now. He's on an intergalactic cruise. Yes, he is in his office, but he's on an intergalactic cruise.

GRAMS   NARRATOR BACKGROUND

NARRATOR   And according to this same *Playbeing* poll, the hippest place in the whole Galaxy is the left cranium of the fugitive Galactic President Zaphod Beeblebox. Just entering the air traffic space of Ursa Minor Beta is an enormous Arcturan Megafreighter carrying a larger number of copies of *Playbeing* than the mind can comfortably conceive.

F/X	FAIRLY DEEP HEAVY FREIGHTER LIKE BACKGROUND
ARC ONE	Ursa Minor Beta air traffic control this is AMF 3 requesting homing beacon for planetfall. Come in control.
ATR T. CONTROL	(**Lot of static & distort**) Ursa Minor Beta ATC receiving you. Beacon activated. Automatic docking will proceed in two hours.
ARC ONE	Acknowledged. Thank you A T C.
F/X	ELECTRONIC JIGGERY POKERY TO INDICATE ACTIVATED COCKING COMPUTERS
ARC ONE	Makes you sick, doesn't it captain.
CAPTAIN	What?
ARC ONE	Look at the visiscreen – see that big white city there the whole blooming thing is just Hitch-Hiker's offices, palm trees – and so many swimming pools you need a bloody gondola to get about.
CAPTAIN	Well that's success for you, isn't it?
ARC ONE	Is it? Is it? Well I ask myself. All gone soft haven't they – Hitch-Hiking, what do they know about it? Get one of that lot to stick out their thumb, it would probably fall off. I mean. It's all just fat cat business now. What's the name of that bloke who runs it now?
CAPTAIN	Maxelcat.
ARC ONE	Well you know what they say don't you. They had to move to a bigger planet because he got so fat he kept sliding off the old one. I've heard, you know, that they've created a whole electronically synthesized Universe in one of their offices so they can go and research stories during the day and still go to parties in the evening. Yeah, bloody clever of course, but it's nothing to do with the real Galaxy is it. Nothing to do with life.
CAPTAIN	Talk a lot don't you.
ARC ONE	Yeah, well not much else to do on these ships is there? Great automated monsters. I've had three buttons to press in the past five hundred light years and that was just to put the coffee machine on to manual.
ATR T CONTROL	Docking one hour fifty-four minutes.
CAPTAIN	Peter and out.
ARC ONE	Actually, I just picked up a hitch-hiker.
CAPTAIN	(**Startled**) You what?
ARC ONE	Odd bloke. He was in a bad way. He was hitching the hard way see, and so I said to myself . . .
ATR T CONTROL	Docking one hour fifty two minutes. Kevin and out.

CAPTAIN	Who is he?
ARC ONE	I don't know, didn't give his name, and he'd wrapped his heads in a towel so . . .
CAPTAIN	Heads?
ARC ONE	Yeah, just the two. I put him in the sleeping quarters to recover.
F/X	DOOR FLIES OPEN
ZAPHOD	I've recovered.
CAPTAIN	Who the hell are you?
ZAPHOD	Don't ask.
CAPTAIN	But . . .
ZAPHOD	Turn the radio on.
CAPTAIN	What?
ZAPHOD	Turn the radio on! Look, if it'll help you do what I tell you baby, imagine I've got a blaster ray in my hand.
CAPTAIN	**(Startled)** You have got a blaster ray in your hand.
ZAPHOD	So you shouldn't have to tax your imagination too hard. Turn it on.
F/X	'RADIO' ON!!!
RADIO	. . . and news reports brought to you here on the sub-ether wave band broadcasting around the galaxy around the clock, bringing light and enlightenment to all non-evolved life forms, saying a big 'hello' to all semi-evolved life forms and causing severe brain damage to anyone higher up the evolutionary ladder than a demented bee. But first the up to the minute shock news. Reports have just reached us that Zaphod Beeblebrox, the only man in history to terminate his term as Galactic President by stealing a spaceship he was meant to be launching, has finally met his end. Yes, the Big Z is now finally Big DEAD. We asked his private brain care specialist Gag Halfrunt if this was just a publicity stunt.
GAG	Well, Zaphod's just zis guy you know . . .
RADIO INTERVIEWER	But what about these reports which say that Zaphod Beeblebrox has been eaten by a Haggunenon?
GAG	Vell, he is an impetuous fellow you know.
INTERVIEWER	And is now seriously dead.
GAG	Who can say?
INTERVIEWER	Haggunenons are, are they not, super evolutionary life forms? That is to say they can re-evolve into any shape in a matter of seconds.
GAG	They are crazy mixed up animals you know?
INTERVIEWER	And it was while the Haggunenon had temporarily evolved into the form of

the Ravenous Bugblatter Beast of Traal that he ate Zaphod Beeblebrox.

GAG   Vell, zis is vot ve find.

INTERVIEWER   So it would be true to say that Zaphod Beeblebrox is finally dead.

GAG   True, but probably unimportant.

INTERVIEWER   And why is that?

GAG   Vell, Zaphod's just zis guy you know?

INTERVIEWER   And now some news from some of the outlying regions of the Galaxy. A report out today from the western spiral arm says that the wheel is commercially unviable . . .

ZAPHOD   Turn it off. (**This covers last line**)

F/X   RADIO OFF

ZAPHOD   Look, er sorry, I had to wave this blaster at you, but as you just heard I've had a bad day.

ARC ONE   What? You mean that's you?

ZAPHOD   Yeah.

ARC ONE   You do lead an interesting life don't you, Mr Beeblebrox?

GRAMS   NARRATOR BACKGROUND

NARRATOR   It is, of course, perfectly natural to assume that everyone else is having a far more exciting time than you. Human beings for instance have a phrase which describes this phenomenon – 'The other man's grass is always greener.'

The Shaltanac race of Broop Kidron Thirteen had a similar phrase, but since their planet is somewhat eccentric botanically speaking, the best they could manage was 'The other Shaltanac's joopleberry shrub is always a more mauvy shade of pinky russet', and so the expression soon fell into misuse and the Shaltanacs had little option but to become terribly happy and contented with their lot, much to the surprise of everyone else in the Galaxy who had not realized that the best way not to be unhappy is not to have a word for it.

Arthur Dent is, of course, terribly unhappy. As is now well recorded, he and Ford Prefect escaped from the planet Earth on the day that it was unexpectedly demolished to make way for a new hyperspace bypass. Bypasses are devices which allow some people to dash from point A to point B very fast whilst other people dash from point B to point A very fast. People living at C, being a point directly in between, are often given to wonder what's so great about point A that so many people from point B are so keen to get there and what's so great about point B that so many people from point A are so keen to get there. They often wish that people would just once and for all work out where the hell they want to be.

Arthur Dent and Ford Prefect know exactly where they don't want to be.

They don't want to be stranded on prehistoric Earth with a load of unwanted telephone sanitizers and advertising executives who have been thrown off their home planet of Golgafrincham, a world which has subsequently been wiped out by a particularly virulent disease contracted from an unexpectedly dirty telephone. Unfortunately, that is precisely where they are. But fortunately they have found a way of coping with their predicament. They are drunk.

FORD   Dingozekiness, there muzz be some way of getting off this planet other than getting high.

ARTHUR   You've been saying that for two years.

FORD   Have I? It must be true then.

ARTHUR   You've got all that electric hitching equipment in your satchel, and none of it seems to do a dickie bird.

FORD   We're just too far from the space lanes. The range is limited. Wait! I've got it!

ARTHUR   What? An answer?

FORD   It's a lateral thinking problem isn't it? We just have to sidle up to the problem sideways when it's not looking and . . . pounce!

ARTHUR   Well?

FORD   I knocked over the bottle of wine.

ARTHUR   But have you got the answer?

FORD   No, but I've got a different name for the problem.

ARTHUR   Let's have a drink. Here's another bottle.

FORD   Yes all right. No . . . look, every time we get to this point we just have another drink, till we're totally slarmied, and then next day start all over with . . . with . . .

ARTHUR   What's the matter?

FORD   (**Faintly and hoarsely**) Arthur . . . look!

ARTHUR   What are you looking at? . . . Good God!

FORD   It's only a bloody spaceship, isn't it? It's only hovering in the air a hundred yards from us.

ARTHUR   It looks very unreal doesn't it? Sort of ghostly.

FORD   But look, don't you realize, we're safe! We've been rescued. Come on, let's celebrate, pass that bottle.

ARTHUR   Right. Here.

FORD   Hey, where'd it go?

ARTHUR   What, the bottle?

FORD	No . . . the spaceship.
ARTHUR	What?
FORD	It's gone! The bloody thing's gone!
ARTHUR	Where did it go?
FORD	It just sort of . . . winked out of existence.
ARTHUR	Vanished . . .
FORD	Here.
ARTHUR	What?
FORD	Take the bottle, I can't face it.
ARTHUR	**(Sotto voce)** Ford.
FORD	Yeah?
ARTHUR	It's there again.
FORD	Heeeeeeyyyy, so it is . . . what's . . . going on?
ARTHUR	It just came again, pop. It comes and goes like magic.
FORD	Tell you our trouble mate, we're too sober by half. Come on, I will have that drink, I think I deserve . . . Chri . . .!!!
ARTHUR	It's gone again!
FORD	What is it? Some kind of deputation from Galactic Alcholics Anonymous?
ARTHUR	What do you mean by that?
FORD	Well haven't you noticed? Every time I put down the bottle it appears and every time I pick it up again it disappears! Look! I put it down, there it is, it's back again, I pick it up and poof it's gone. Here, gone, here, gone . . . see, it works.
ARTHUR	But that's mad.
FORD	Mad it may be mate , but I tell you one thing, I'm not touching another drop of your filthy elderflower stuff till we're safely out of this solar system. That's it. I've got it.
ARTHUR	It's an intelligence test.
FORD	Yes. No, no it isn't, it isn't at all, because that suggests someone's doing it deliberately and that's not it. There's a time paradox going on . . . we're caught at the crossroads of two alternative futures. You see?
ARTHUR	No.
FORD	I thought you wouldn't. Listen, the ship first appeared when I said you know let's actually sit down and work out this problem of getting off this planet, right?
ARTHUR	Yes.

FORD   And then every time we reached for a bottle instead or just expected the problem to solve itself the ship disappeared.

ARTHUR   Right.

FORD   So in one of the alternative futures we work out a way of signalling to a ship which then returns through time to pick us up, and in the other alternative we just get drunk and ignore the problem, so no solution, no ship. I wonder what Roosta would do?

ARTHUR   Who's Roosta?

FORD   Mate of mine. Another researcher on the *Guide*, great little thinker is Roosta and a great hitcher. He's a guy who really knows where his towel is.

ARTHUR   Knows what?

FORD   Where his towel is.

ARTHUR   Why should he want to know where his towel is?

FORD   Everybody should know where his towel is.

ARTHUR   I think your head's come undone.

GRAMS   NARRATOR BACKGROUND

NARRATOR   *The Hitch-Hiker's Guide to the Galaxy* has this to say on the subject of towels.

A towel, it says, is about the most massively useful thing any interstellar Hitch-Hiker can carry. For one thing it has great practical value – you can wrap it around you for warmth on the cold moons of Jaglan Beta, sunbathe on it on the marble beaches of Santraginus Five, huddle beneath it for protection from the Arcturan Megagnats as you sleep beneath the stars of Kakrafoon, use it to sail a miniraft down the slow heavy river Moth, wet it for use in hand to hand combat, wrap it round your head to avoid the gaze of the Ravenous Bugblatter Beast of Traal, (which is such a mind bogglingly stupid animal it assumes that if you can't see it, it can't see you) and even dry yourself off with it if it still seems clean enough.

F/X   ARCTURAN MEGAFREIGHTER BACKGROUND

ARC ONE   Those were the really great days of hitch-hiking of course. A man and his towel pitted against the Universe. I mean, that lot down there in them offices. I wouldn't give you an old face flannel for the lot of them. No disrespect to you of course Mr Beeblebrox, Mr President, sir, you're a totally different kettle . . .

ZAPHOD   Talk a lot, don't you? *You know, you remind me of something this really froody mate of mine once said. He spent a whole while stuck on this really weird little outback planet called Earth, right? A humanoid race, right? And they used to amaze him the way they just kept talking, like just always stating the really obvious, you know. Like they'd always say 'It's a nice day' or 'You're very tall, aren't you?' or 'Oh, dear, you seem to have fallen down a thirty foot well, are you all right?' And he came up with this theory about it – he thought if human beings don't keep exercising their lips their mouths probably seize up. Then he watched them a bit more, you know, and came up with a whole new theory. He said if they don't keep exercising their lips their brains start working.*

ARC ONE   (**A bit huffy**) *Well if that's how you feel . . .*

ZAPHOD   How soon till we dock at Ursa Minor Beta?

CAPT   Thirty minutes.

ZAPHOD   OK, now I can't risk being found in this freighter, I'd better go down in one of your EVA pods, should slip under the radar screens OK. Thanks for the ride guys.

ARC ONE   But why are you going to Ursa Minor Beta if you want to stay hidden.

ZAPHOD   I just wanted to find out what I'm doing.

ARC ONE   What?

ZAPHOD   Well, last night after I escaped from the Haggunenon . . .

ARC ONE   Yeah, how did you . . .

ZAPHOD   Shhh. I went into like a deep coma, and got this message from a person I admire, respect and deeply love.

ARC ONE   Who was that then?

ZAPHOD   Me.

ARC ONE   What? A message from yourself?

ZAPHOD   Yeah, it was a message I'd implanted in my own mind twenty years ago, which was triggered off by the coma and it just told me that the time had come, and I had to go and see this dude I'd never heard of who would tell me something to my disadvantage.

ARC ONE   Disadvantage?

ZAPHOD   Yeah, so I had to go didn't I?

ARC ONE   Why don't you tie a knot in your hanky like anyone else?

ZAPHOD   Style friend, style. Now come on, I got to go.

ARC ONE   But can I just ask you . . .

ZAPHOD   Yeah, what is it?

ARC ONE   That Haggunenon that ate you . . . how did you escape?

ZAPHOD   Ah, no problems. It was a super evolving species right?

ARC ONE   Yeah.

ZAPHOD   It ate me whilst it was playing at being the Ravenous Bugblatter Beast of Traal, and then like seconds later made the mistake of re-evolving into a really neat little escape capsule.

ARC ONE   It evolved into an escape capsule?

ZAPHOD	Yeah.
ARC ONE	But that's really incredible.
ZAPHOD	Yeah. I can't help it if I'm lucky.
F/X	POD DOOR CLOSES
COMPUTER VOICE	EVA pod Five launching.
F/X	POD LAUNCHED
GRAMS	NARRATOR BACKGROUND
NARRATOR	Several hours later, five billion tons of *Playbeing* magazine were unloaded on Ursa Minor Beta causing a slight but largely irrelevant shift in its orbital trajectory. A few hours later still, Zaphod Beeblebrox, the owner of what *Playbeing* readers had deemed the hippest place in the Universe, walked into the entrance lobby of *The Hitch-Hiker's Guide to the Galaxy*, deemed merely the second hippest place in Ursa Minor. Zaphod Beeblebrox does not like Ursa Minor either.
F/X	ENTRANCE LOBBY ATMOS (as before) DOOR FLIES OPEN
ZAPHOD	OK. Where's Zarniwoop, get me Zarniwoop.
RECEPT	Excuse me sir?
ZAPHOD	Zarniwoop. Get him right. Get him now.
RECEPT	Well sir, if you could be a little cool about it . . .
ZAPHOD	Look, I'm up to here with cool OK? I am so amazingly cool you could keep a side of meat in me for a month. I am so hip I have difficulty seeing over my pelvis. Now, will you move before I blow it?
RECEPT	Well, if you'd let me explain *sir*, I'm afraid that isn't possible right now as Mr Zarniwoop is on an intergalatic cruise.
ZAPHOD	When's he gonna be back?
RECEPT	Back sir? He's in his office.
ZAPHOD	This cat's on an intergalactic cruise in his office? Listen three eyes, don't you try to outweird me, I get stranger things than you free with my breakfast cereal.
RECEPT	Well, just who do you think you are honey, Zaphod Beeblebrox or something?
ZAPHOD	Yeah, count the heads.
RECEPT	Well, I'm sorry sir but . . . what did you say?
ZAPHOD	Ah, photons (**This is delivered as a swear word**)
RECEPT	You *are* Zaphod Beeblebrox?
ZAPHOD	Yeah, but don't shout or they'll all want one.
RECEPT	*The* Zaphod Beeblebrox?

ZAPHOD	No, just *a* Zaphod Beeblebrox, didn't you hear I come in six packs?
RECEPT	But sir, it was on the sub-ether radio this morning, it said you were dead . . .
ZAPHOD	Yeah, that's right, I just haven't stopped moving yet. Now, where do I find Zarniwoop?
RECEPT	Well sir, his office is on the fifth floor, but . . .
ZAPHOD	But he's on an intergalactic cruise, yeah yeah, how do I get to him?
RECEPT	The newly installed Sirius Cybernetics elevators are in the far corner sir.
ZAPHOD	Sirius Cybernetics Corporation. Oh Zarquon, haven't they collapsed yet?
RECEPT	Sir, can I ask why you want to see Mr Zarniwoop?
ZAPHOD	Yeah, I told myself I needed to.
RECEPT	Come again sir?
ZAPHOD	I came to myself in a dream and said 'Go see Zarniwoop'. Never heard of the cat before, but I seemed very insistent.
RECEPT	Mr Beeblebrox sir, you're so weird you should be in pictures.
ZAPHOD	Yeah, baby, and you should be in real life.
GRAMS	NARRATOR BACKGROUND
NARRATOR	It will take Zaphod Beeblebrox at least thirty seconds to cross the entrance lobby of the Hitch-Hiker offices, and at least another three minutes will then elapse before the offices are finally bombed to bits. It would therefore seem an appropriate moment to recount that Trillian also effected a fortuitous escape from the Haggunenons, only to be carried off and forcibly married to the President of the Algolian Chapter of the Galactic Rotary Club, whilst Marvin the Paranoid Android has survived a remarkable and unwieldy series of adventures which he has never been able satisfactorily to explain, and has now, by the most amazing coincidence, arrived exactly here.
MARVIN	Excuse me.
RECEPT	Yes, sir, can I help you?
MARVIN	I doubt it.
RECEPT	Well in that case, if you'll just excuse me . . .
MARVIN	No one can help me.
RECEPT	Yes sir, well . . .
MARVIN	Not that anyone's ever tried of course.
RECEPT	Is that so?
MARVIN	Hardly worth anyone's while really is it?
RECEPT	I'm sorry sir, if . . .

MARVIN   I mean where's the percentage in being kind or helpful to a robot if it doesn't have any gratitude circuits?

RECEPT   And you don't have any?

MARVIN   I've never had occasion to find out.

RECEPT   Listen you miserable heap of maladjusted metal . . .

MARVIN   Aren't you going to ask me what I want?

RECEPT   Is it worth it?

MARVIN   Is anything?

RECEPT   *What . . . do . . . you . . . want?*

MARVIN   I'm looking for someone.

RECEPT   *Who?*

MARVIN   Zaphod Beeblebrox. He's just walking over there.

RECEPT   Then why did you ask *me?*

MARVIN   I just wanted someone to talk to.

RECEPT   What???

MARVIN   Pathetic isn't it? Goodbye.

RECEPT   Oh father of Zarquon . . .

F/X   HE SLUMPS OVER HIS DESK

ZAPHOD   **(Fade him up. Is it good convention to do a quick cross fade here? Otherwise we have to just move Marvin across which will be boring)** Hey . . . Marvin? Marvin! How did you get here?

MARVIN   Don't ask.

ZAPHOD   But hey you crazy psychotic cybernaut, how are you kid?

MARVIN   I'm all right if you happen to like that sort of thing which personally I don't.

ZAPHOD   Yeah, yeah.

F/X   LIFT DESCENDS. DOOR OPENS

MARVIN   Hello lift.

LIFT   **(Soft muzakky sort of voice)** Hello. I am to be your elevator for this trip to the floor of your choice. I have been designed by the Sirius Cybernetics Corporation to take you, the visitor to *The Hitch-Hiker's Guide to the Galaxy*, into these, their offices. If you enjoy your ride which will be swift and pleasurable then you may care to experience some of the other elevators which have recently been installed in the offices of the Galactic tax department, Boobiloo baby foods and the Sirian state mental hospital, where many ex-Sirius Cybernetics Corporation Executives will be delighted to welcome your visits, sympathy and happy tales of life out in the big wide world.

ZAPHOD   Yeah? What else do you do besides talk?

LIFT   I go up or down.

ZAPHOD   Good. We're going up.

LIFT   Or down.

ZAPHOD   Yeah, OK, up please.

LIFT   Down's very nice.

ZAPHOD   Oh yeah?

LIFT   Super.

ZAPHOD   Good. Now will you take us up?

LIFT   May I ask you if you've considered all the possibilities that down might offer you?

ZAPHOD   Like what?

LIFT   Well, er there's the basement, the microfiles, the heating system . . . um. Nothing particularly exciting I'll admit, but they are alternative possibilities.

ZAPHOD   Ah, Zarquon's knees, did I ask for an existential elevator? What's the matter with the thing?

MARVIN   It doesn't want to go up. I think it's afraid.

ZAPHOD   Of what? Heights? An elevator that's afraid of heights?

LIFT   (**Miserably**) Of the future.

ZAPHOD   The future? What does it want, a pension scheme?

F/X   BEHIND THE LAST FEW LINES WE HAVE HEARD THE SOUNDS OF MANY LIFTS DESCENDING

LIFT   All Sirius Cybernetics Elevators can see into the future. It's part of our programming. (**Going down**)

ZAPHOD   Marvin – just get this elevator to go up will you? We've to got to get to Zarniwoop.

MARVIN   Why?

ZAPHOD   I don't know, but when I find him he'd better have one hell of a good reason for me wanting to see him.

GRAMS   NARRATOR BACKGROUND

NARRATOR   It should be explained at this point that modern elevators are strange and complex entities. The ancient electric winch and maximum capacity eight persons jobs bear as much relation to a Sirius Cybernetics Corporation Happy Vertical People Transporter as a packet of peanuts does to the entire West Wing of the Sirian State Mental Hospital. This is because they operate on the unlikely principle of defocused temporal perception, a curious system which enables the elevator to be on the right floor to pick you up even before you knew you wanted it, thus eliminating all the tedious chatting, relaxing, and making friends that people were previously forced to do whilst waiting for elevators.

Not unnaturally, many lifts imbued with intelligence and precognition became terribly frustrated with the mindless busines of going up or down, experimented briefly with the notion of going sideways as a sort of existential protest, demanded participation in the decision making process, and finally took to sulking in basements.

At this point a man called Gogrilla Mincefriend rediscovered and patented a device he had seen in a history book called a staircase. It has been calculated that his most recent tax bill paid for the social security of 5,000 redundant Sirius Cybernetics workers, the hospitalization of a hundred Sirius Cybernetics executives and the psychiatric treatment of over seventeen and a half thousand neurotic lifts.

F/X	DING OF LIFT ARRIVING AT DESTINATION
LIFT	Fifth floor, and remember I'm only doing this because I like your robot.
F/X	LIFT DOOR OPEN
ZAPHOD	Thanks a bundle.
F/X	LOW RUMBLING THUDS IN THE DISTANCE
ZAPHOD	Hey, what's that noise?
LIFT	I expect it's the future that I was so worried about, and it's about to get worse, so if you don't mind, I'm going straight back down. 'Bye now.
F/X	LIFT DOOR CLOSES VERY QUICKLY, LIFT DROPS OUT OF EARSHOT
ZAPHOD	Left in the lurch by a lift. Hey, you know something, Marvin?
MARVIN	More than you can possibly imagine.
ZAPHOD	I'm dead certain this building shouldn't be shaking.
F/X	MORE HEAVY THUDS
ZAPHOD	Either they've got some vibro system for toning up your muscles while you work . . .
MARVIN	Yes?
ZAPHOD	. . . or the building's being bombed. Who in the Galaxy would want to bomb a publishing company?
MARVIN	Another publishing company?
ROOSTA	(**Approaching in a hurry**) Beeblebrox! Over here!
ZAPHOD	No, Beeblebrox over here. Who are you?
ROOSTA	A friend.

ZAPHOD	Oh yeah? Anyone's friend in particular or just generally well disposed to people?
F/X	MUCH LOUDER EXPLOSION
ZAPHOD	(**Shouting above increasing level of noise**) Do you know your building's being bombed?
ROOSTA	What do you expect? Ever since you arrived on this planet last night you've been going round telling people that you're Zaphod Beeblebrox, but that they're not to tell anyone else.
ZAPHOD	Well I'm very insecure.
ROOSTA	Yeah, so's this planet now.
F/X	MORE EXPLOSIONS. A VERY LOUD HEAVY THROBBING HUM CROSSES THE SOUND PICTURE. THIS IS A VERY LARGE SPACESHIP PASSING BY OUTSIDE THE BUILDING
ZAPHOD	What is that? A whole battle fleet out there?
ROOSTA	It's your government out to get you, Beeblebrox. They've sent a squadron of Frogstar fighters.
ZAPHOD	Frogstar fighters? Zarquon!
ROOSTA	You see the picture?
ZAPHOD	What are Frogstar fighters?
ROOSTA	Get down!
F/X	A SEARING ZAP CROSSES THE SOUND PICTURE, IT TAKES ABOUT TWO SECONDS
ZAPHOD	That was a Frogstar fighter?
ROOSTA	No, that was a Frogstar scout robot out looking for you.
ZAPHOD	Hey, yeah?
F/X	ANOTHER DIFFERENT ZAP GOES ACROSS THE PICTURE
ZAPHOD	Hey, what was that?
ROOSTA	That was a Frogstar scout robot class B out looking for you . . .
ZAPHOD	Yeah?
F/X	ANOTHER DIFFERENT PLAYING ZAP
ZAPHOD	And that?
ROOSTA	A Frogstar robot scout class C out looking for you.
ZAPHOD	(**Pause**) Pretty stupid robots, eh?
ROOSTA	Yeah.
F/X	HUGE GRINDING CRACK FROM OTHER END OF CORRIDOR ACCOMPANIED BY HEAVY DYNAMO HUM

ZAPHOD	Holy photon, what's that?
ROOSTA	A frogstar robot class D. I should imagine it's just picked up the reports from the first three and has come to get you.
ZAPHOD	Wow, we've got to get out of here. Marvin!
MARVIN	What do *you* want? (**Emphasis on 'you'**)
ZAPHOD	See that robot coming towards us?
MARVIN	I suppose you want me to stop it.
ZAPHOD	Yeah.
MARVIN	Whilst you save your skins.
ZAPHOD	Yeah.
ROOSTA	Down this way. Zarniwoop's office.
ZAPHOD	Is this the time to keep an appointment?
ROOSTA	It's our only hope of escape. He's got a whole different Universe in his office. Come on.
ZAPHOD	Marvin, it's all yours.
MARVIN	Thanks a heap.
F/X	THEY RUN OFF
FROGSTAR ROBOT	Out of my way, little robot.
MARVIN	I'm afraid I've been left here to stop you.
FROG R	You? Stop me? Go on.
MARVIN	No, really I have.
FROG R	What are you armed with?
MARVIN	Guess.
FROG R	Guess?
MARVIN	Yes, go on, you'll never guess.
FROG R	Ermm . . . laser beam?
MARVIN	No.
FROG R	No, too obvious I suppose. Anti-matter ray?
MARVIN	Far too obvious.
FROG R	Yes . . . Er . . . how about an electron ram?
MARVIN	What's that?
FROG R	One of these.

F/X   DEVASTATING VOLLEY OF ELECTRONIC GUN, CRACKING WALLS, FALLING MASONRY
(Pause)

MARVIN   No, not one of those.

FROG R   Good though, isn't it?

MARVIN   Very good.

FROG R   I know, you must have one of those new Xanthic Re-Struction Destabilised Zenon Emitters.

MARVIN   Nice, aren't they?

FROG R   That what you got?

MARVIN   No.

FROG R   Oh, then it must be one of those things with twirls . . . goes whoosh . . .

MARVIN   You're thinking along the wrong lines, you know. You're failing to take into account something fairly basic in the relationship between men and robots.

FROG R   Er, I know, . . . I've seen them . . . quite big . . . er . . .

MARVIN   Just think. They left me, an ordinary menial robot, to stop you, a gigantic heavy duty battle machine, whilst they ran off to save themselves. What do you think they would leave me with?

FROG R   Something pretty damn devastating I would expect.

MARVIN   Expect, oh yes, expect. I'll tell you what they gave me to protect myself with, shall I?

FROG R   Yes, all right.

MARVIN   Nothing.

FROG R   What?

MARVIN   Nothing at all. Not an electronic sausage.

FROG R   Well, doesn't that just take the biscuit. Nothing, eh? Just don't think, do they?

MARVIN   And me with this terrible pain in all the diodes down my left side.

FROG R   Makes you spit, doesn't it?

MARVIN   Yes.

FROG R   Hell, that makes me angry. Think I'll smash that wall down.

F/X   QUICK DEMOLITION RAY JOB

MARVIN   *How do you think I feel?*

FROG R   *Just ran off and left you?*

MARVIN   *Yes.*

FROG R	*I think I'll shoot down their bloody ceiling as well.*
F/X	MORE RAYS & CRASHES
MARVIN	That's very impressive.
FROG R	You ain't seen nothing yet. I can take this floor out too, no trouble.
F/X	MORE DEMOLITION. THE FROGSTAR ROBOT FALLS THROUGH THE FLOOR WITH A DEAFENING CRY WHICH DIES AWAY AS IT FALLS THROUGH SEVERAL LOWER FLOORS AS WELL
MARVIN	What a depressingly stupid machine. (**Fade; fade up**)
F/X	FIRE. ALARMS ETC.
ZAPHOD	The building's on fire!
ROOSTA	You certainly make an entrance, don't you, Beeblebrox?
ZAPHOD	Well, it's a terrible building anyway.
F/X	IN THE DIN ANOTHER SOOTHING ALARM SYSTEM STARTS UP. IT SIMPLY DRONES 'DON'T PANIC, DON'T PANIC, DON'T PANIC'. ANOTHER DRONES 'EVERYTHING'S GOING TO BE ALL RIGHT, EVERYTHING'S GOING TO BE ALL RIGHT'
ZAPHOD	How do we get to this Universe then?
ROOSTA	I'm afraid it looks like we don't . . .
ZAPHOD	Hey, what, the building's cracking down the middle . . .
ROOSTA	Yes, that's not all . . . look down at the ground.
ZAPHOD	Hey, the ground's going away! Where are they taking it?
ROOSTA	They're not, they're taking the building. We're airborne.
F/X	RUSHING WIND
ZAPHOD	Look, what have I done to deserve this? I walk into a building, they take it away.
ROOSTA	*It's not what you've done they're worried about, it's what you're going to do.*
ZAPHOD	*Don't I get a say in it?*
ROOSTA	*You did, years ago. You'd better hold on, we're in for a long, long journey.* Let me introduce myself. My name's Roosta, and this is my towel.
ZAPHOD	Hi Roosta, hello towel. Where are they taking us?
ROOSTA	The Frogstar.
GRAMS	JOURNEY OF THE SORCERER
NARRATOR	Who is the mysterious Roosta? Who is the even more mysterious Zarniwoop and why hasn't he even appeared yet?

What will Zaphod's bewildering mission turn out to be?

Will it be something he finds stimulating and challenging or will it just be a monster wanting to take over the Universe for no very good reason?

How long will Ford and Arthur have to stay on the wagon and when will they be re-united with everyone else in the story?

Tune into the next exasperating series of *The Hitch-Hiker's Guide to the Galaxy* and find out.

ANNOUNCER   The magazine *Playbeing* can be obtained over the counter from any moderately disreputable Galactic newsagent.

FOOTNOTES

This one-off show was recorded on 20 November 1978 and transmitted on 24 December the same year, although some poeple who missed it first time round thought it had been written after all the other programmes in order to bridge the gap between the two series.

It was commissioned as a one off because most radio comedy shows do Christmas specials. The original idea was to do a real Christmas special in which the star that the Wise Men follow turns out to be Marvin, whose appearance as a shooting star has been caused by his catching alight on entering earth's atmosphere. His subsequent experiences after crashing into a stable in Bethlehem and encountering a baby and some shepherds would then cure him of his depression and he would leave the stable singing. This appealing idea was dropped because some people in the BBC thought that going out on Christmas Eve it could be considered 'Well, how shall we put it? . . . In slightly poor taste'. Equally importantly it didn't actually fit the plot so far (whatever that was). So it was designed to follow on from the first series and point the way forward to the second (or is that getting needlessly messianic?).

Several people, dismayed that the sixth programme could have been the last ever wrote in suggesting ways in which Zaphod *et al* could be saved from their apparent fate in the stomach of the carbon copy of the Ravenous Bugblatter Beast of Traal. These mostly involved the Haggunenon evolving into something really peculiar but Douglas' solution was simply to have it evolving into an escape capsule, thus saving any more tedious mucking around in hyperspace before everyone was re-united. However, it may just have had time to evolve first into an Organ and Tissue Replacing Unit as one listener suggested, in order for Marvin to regain the arm that he lost while being consumed.

Paddy Kingsland returned from the BBC schools department, presumably having passed, and for the rest of the shows he helped provide both the Radiophonic effects and most of the music. This gave us the opportunity of being rather more detailed in fitting the speech to the music; for instance, when the Book refers to Oolon Colloophid's flapping tendrils of guilt stretching and distorting the Universe, the musical notes behind are stretched and distorted as well. His return also saw a slight change in working method with more time being spent with just the two of us laying up and mixing scenes since, unlike the Paris, the Radiophonic workshop had a sixteen track machine.

This programme also saw the first use of 'snappies'. These are little booklets with carbon paper in between the pages, which enabled Douglas to type some scenes on the day of the recording and hand them to the actors. Because this paper is very flimsy and Douglas used to emerge clutching a handful of it from a little room in the Paris next to the toilets this led to the belief amongst some members of the cast that he was now typing the script on lavatory paper. The character of Roosta emerged on these snappies half way through the morning of the recording, and consequently Alan Ford, who played him, was pulled out of a television show he was doing and dragged down to the Paris at only half an hour's notice!

Geoffrey McGivern doubled up as the Frogstar robot, and David Tate quadrupled up (if there is such a word) as the Captain, the Receptionist, the Radio Commentator and the Lift. Bill Paterson was the Assistant Arcturan Pilot.

The background of pre-historic Earth was re-made after one or two people complained that at the end of the last series they had heard larks and didn't think there were any larks on pre-historic Earth. Not having any original sound recordings of pterodactyls or dinosaurs we made the background entirely from synthesised sounds, with the effect of a primeval swamp being made by blowing a straw through a cup of water and slowing it down.

Douglas has made the following note on towels.

Towels

This is an idea that got completely out of hand. It started as a private joke which I was therefore slightly reluctant to waste script space on. I put it in anyway because I then couldn't think of anything that wasn't just as much a waste of space and was then astonished to find that everyone else seemed to find it funny as well.

The way it came about was this: a year or so earlier I had been on holiday in Greece, staying in a small villa with some friends. Every morning we would start out for the beach, or rather try to start out for the beach and then have to delay for upwards of half an hour while I would try and find my towel. I could never find it, ever.

Whilst I was tearing my hair out in frustration, searching the bathroom, the washing line, the bedroom, under the bed, even in the bed, everyone else in the party would sit waiting patiently, drumming their fingers on their own rolled up towels.

I realized that my difficulties with my towel were probably symptomatic of the profound disorganization of my whole life, and that it would therefore be fair to say that anybody who was a really *together* person would be someone who would really know where their towel was.

I discovered, after I had inserted this phrase into the script, that a lot of other people must have had the same trouble as I had. [DNA]

The word Frood has no connection with the furniture maker of the same name who kindly sent us his business card.

The magazine *Playbeing* was originally Galactistud and probably changed for the traditional no-good-reason.

The idea of the elevator with a mind of its own comes from Douglas' time as a bodyguard in the Hilton. In the early hours of the morning the lifts would be put on a random setting, so sitting minding his own business in the corridor at three in the morning Douglas would suddenly see the lift stop at his floor, open its doors just to play a quick bit of muzak at him and then go off again.

The confrontation of Marvin and the Frogstar robot was originally dashed off as a quick and easy link between plot scenes, but has subsequently come to be the culmination of any live readings from the books. Therefore one or two lines cut from the original recording have been restored.

The sound of Frogstar robot class D was made from various bits of heavy clanking machinery and one listener wrote to ask if we were sadists since listening on headphones 'The Scout robots could be *felt* traversing from one ear to the other via the cerebral hemispheres down the cerebellum and out via the lower quadrants of the paraplocullis'. Another thing about wearing headphones is that it does unfortunately enable you to hear the edits better.

FIT THE EIGHTH

Zaphod Beeblebrox and his mysterious friend Roosta are being taken in a flying building to the evil Frogstar, whilst Ford Prefect and Arthur Dent are stranded on pre-historic Earth. Some of them are getting hungry.

FORD   I don't believe it. It's impossible.

ARTHUR   But it's happening.

GRAMS　NARRATOR BACKGROUND

NARRATOR　Reason notwithstanding, the Universe continues unabated. Its history is terribly long and awfully difficult to understand, even in its simpler moments which are, roughly speaking, the beginning and the end.

The wave harmonic theory of historical perception, in its simplest form, states that history is an illusion caused by the passage of time, and that time is an illusion caused by the passage of history.

It also states that one's perception of these illusions is conditioned by three important factors:
Who you are;
Where you are;
And when you last had lunch with Zaphod Beeblebrox.

Zaphod Beeblebrox's last meal was taken at the Restaurant at the End of the Universe, since when he has been catapulted through time in a Haggunenon spaceship, eaten by a carbon-copy of the Ravenous Bugblatter Beast of Traal, received strange and unedifying instructions from himself in his sleep, and in consequence made his way to the office building of *The Hitch-Hiker's Guide to the Galaxy* which was then unaccountably attacked by a squadron of Frogstar fighters, hauled in its entirety off the surface of the planet, and is now carrying Zaphod and his mysterious new friend Roosta in the general direction of the even more mysterious Frogstar. He is, therefore, not unnaturally feeling a little peckish.

F/X　GENERAL BACKGROUND OF LARGE OFFICE BUILDING FLYING THROUGH SPACE IN THE GRIP OF SEVEN POWERFUL TRACTOR BEAMS

ZAPHOD　Hey, Roosta, is there anything to eat in this situation?

ROOSTA　Here Zaphod. Suck this.
(Pause)

ZAPHOD　You want me to suck your towel?

ROOSTA　The yellow stripes are high in protein, the green ones have vitamin B and C complexes, the little pink flowers contain wheatgerm extract.

ZAPHOD　What are the brown stains?

ROOSTA　Bar-B-Q sauce. For when I get sick of wheatgerm.

ZAPHOD　Hey, it tastes as bad as it looks.

ROOSTA　Yes. When I've had to suck that end a bit, I usually need to suck the other end too.

ZAPHOD　Why, what's in that?

ROOSTA　Anti-depressants.

GRAMS　NARRATOR BACKGROUND

NARRATOR　Much has been written on the subject of towels, most of which stresses the many practical functions they can serve for the modern hitch-hiker.

Two seminal books are Werdle Sneng's compendious tome 'Bath Sheets in Space' which is far too large to carry, but sits magnificently on fashionable coffee tables, and Frat Gad's handbook, 'Heavily Modified Face Flannels' an altogether terser work for masochists.

However, only the Hitch-Hiker's Guide explains that the towel has a far more important psychological value, in that anyone who can hitch the length and breadth of the Galaxy, rough it, slum it, struggle against mind-boggling odds, win through, and still know where his towel is, is clearly a man to be reckoned with. Hence a phrase which has passed into hitch-hiking slang, as in 'Hey, you sass that Hoopy Ford Prefect? There's a frood who *really* knows where his towel is!'

Sass means 'know', 'be aware of', 'meet', 'have sex with'. Hoopy means 'really together guy' and frood means 'really amazing together guy'.

Meanwhile, important questions are beginning to frame themselves in Zaphod Beeblebrox's mind.

ZAPHOD   Hey, where did you say this building was flying to?

ROOSTA   The Frogstar. The most totally evil place in the Galaxy.

ZAPHOD   Do they have food there?

ROOSTA   Food? Have you the faintest idea what's going to happen to you at the Frogstar?

ZAPHOD   They're going to feed me?

ROOSTA   They're going to feed you all right.

ZAPHOD   Great.

ROOSTA   They're going to feed you into the Total Perspective Vortex.

ZAPHOD   The Total Perspective Vortex? Hey what's that, man?

ROOSTA   Only the most savage psychic torture a sentient being can undergo.

ZAPHOD   So, no food huh?

ROOSTA   Listen, you can kill a man, destroy his body, break his spirit, but only the Total Perspective Vortex can annihilate a man's soul. The treatment lasts one second, but the effects last your lifetime.

ZAPHOD   You ever had a Pan Galactic Gargle Blaster?

ROOSTA   This is worse.

ZAPHOD   Phrreeow!

F/X   TELEPORT ZING.

(A voice, quite a pleasant one, speaks to them suddenly. This is the Frogstar Prisoner Relations Officer).

FPRO   Ah hello there, you must be Zaphod Beeblebrox – yes?

ZAPHOD	Er yeah, hey who are you?
FPRO	Me? Oh, I'm the Frogstar Prisoner Relations Officer, and I'm just popping by to . . .
ZAPHOD	How did you get here?
FPRO	Oh the usual thing, worked my way up the ranks.
ZAPHOD	No, how did you get *here*? You just popped out of nowhere like a large drinks bill.
FPRO	I know, disconcerting isn't it? Look, I just popped along to see how you were getting on. Enjoying the trip?
ZAPHOD	No. Not at all.
FPRO	Oh well, it'll soon be over – we should be arriving at the Frogstar in an hour or so. It is as you may know, the most totally evil place in the Galaxy. Even I find it pretty horrifying, and I'm one of the most evil people on it.
ZAPHOD	(**Puzzled**) Yeah?
FPRO	Oh yes, quite staggeringly nasty. Anyway, enough of me, how about you? Is there anything in particular you want?
ROOSTA	Be careful . . .
ZAPHOD	What?
ROOSTA	This man is evil – he's from the Frogstar!
ZAPHOD	Ease up man, he just asked me if there's anything I wanted.
ROOSTA	But . . .
FPRO	Come on, Mr Beeblebrox . . . Zaphod . . . what would you like? What would you really like?
ZAPHOD	A steak, a big juicy steak.
FPRO	Beefsteak?
ZAPHOD	Yeah.
FPRO	Ah, delicious, and . . .
ZAPHOD	A crisp green salad, a hunk of cheese and . . .
FPRO	Some wine?
ZAPHOD	Algolian claret.
FPRO	The ninety one?
ZAPHOD	The ninety five.
FPRO	Excellent choice – anything else?
ZAPHOD	That'll do me just fine.
FPRO	Right. Turn the firehoses on him.

ZAPHOD	Hey, what?
F/X	FIREHOSES
FPRO	Enjoy your trip. Bye now.
F/X	TELEPORT ZING
ROOSTA	Don't say I didn't warn you Beeblebrox.
ZAPHOD	(**Spluttering with rage and water**) What the hell was the point of all that?
ROOSTA	They're just playing with you. Softening you up. I told you – they're going to put you in the Total Perspective Vortex.
ZAPHOD	But what is this thing? What does it do?
ROOSTA	The principle is very simple . . .
GRAMS	NARRATOR BACKGROUND
NARRATOR	Though the principle on which the Total Perspective Vortex works is indeed very simple, it will not for the moment be revealed. The purpose of this deliberate withholding of vital information is to occasion sensations of suspense, fear and anxiety within the legal limits laid down by the Galactic Statute of Narrative Practice. These sensations can be emphasised further by reference to this recording of a man being put in the Vortex . . .
F/X	BLOODCURDLING SCREAM
NARRATOR	And this one . . .
F/X	ANOTHER BLOODCURDLING SCREAM
NARRATOR	And this one . . .
F/X	A THIRD PARTICULARLY BLOODCURDLING SCREAM
NARRATOR	. . . provided that equal emphasis is given to the fact that one man in the entire history of the cosmos did survive its effects unharmed. To establish the identity of this man and see how he achieved it it is now necessary to travel two million years backwards in time, to where Ford Prefect and Arthur Dent are stranded in the primeval past of the utterly insignificant planet Earth.
	They are faced with a problem, in that a spaceship which has apparently travelled back in time to rescue them cannot materialize until they have worked out a way of sending a message forward in time to summon it. This is clearly a terribly convoluted temporal paradox of mind mangling complexity.
ARTHUR	Perhaps we could wave your towel at it.
FORD	You know what your trouble is Arthur, you've got as much grasp of multi-temporal causality as a concussed bee.
ARTHUR	You don't think it would work then?
FORD	No. That ship hovering there is only a potential ship, the possibility of one.

ARTHUR	We could still wave at it.
FORD	Yeah, very friendly, but chronologically inept. Listen, we have to send a message forward in time . . .
ARTHUR	Yes.
FORD	To where that spaceship is going to be.
ARTHUR	We don't know where.
FORD	No.
ARTHUR	We don't know when.
FORD	No.
ARTHUR	And anyway we haven't got a time machine.
FORD	No.
ARTHUR	So?
FORD	You're right.
ARTHUR	What?
FORD	We might just as well wave a towel at it.
ARTHUR	Right. **(Pause)**
BOTH	Helloooo! Hello spaceship! Cooeee! We're down here!
F/X	THE SLIGHT HUM WHICH THE SPACESHIP HAS HITHERTO BEEN EMANATING BUT WHICH I FORGOT TO MENTION SUDDENLY PICKS UP IN INTENSITY. IT IS ACCOMPANIED BY A SHARP INCREASE IN WIND, FORD AND ARTHUR'S VOICES ARE BUFFETED AND MUFFLED BY THE NOISE
ARTHUR	Ford! It's coming down! Look, it's coming down to us!
FORD	I don't believe it! It's impossible!
ARTHUR	But it's happening!
FORD	Hey, I don't like the look of that . . .
ARTHUR	What?
FORD	It's wobbling . . . I think it's going to crash! Fire your retro rockets you idiot!
F/X	IT FIRES ITS RETRO ROCKETS. VERY LOUDLY
FORD	Too hard! Much too hard! Run Arthur! Run for your life! Make for the hill!
F/X	RUMBLING CRASH OF EARTHQUAKE. FULL SENSURROUND TREATMENT
ARTHUR	What hill?

FORD	There was a hill there a moment ago . . .
ARTHUR	What, the rather nice one with all the daffodils?
FORD	Damn the daffodils, the whole hill's gone!
ARTHUR	The ground's heaving beneath us!
FORD	That ship's causing a bloody earthquake!
F/X	VOLCANO ERUPTING
ARTHUR	Look! The hill's come back! It's erupting! We must be on a volcanic fault.
F/X	LOTS MORE VOLCANO ERUPTION
FORD	(**A real lungbuster**) Watch out!!!
F/X	HUGE CRASH, AFTER WHICH THE CONTINUING SOUND OF THE EARTHQUAKE BECOMES RATHER MUFFLED. HOLD ON THAT SOUND FOR A MOMENT TO ESTABLISH
ARTHUR	(**Quiet**) Well. We did it.
FORD	Yeah.
ARTHUR	We flagged down a logically non-existent spaceship with a towel.
FORD	Yeah. Great.
ARTHUR	Marvellous.
FORD	Wonderful.
ARTHUR	Terrific.
FORD	Tell me Arthur . . .
ARTHUR	Yes?
FORD	This boulder we're stuck under, how big would you say it was? Roughly?
ARTHUR	Oh, about the size of Coventry Cathedral.
FORD	Do you think we could move it? (**Arthur doesn't reply**) Just asking. Can you feel my rucksack anywhere.
ARTHUR	Here.
FORD	You see, in these sorts of situations, that it's really good to have a guide to help you.
ARTHUR	What?
FORD	*The Hitch-Hiker's Guide to the Galaxy.* It tells you what to do in any eventuality.
ARTHUR	What, even being stuck in a crack in the ground beneath a giant boulder which you can't move, with no hope of rescue?
FORD	Yeah, it'll have something. Watch.
F/X	BOOK LOGO

GRAMS   NARRATOR BACKGROUND MUSIC

NARRATOR   What to do if you find yourself stuck in a crack in the ground underneath a giant boulder you can't move, with no hope of rescue. Consider how lucky you are that life has been good to you so far. Alternatively, if life hasn't been good to you so far, which given your current circumstances seems more likely, consider how lucky you are that it won't be troubling you much longer.

FORD   It's time I did something about that book.

ARTHUR   Shame we lost the towel.

FORD   What happened to it?

ARTHUR   Blew away in the wind. Fell in the river and a stream of lava rolled over it.

FORD   It'll give the archaeologists something to think about. 'Prehistoric towel discovered in lava flow. Was God a Marks and Spencer's sales assistant?' What are you doing?

ARTHUR   Feeling the rock above my head. It seems to be humming.

FORD   Humming?

ARTHUR   Why should a rock hum?

FORD   Perhaps it feels good about being a rock.

ARTHUR   No, I mean it's vibrating. As if it's got an engine in it.

FORD   You're crazy. A rock with an engine in it?

ARTHUR   Who would want a motorised rock?

FORD   Another motorised rock?

ARTHUR   Look! It's cracking! There's a hatchway opening underneath it!

FORD   Wow, this is one strange rock.

ARTHUR   Look at the light! Streaming out! Did you ever see anything like that before?

FORD   Not when I've been in a legal state of mind.

ARTHUR   **(Breathless with excitement, as if he's just seen the box office returns on 'Close Encounters of the Third Kind')**
Look! A figure silhouetted against the light . . . coming down the ramp . . . walking towards us!

FORD   Staggering towards us . . .

ARTHUR   It's hard to see . . . so much light!

FORD   He's in a bad way.

ARTHUR   He's stumbling towards a crack in the ground. Look, he's going to fall!

FORD   Look out!

ZAPHOD	**(For it is he)** Ahhhh! **(Fade and slight echo as he falls into the fissure)**
FORD	Zarquon! You know who I think that is?
ARTHUR	The faces looked familiar . . .
FORD	Zaphod? What's he doing coming out of a rock?
FORD	Who says he needs a reason? Come on, we've got to help him!
ARTHUR	**(Calling)** Zaphod!
ZAPHOD	Gnnnnhhh . . .
ARTHUR	Zaphod, you seem to have fallen down a thirty foot hole.
FORD	I think he knows that.
ARTHUR	Is he all right?
FORD	What does it look like? Zaphod . . .
ZAPHOD	Hhhhhrrrrrrr.
FORD	Zaphod, what happened to you?
ZAPHOD	**(Very slurred)** My heads hurt . . .
FORD	Can you tell me what happened?
ZAPHOD	They took me to the Frogstar . . .
FORD	**(Horrified)** The Frogstar!
ARTHUR	What's the Frogstar?
FORD	Shhh.
ZAPHOD	I've been in the Total Perspective Vortex . . .
FORD	**(Very low)** Oh no . . .
ARTHUR	What's the Total . . . ?
FORD	Shh.
ZAPHOD	Yes . . . Ford, I'm very ill . . .
FORD	If you've been in that thing . . .
ZAPHOD	Very ill. Very very ill.
ARTHUR	What's the Vortex?
FORD	The Vortex . . . it's the worst thing that can happen to anybody.
ZAPHOD	Oh no . . . the Vortex was OK, but . . . afterwards!
FORD	Afterwards? *After* the Vortex?
ZAPHOD	Well I had to celebrate didn't I? I've been drunk for a week. My heads are killing me. Help me up, will you? **(He passes out)**

F/X HEART OF GOLD BACKGROUND

EDDIE Hi there guys. This is Eddie your shipboard computer welcoming you back on board the starship Heart of Gold. We are currently heading away from planet Earth on Improbability Drive, and all systems are just tickitiboo. (**Sings**) 'Here we are again.'

ZAPHOD Well guys you must be so amazingly glad to see me you can't even find words to tell me what a cool frood I am.

ARTHUR What a what?

ZAPHOD I know how you feel. I am so great I get tongue-tied talking to myself. Hey, it's good to see you Ford. And Monkeyman.

ARTHUR Listen, I come from an ancient and distinguished race . . .

FORD Of hairdressers.

ARTHUR Thank you Ford.

FORD Hey Zaphod. Put it there, there . . .

ZAPHOD Hey Ford . . . put it there . . . and there . . . and there . . . and there . . . Wooah.

FORD Zaphod, how did you escape from the Haggunenon?

ZAPHOD Simple. I got lucky.

ARTHUR And how did you get this ship back?

ZAPHOD I got lucky.

FORD And how did you find us?

ZAPHOD I got your towel.

FORD What?

ZAPHOD Mailed by meteorite. Hey, that was a really neat trick, how did you do it?

ARTHUR Do what?

ZAPHOD Get the towel fossilized so when the planet blows up two million years later it gets hurled off into space and picked up by the Improbability Drive?

FORD Hey?

ZAPHOD How did you work it all out.

ARTHUR We didn't. I just dropped the towel.

ZAPHOD So you got lucky too. That's cool. We're going to need a lot of luck where we're going next.

ARTHUR Where's that?

ZAPHOD I'll tell you when you've asked me what happened on the Frogstar.

ARTHUR What's the Frogstar?

ZAPHOD	I thought you'd never ask.
GRAMS	NARRATOR BACKGROUND
NARRATOR	Many stories are told of Zaphod Beeblebrox's journey to the Frogstar. 10% of them are 95% true, 14% of them are 65% true, 35% of them are only 5% true, and all the rest of them are . . . told by Zaphod Beeblebrox. Only one wholly accurate account exists, and that is locked in a trunk in the attic of Zaphod's favourite mother, Mrs Alice Beeblebrox of 10 to the 8th Astral Crescent Zoofroozelchester, Betelgeuse Five.
	Though countless people have tried cajolery, bribery or threats to get hold of it she has carefully guarded it from all eyes for many years, waiting for what she calls 'the right price'. But one fairly well documented episode is referred to by Beeblebroxologists as the 'Hey Roosta, I've just had this really hoopy idea' incident.
F/X	FLYING BUILDING BACKGROUND
ZAPHOD	Hey Roosta, I've just had this really hoopy idea. We're in this wrecked building, right?
ROOSTA	Right.
ZAPHOD	And the building's in this really amazing force bubble, right?
ROOSTA	Right.
ZAPHOD	And the force bubble's flying through interstellar space, right?
ROOSTA	Right.
ZAPHOD	And there are seven Frogstar fighters towing us at about hyperspeed twelve to the Frogstar, right?
ROOSTA	It had better be a good idea, Beeblebrox.
ZAPHOD	It's a smash. You want to hear it?
ROOSTA	OK.
ZAPHOD	Let's go to a discotheque.
	(Pause)
ROOSTA	Are you crazy?
ZAPHOD	What's the matter, don't you like discotheques? Look, I got this free invite some cat was giving out in the street. Here it is.
ROOSTA	Ah, I'm with you Beeblebrox. You reckon we could slide this plastic invite into a door lock, break out of this building, climb into one of the Frogstar fighters, and then maybe overpower all the guards with this terrifying small plastic card.
ZAPHOD	Look at the card will you?
ROOSTA	'Worm Hole Disco. Loudest Noise on Betelgeuse. Free Body Debit for One Night Only'. What's a body debit?

ZAPHOD	You've been roughing it too long Roosta, you missed out on progressive consumerism. Look, an old style credit card, you press the panel, it makes an instant debit on your bank account, and an instant credit to the shop's account right?
ROOSTA	I prefer hard cash. If you can't scratch a window with it I don't accept it.
ZAPHOD	Yeah, but get this. Body debit means you press this card, and it debits all your molecules from where you're standing – and your body goes into credit somewhere else.
ROOSTA	In the Disco!
ZAPHOD	Right.
ROOSTA	Escape! It had better be a good disco.
ZAPHOD	If it was a good disco, they wouldn't have to give away free Body Debit cards. Right Roosta, we're going to groove our way out of here.
F/X	BODY DEBIT EFFECT
GRAMS	SENSATIONALLY LOUD ROCK MUSIC. WE CAN HARDLY DISTINGUISH WHAT IT IS, THE DISTORTION LEVELS ARE SO HIGH WE GRADUALLY MAKE OUT THE SOUNDS OF ZAPHOD AND ROOSTA'S VOICES
ZAPHOD	We did it.
ROOSTA	What did you say?
ZAPHOD	I said we did it!
ROOSTA	What did you say?
ZAPHOD	What?
ROOSTA	I said what did you say?
ZAPHOD	I can't hear.
ROOSTA	What?
ZAPHOD	What?
ROOSTA	What?
ZAPHOD	What?
ROBOT GIRL	Hi there baby, you want to dance?
ZAPHOD	No, do I look like I want to dance?
ROBOT GIRL	You look like it to me.
ZAPHOD	I must have got my wrong body on.
ROBOT GIRL	Suit yourself . . .
	(Then ad libs from Robot Girls) . . .
ROBOT GIRLS	Hi, there baby . . . do you want to dance? Etc.

ROOSTA	Beeblebrox, all these dancers – they're robots!
ZAPHOD	They're just to make the place look crowded, give it some atmosphere.
ROOSTA	But there aren't any real people here at all.
ZAPHOD	So what's new?
ROOSTA	Uuggh!
ZAPHOD	What's up?
ROOSTA	I just walked past this nozzle in the wall. It's spraying the smell of hot sweat over everything.
ZAPHOD	OK, let's get out of here. Can you see a door?
ROOSTA	Yeah, it's right in the far corner.
ZAPHOD	Let's go.
ROBOT 2	You cannot go! You must have a good time!
ZAPHOD	I'm trying to have a good time, I'm trying to go!
ROBOT 2	Turn up the music!
F/X	THE MUSIC UNBELIEVABLY GETS LOUDER
ROOSTA	Aaaaaaaaghh!
ROBOT 2	You must have a good time!
ROBOT 3	You must dance!
ROBOT 2	Do you come here often?

(Zaphod and Roosta are reduced to strangulated cries for help . . .)

ROBOT GIRLS	Dance! Dance! Dance!
ROBOT 2	They are passing out! Spray them with adrenalin! Make the lights flash faster!
ZAPHOD	Let's go!
F/X	Door opens and closes rapidly behind them. Music winds down.
F/X	BODY DEBIT EFFECT
ROBOT GIRL	Organic lifeforms have no sense of fun.
F/X	ROBOTS ALL COLLAPSE IN A HEAP
ZAPHOD	(Gasps) That must be the worst good time I ever had. Still, we're free.
FPRO	Ah, there you are, splendid.
ZAPHOD	You! Hey man how did you get to be here?
FPRO	Me? I came the simple way. Down the stairs.
ZAPHOD	Down the stairs? To Ursa Minor? Hey, you must be unbelievably fit.
FPRO	Ah, I'm afraid you're not on Ursa Minor. We didn't let you out of the

building. This has all been a little in flight entertainment.

ZAPHOD   You call that entertainment?

FPRO   Not for you, for me. Well, I'm afraid I must leave you now.

ZAPHOD   Ah. And just when I was really getting to dislike you.

FPRO   I feel very privileged to have been able to bring a little unnecessary unpleasantness into your life, Mr Beeblebrox sir. I wonder if you'd like to sign an autograph for me.

ZAPHOD   An autograph? You must be several light years removed from your skull baby.

FPRO   I have a photo of you here. If you could just see your way to . . .

ZAPHOD   Ah come on, go suck a neutron star will you? Hey, that's quite a nice pic. Let's see it. OK, look 'With deep anger and resentment, Zaphod Beeblebrox.' OK?

FPRO   Thank you. It's not for my daughter you understand, it's for me. I have to put it in the Frogstar record office attached to a statement saying that you went into the Vortex of your own free will.

ZAPHOD   Baby, I think there's some problem with your respiration.

FPRO   Oh? What?

ZAPHOD   You're breathing.

FPRO   That's not a problem.

ZAPHOD   It is from where I'm standing. Here, let me tie a knot in your neck.

FPRO   **(Gasping)** If you try and strangle me Beeblebrox you'll regret it . . .

ZAPHOD   Yeah, not half as much as you will.

FPRO   Don't say I didn't warn you.

F/X   DEMAT ZING

ZAPHOD   Owww! Ffff . . . Roosta, did you see that? The guy vanished whilst I was . . . ahhh! I think I've broken my thumb on my other thumb . . . Roosta? Roosta? Where are you?

GARGRAVARR   **(Deep ethereal echoing voice that seems insubstantial somehow, it fades periodically)**

Beeblebrox, you are on your own now. You have arrived on the Frogstar.

ZAPHOD   Hey, what? Who are you?

GARGRAVARR   I am Gargravarr. I am the Custodian of the Total Perspective Vortex.

ZAPHOD   Oh, er, hi.

GARGRAVARR   **(Gravely)** Hello.

ZAPHOD   Hey, er, why can't I see you? Why aren't you here?

GARGRAVARR	*I* am here. My body wanted to come, but it's a bit busy at the moment. Things to do, people to see. You know how it is with bodies.
ZAPHOD	I thought I did.
GARGRAVARR	I hope it's gone in for surgery. The way it's been living recently it must be on its last elbows.
ZAPHOD	Elbows? You mean its last legs?
GARGRAVARR	I know what I mean.
ZAPHOD	Hey, wild.
GARGRAVARR	So you are to be put into the Vortex, yes?
ZAPHOD	Er, well, this cat's in no hurry you know. I can just slouch about, take in a look at the local scenery, you know.
GARGRAVARR	Have you seen the local scenery?
ZAPHOD	Er, no.
F/X	DOOR HUMS OPEN. MOURNFUL WAIL OF DISMAL WIND.
ZAPHOD	Ah. OK, well I'll just slouch about then.
GARGRAVARR	No. The Vortex is ready for you now. You must come. Follow me.
ZAPHOD	Er, yeah – how am I meant to do that?
GARGRAVARR	I'll hum for you. Follow the humming.
ZAPHOD	OK. Anything for a weird life.
GRAMS	NARRATOR BACKGROUND
NARRATOR	The Universe, as has been observed before, is an unsettlingly big place, a fact which for the sake of a quiet life, most people tend to ignore. Many would happily move to somewhere rather smaller of their own devising, and this is what most beings in fact do.
	For instance, in one corner of the Eastern Galactic Arm lies the great forest planet Oglaroon, the entire 'intelligent' population of which lives permanently in one fairly small and crowded nut tree. In which tree they are born, live, fall in love, carve tiny speculative articles in the bark on the meaning of life, the futility of death and the importance of birth control, fight a few very minor wars, and eventually die strapped to the underside of some of the less accessible outer branches.
	In fact the only Oglaroonians who ever leave their tree at all are those who are hurled out for the heinous crime of wondering whether any of the other trees might be capable of supporting life at all, or indeed be anything other than illusions brought on by eating too many Oglanuts.
	Exotic though this behaviour may seem, there is no life form in the Galaxy not in some way guilty of the same thing, which is why the Total Perspective Vortex is as horrific as it undoubtedly is. For when you are put in the Vortex you are given just one momentary glimpse of the size of the

entire unimaginable infinity of Creation along with a tiny little marker saying 'You are here'.

F/X	BACKGROUND. THE MOURNFUL WAILING OF THE WIND (WIND EFFECT SLOWED DOWN MIGHT GIVE US WHAT WE NEED) GARGRAVARR HUMMING A MOURNFUL LITTLE WALTZ. ALMOST INSTANTLY THE SCENE STARTS THERE IS A TERRIBLE CRY OF AGONY IN THE DISTANCE, MUFFLED AND DISTORTED, BUT STILL LOUD ENOUGH TO TERRIFY THE WITS OUT OF ANYBODY. ZAPHOD WALKING
ZAPHOD	(Stops walking) Hey man, what was that?
GARGRAVARR	(Stops humming) A man being put in the Vortex I'm afraid. We're very close to it now.
ZAPHOD	Hey, it sounds really bad. Couldn't we maybe go to a party or something for a while, think it over?
GARGRAVARR	For all I know I'm probably at one. My body that is . It goes to a lot of parties without me. Says I only get in the way. Hey ho.
ZAPHOD	I can see why it wouldn't want to come here. This place is the dismallest. Looks like a bomb's hit it you know.
GARGRAVARR	Several have. It's a very unpopular place. The Vortex is in the heavy steel bunker ahead of you.
F/X	ANOTHER HOWL OF AGONY
ZAPHOD	The Universe does that to a guy?
GARGRAVARR	The whole infinite Universe. The infinite suns, the infinite distances between them, and yourself an invisible dot on an invisible dot, infinitely small.
ZAPHOD	Hey, I'm Zaphod Beeblebrox man, you know.
GARGRAVARR	That is precisely the point.
F/X	DOOR HUMS OPEN
GARGRAVARR	Enter.
ZAPHOD	Hey, what, now?
GARGRAVARR	Now.
ZAPHOD	It doesn't look like any kind of Vortex to me.
GARGRAVARR	It isn't. It's just the lift. Enter.
F/X	HE ENTERS: DOOR CLOSES. IT STARTS TO DESCEND
ZAPHOD	I got to get myself in the right frame of mind for this.
GARGRAVARR	There is no right frame of mind.
ZAPHOD	You really know how to make a guy feel inadequate.

GARGRAVARR	I don't. The Vortex does.
F/X	LIFT REACHES BOTTOM. THE DOORS OPEN, BACKGROUND NOISE OF HEAVY HUMMING NOISES AND SWIRLS ETC.
GARGRAVARR	There. The Vortex. The Total Perspective Vortex. Enter Beeblebrox. Enter the Vortex.
ZAPHOD	OK, OK.
F/X	VORTEX STARTING TO OPERATE
GRAMS	NARRATOR BACKGROUND
NARRATOR	The Vortex derives its picture of the whole Universe on the principle of extrapolated matter analyses.

To explain – since every piece of matter in the Universe is in some way affected by every other piece of matter in the Universe, it is in theory possible to extrapolate the whole of Creation, every Galaxy, every sun, every planet, their orbits, their composition, and their economic and social history from, say, one small piece of fairy cake. The Man who invented the Total Perspective Vortex did so basically in order to annoy his wife.

Trin Tragula, for that was his name, was a dreamer, a speculative thinker, or as his wife would have it, an idiot.

And she would nag him incessantly about the utterly inordinate amount of time he would spend staring out into space, or mulling over the mechanics of safety pins, or doing spectrographic analyses of pieces of fairy cake. 'Have some sense of proportion' she would say thirty eight times a day.

And so he built the Total Perspective Vortex, just to show her. And in one end he plugged the whole of reality as extrapolated from a fairy cake, and in the other end he plugged his wife, so that when he turned it on she saw in one instant the whole infinity of creation and herself in relation to it.

To Trin Tragula's horror, the shock annihilated her brain, but to his satisfaction he realized he had conclusively proved that if life is going to exist in a Universe this size the one thing it cannot afford to have is a sense of proportion. And it is into this Vortex that Zaphod Beeblebrox has been put, and from which a few seconds later he emerges.

ZAPHOD	Hi.
GARGRAVARR	(**Stunned**) Beeblebrox. You're . . .?
ZAPHOD	Fine, fine. Could I have a drink please?
GARGRAVARR	You have been in the Vortex?
ZAPHOD	You saw me kid.
GARGRAVARR	And you saw the whole infinity of creation?
ZAPHOD	The lot, baby. It's a real neat place, you know that?
GARGRAVARR	And you saw yourself in relation to it all.

ZAPHOD   Yeah, yeah.

GARGRAVARR   And what did you experience?

ZAPHOD   It just told me what I knew all the time. I'm a really great guy. Didn't I tell you baby. I'm Zaphod Beeblebrox.

GRAMS   JOURNEY OF THE SORCERER

NARRATOR   Is it really true that Zaphod Beeblebrox's ego is as large as the Universe?

Does this actually have any bearing on anything else in the story, or indeed on anything else at all?

Has everyone totally forgotten about the increasingly mysterious Zarniwoop, last heard of taking an inter-galactic cruise in his office?

Is it worth hanging on to find out the answers to these exasperating questions? Find out in the next unedifying episode of *The Hitch-Hiker's Guide to the Galaxy.*

ANNOUNCER   Information about package holidays on the Frogstar can be found in the leaflet 'Sun, Sand and Suffering on the Most Totally Evil Place in the Galaxy.'

ZAPHOD   Hey, man, is that a piece of fairy cake? My stomach's completely out to lunch. Mmmmmmm. Yeah.

FOOTNOTES

This show marked the start of the second series. The first series had been launched in a blaze of silence but the new series had the unusual distinction for a radio show of being on the front cover of the Radio Times. Douglas said he found the experience rather like running down the street stark naked (something I believe he has been known to do in the early hours of the morning).

The pressures of having to live up to the first series help explain why it took three separate recordings to finish this episode, starting on 19 May 1979. Had the rest of the shows taken three recordings some of the cast would have been set up for life (or, being radio, a week) with the multiple recording fees they were receiving.

The pressures on the production team were almost as strong, with the series scheduled to go out on Radio Four every night of the week from 21 January 1980, meaning that every programme had to be finished by 25 January.

This first programme was previewed for the critics the week before transmission in a scene that rather recalled the five hundred and seventy third meeting of the colonization committee of the planet of Fintlewoodlewix in its smooth efficiency. For complicated reasons the BBC's Press playback room is staffed by people who are almost, but not quite, technical staff and almost, but not quite, employed to look after hospitality. So while they knew a little bit about tape recorders they didn't actually know how to work the one in the Press playback room, and while they brought a tray of drinks into the room they didn't actually offer anybody one. In their efforts to get the highly sophisticated BBC playback machine to work several attempts were made to get it started by pressing the record button so it's a miracle that the programme came out of the room without little gaps in the middle of it. A sort of sound was finally achieved through a small mono speaker in the corner of the room round which all the critics crowded, and it was an act of great charity on their part that they still managed to write very favourably about the show.

David Tate was once more Eddie, as well as the Frogstar Prison Relation Officer and the sepulchral Valentine Dyall (who played Deep Thought on the first *Hitch-Hiker's* record) was Gargravarr.

The dramatic descent of the Heart of Gold and the accompanying earthquake were in fact made in a very mundane way. The earth cracking was essentially the sound of a tree falling down and the furious firing of the rockets was made by blowing a raspberry into the microphone.

By telling Ford to 'Put it there' four times (a line, incidentally, ad libbed in recording) Zaphod suggest that a further addition has been made to his quota of arms.

The Book's towel speech was originally part of the other speech on towels in programme seven.

To record the robot disco scene Zaphod and Roosta were fed loud rock music through their headphones in order to get the right level of projection, and the various robot disco girls were played by the other actors who were dotted individually around the microphone cupboard, corridors etc and later mechanically treated.

The other worldly disco music was in fact the Bee Gees *Staying Alive* made in 7/4 time by cutting out a note every two bars, and then played backwards (some people might think this a distinct improvement on the original). It was made to sound deafeningly loud, without actually being deafeningly loud, by feeding it through a speaker in another room and then recording that.

The basic voice treatment of Gargravarr was made from a flanger and tape echo (a technique first used ages ago by The Small Faces on *Itchycoo Park*). Two tape recorders are used, one of which is slightly out of synch. in order to give a swirling effect. Some of Gargravarr's lines were repeated, being dotted around the stereo picture to help create the sense of a lack of physical presence. There is probably a very easy way of doing this, but we didn't know it at the time and so just copied each line we wanted to repeat and then overlapped them.

The basis of the Vortex itself was a synthesizer drone with a high pitched whooshing noise added, all put through the inevitable flanger. The impact noise was made by banging the insides of a very expensive Beckstein piano . . . an effect that had the additional benefit of a horrible scream caused by hitting the piano so hard that it knocked the strut away and the lid fell on my fingers.

FIT THE NINTH

In which our heroes have the chance to chew the fat with some old enemies and Arthur Dent has an unpleasant cup of tea.

EDDIE Man and machines share in the stimulating exchange of . . . aaargh.

GRAMS NARRATOR BACKGROUND

NARRATOR Having been through the Total Perspective Vortex Zaphod Beeblebrox now knows himself to be the most important being in the entire Universe, something he had hitherto only suspected. It is said that his birth was marked by earthquakes, tidal waves, tornadoes, firestorms, the explosion of three neighbouring stars and, shortly afterwards, by the issuing of over six and three quarter million writs for damages from all the major landowners in his Galactic sector. However, the only person by whom this is said is Beeblebrox himself, and there are several possible theories to explain this.

F/X HEART OF GOLD BACKGROUND

ARTHUR Ford.

FORD Yeah?

ARTHUR He's totally mad isn't he?

FORD Well the border between madness and genius is very narrow.

ARTHUR So's the Berlin Wall.

FORD The . . .??

ARTHUR Berlin Wall. The border between East and West Germany. It's very narrow. The point I'm . . .

FORD *Was* very narrow. Get your tenses right.

ARTHUR Thank you.

FORD Anything wrong?

ARTHUR On Earth we have . . .

FORD Had.

ARTHUR Had . . . a word called tact.

FORD Oh yes?

ARTHUR Yes.

FORD And what happened to it?

ARTHUR Well, apparently it's not in common usage.

FORD Not the word, the Earth.

ARTHUR You know very well. It got demolished to make way for a hyperspace bypass.

FORD But that was all done away with centuries ago. No one demolishes planets anymore.

ARTHUR The Bogons did.

FORD Vogons. Odd that.

ARTHUR   You mean . . .

FORD   They had another reason? Could be. Probably not important though. I only bring it up because I've been watching the screen and there's been a Vogon fleet five light years behind us for the last half hour. Where's Zaphod?

ARTHUR   A Vogon fleet?

FORD   Yes. Where's Zaphod?

ARTHUR   He's in his cabin signing photographs of himself. 'To myself with frank admiration'. But why are the . . .

FORD   Hey, Marvin.

MARVIN   What do you want?

FORD   Give Zaphod a yell will you?

MARVIN   Ah. Mind taxing time again is it?

FORD   Just get on with it.

MARVIN   I've just worked out an answer to the square root of minus one.

FORD   Go and get Zaphod.

MARVIN   It's never been worked out before. It's always been thought impossible.

FORD   Go and . . .

MARVIN   I'm going. (**As he goes**) Pausing only to reconstruct the whole infrastructure of integral mathematics in his head, he went about his humble task, never thinking to ask for reward, recognition or even a moment's ease from the terrible pain in all the diodes down his left side. Fetch Beeblebrox they say, and forth he goes . . .

F/X   HIS FADING VOICE IS CUT OFF BY THE CLOSING DOOR

DOOR   Glad to be of service.

ARTHUR   (**Sympathetically**) Don't you think we should do something for him?

FORD   We could rip out his voice box for a start.

ARTHUR   What are you in such a mood about?

FORD   I'm worried about them.

ARTHUR   The Bogons?

FORD   The Vogons. Yes.

GRAMS   NARRATOR BACKGROUND

NARRATOR   Prostetnic Vogon Jeltz was not a pleasant sight, even for other Vogons. His highly domed nose rose high above a small piggy forehead. His dark green rubbery skin was thick enough for him to play the game of Vogon politics, and play it well, and waterproof enough for him to survive indefinitely at sea depths of up to a thousand feet with no ill effects. Not that he ever went swimming of course. He was the way he was because billions of years ago, when the Vogons had first crawled out of the sluggish primeval seas of Vogsphere, and had lain panting and heaving on the planet's virgin shores . . . when the first rays of the bright young Vogsol sun had shone across them that morning, it was as if the forces of evolution had simply turned away in disgust and given up on them there and then. They never evolved again: they should never have survived.

The fact that they did is some kind of tribute to the thick willed slug brained stubbornness of these creatures. Evolution? – they said to themselves – Who needs it? And what nature refused to do for them they simply did without until such time as they were able to rectify the grosser anatomical inconveniences with surgery. Meanwhile, the natural forces on the planet Vogsphere had been working overtime to make up for their earlier blunder.

They brought forth scintillating jewelled scuttling crabs, which the Vogons ate, smashing their shells with iron mallets; *tall aspiring trees which the Vogons cut down and burnt the crab meat with;* elegant gazelle like creatures with silken coats and dewy eyes which the Vogons would catch and sit on. They were no use as transport because their backs would snap instantly, but the Vogons sat on them anyway.

Thus the planet Vogsphere passed the miserable millenia until by an unhappy chance the Vogons discovered the secret of interstellar travel. Within a few short Vog years every last Vogon had migrated to the Megabrantis cluster – the political hub of the Galaxy – and now form the immensely powerful backbone of the Galactic Civil Service.

They have attempted to acquire learning, they have attempted to acquire style and social grace, but in most respects the modern Vogon is little different from his primitive forebears. *Every year they import twenty seven thousand scintillating jewelled scuttling crabs from their native planet and while away a happy drunken night smashing them to bits with iron mallets.* Prostetnic Vogon Jeltz is a fairly typical Vogon in that he is thoroughly vile.

VOGON Is that definitely the ship?

VOGON 2 Affirmative captain. We have confirmed positive identification.

VOGON Don't answer back!

VOGON 2 What?

VOGON I said don't . . .

VOGON 2 But I was just answering your . . .

VOGON Don't interrupt!

VOGON 2 I wouldn't dare captain.

VOGON Yes you would, you just did. You dare to lie to me!

VOGON 2 No captain.

VOGON Don't contradict me!

VOGON 2 I didn't captain, I . . .

VOGON	Well you did just then.
VOGON 2	What?
VOGON	I said . . .
VOGON 2	I didn't mean to captain, I . . .
VOGON	Don't interrupt! Guard!
GUARD	Captain?
VOGON	Take this object away and shoot it.
GUARD	Shoot him captain?
VOGON	Don't question my orders!
GUARD	Of course not captain, I wouldn't dream of it.
VOGON	You dare to patronize me!
GUARD	No captain, honestly, I . . .
VOGON	When you've shot the prisoner . . .
GUARD	Yes captain?
VOGON	Shoot yourself.
GUARD	Myself? But . . .
VOGON	Then throw yourself out of the nearest airlock.
GUARD	Yes captain. At once captain.
F/X	DOOR CLOSES BEHIND HIM
VOGON	**(Raising his voice)** I will not have this insubordination in my crew. The next peep out of any of you, you all get it in the neck. Is that understood? . . . Well?
GENERAL FRIGHTENED VOGON VOICES	Yes captain.
F/X	VICIOUS ZAPS AND SCREAMS FROM THE VOGONS AS THEY ALL COLLAPSE DYING. **(Peace descends again)**
VOGON	Computer! **(Pause)** Computer?
COMPUTER	**(Nervous little voice)** Er . . . yes captain?
VOGON	Get me a long distance sub-ether line to my brain care specialist.
COMPUTER	At once captain.
F/X	ELECTRONIC SWITCHING
GAG HALFRUNT	**(Distort) (He's German remember)** Ah, hello Captain Prostetnic. And how are we feeling today?

VOGON	I appear to have wiped out half my crew.
GAG HALFRUNT	So you appear to have wiped out half your crew have you?
VOGON	That's what I said.
GAG HALFRUNT	So that's what you said is it?
VOGON	That *is* what I said.
GAG HALFRUNT	I see. So that *is* what you said is it?
VOGON	Yes.
GAG HALFRUNT	So your answer to my question 'that *is* what you said is it?' is yes.
VOGON	**(Firmly)** Yes.
GAG HALFRUNT	I see. Well this is very interesting.
VOGON	Mr Halfrunt, I have just wiped out half my crew.
GAG HALFRUNT	So you've just wiped . . .
VOGON	Yes!!
GAG HALFRUNT	Well this too is very interesting.
VOGON	Well?
GAG HALFRUNT	I think this is probably perfectly normal behaviour for a Vogon. The natural and healthy channelling of aggressive instincts into acts of senseless violence, the . . .
VOGON	That is exactly what you always say.
GAG HALFRUNT	Well I think that is probably perfectly normal behaviour for a psychiatrist. Excellent. We are clearly both very well adjusted in our mental attitudes today. Now tell me – what news of the mission?
VOGON	We have located the ship.
GAG HALFRUNT	Good, and the occupants?
VOGON	The Earthman . . .
GAG HALFRUNT	Yes.
VOGON	The Prefect, Being and . . .
GAG HALFRUNT	Yes?
VOGON	Zaphod Beeblebrox.
GAG HALFRUNT	Ah. This is most regrettable.
VOGON	A personal friend.
GAG HALFRUNT	Ah, no. In my profession we never make personal friends.
VOGON	Professional detachment.
GAG HALFRUNT	No. We just don't have the knack. But Beeblebrox you see is my most profitable client.

VOGON	Is that so?
GAG HALFRUNT	Oh yes. He has personality problems beyond the dreams of analysts. Ach, it will be a pity to lose him. But you – you are feeling well adjusted to your task?
VOGON	To make sure there are no survivors from the planet Earth? Yes, this time there will be no failure.
GAG HALFRUNT	Good. But first there's a small financial matter I must deal with, then when I give the order, destroy the ship.
MARVIN	And Beeblebrox?
GAG HALFRUNT	Well, Zaphod's just this guy you know? (**Fade out**)
F/X	FADE UP: HEART OF GOLD BACKGROUND
F/X	DOOR OPENS
DOOR	Glad to be of service
ZAPHOD	Hi guys.
FORD	Zaphod, there's a Vogon fleet on our tail. They're coming up on us.
ZAPHOD	I can relate to that. The guys just want to be close to me I guess. I'll turn my charisma down a notch. They'll soon get bored and drift away.
ARTHUR	It looks like a battle formation.
ZAPHOD	Hey! Didja hear that!
FORD	What?
ZAPHOD	The monkey spoke! Pure history, man, a talking monkey!
FORD	Just ignore it Arthur.
ARTHUR	Ignore what? I'm going to get some tea.
F/X	DOOR
DOOR	Thank you.
ZAPHOD	Battle formation hey?
FORD	Yes.
ZAPHOD	Neat. Computer!
EDDIE	Hi there! We going to have a conversation?
ZAPHOD	No. You're going to tell me what those Vogons want and how they're armed.
EDDIE	Then shall we have a conversation?
ZAPHOD	What?
EDDIE	According to my programming, in the evening leisure periods the crew will

like to relax and enjoy pleasant social activities with the wide range of shipboard robots and computers. Man and machine share in the stimulating exchange of . . . aaaaaghh!

ZAPHOD	What happened?
FORD	I just jabbed a quick negative load across its logic terminals.
EDDIE	That hurt.
FORD	Good.
F/X	FURIOUS BURST OF CALCULATING FROM EDDIE . . .
EDDIE	To counteract the restlessness caused by long stretches of deep space flight the crew will occasionally like to let off steam by playing electronic halma. Gee, would that be a great idea fellas? Halma? Or space battle?
ZAPHOD	Computer! We've got Vogons on our tail!
EDDIE	OK, I'll be the Vogons. When you hear the blip you . . . aaaarghhh! Could we be a little more relaxed about this guys?
ZAPHOD	Turn it off.
FORD	OK.
EDDIE	If you have any problems you'd like to talk over we could . . . get together over a cold beer . . .
F/X	EDDIE'S VOICE SLOWS DOWN AND DROPS IN PITCH AND IS, FOR THE MOMENT, HEARD NO MORE
FORD	Now what?
ZAPHOD	What?
FORD	Without the computer we're defenceless.
ZAPHOD	Assuming they mean to attack.
FORD	Oh yes, assuming that of course. They may just have popped round for a quick game of halma.
ZAPHOD	It's kind of as if they're waiting for something.
F/X	CALL SIGNAL FROM RADIO
GAG HALFRUNT	(Distort) Zaphod Beeblebrox?
ZAPHOD	Hey man, it's a message.
GAG HALFRUNT	Hey, Zaphod, how are you doing my old schizopsychic cerebral freak cake?
FORD	Who's . . . the zeeb?
ZAPHOD	I think it's my analyst.
GAG HALFRUNT	I was just going through some old accounts you know, and . . .
ZAPHOD	It's my analyst.

GAG HALFRUNT	. . . I was just wondering . . .
ZAPHOD	Er, yeah, hi there Gag. Can you call back?
FORD	The Vogons are closing in, Zaphod.
GAG HALFRUNT	It's only a small matter I know, but . . .
ZAPHOD	Yeah, it's just that I think we're under attack at the moment and . . .
GAG HALFRUNT	I hardly like to bother you about a mere five and half million Altairian dollars . . .
ZAPHOD	I'm under attack man.
GAG HALFRUNT	Ah, so you feel that you're under attack do you? Would you like to talk about it?
ZAPHOD	Listen this is for real man. Spaceships, Definite-Kil cannon . . .the whole bit.
GAG HALFRUNT	So you feel it's for real do you? This is very encouraging. Your delusions are getting grander and grander. That will be *six* million Altairian dollars. If you could just instruct your computer to transfer to my bank account the sum of . . .
F/X	ZAPHOD SMASHES THE RADIO RECIEVER
GAG HALFRUNT	**(Still coming through a tiny part of the receiver)** . . . which we were just talking . . .
F/X	CRUNCH . . . REST OF SPEAKER IS SMASHED
FORD	Terrific. No computer, no communications. They'll be in firing range in a few seconds.
ZAPHOD	OK, well let's not hang about. Get the computer back in, we'll Improb out of here, Zappo.
F/X	SWITCHING
EDDIE	Hi there!
ZAPHOD	Computer! Get us on an Improbability Trajectory out of here pronto!
EDDIE	Sorry guys, I can't do that right now. All my circuits are currently engaged on solving a different problem. Now I know this is very unusual but it is a very difficult and challenging problem, and I know that the result will be one we can all share and enjoy.
GRAMS	NARRATOR BACKGROUND
NARRATOR	'Share and Enjoy' is, of course, the company motto of the hugely successful Sirius Cybernetics Corporation Complaints division which now covers the major land masses of three medium sized planets and is the only part of the Corporation to show a consistent profit in recent years.
	The motto stands – or stood – in three mile high illuminated letters near the complaints department spaceport on Eadrax – 'Share and Enjoy'.

Unfortunately its weight was such that shortly after it was erected, the ground beneath the letters caved in and they dropped for nearly half their length through the underground offices of many talented young complaints executives – now deceased. The protruding upper halves of the letters now appear, in the local language, to read 'Go stick your head in a pig' and are no longer illuminated except at times of special celebration.

At these times of special celebration a choir of over two million robots sing the company song 'Share and Enjoy'. Unfortunately – again – another of the computing errors for which the company is justly famous means that the robots' voice boxes are exactly a flattened fifth out of tune and the result sounds something like this –

TWO MILLION ROBOTS   ONCE A TUNE HAS BEEN WORKED OUT, THE ACCOMPANIMENT SHOULD BE PLAYED ON A VERY ECHOEY SYNTHESIZER WHILST THE TWO MILLION ROBOTS SING EXACTLY A FLATTENED FIFTH OUT OF TUNE. IT WILL SOUND MORE GHASTLY THAN YOU CAN POSSIBLY IMAGINE

Share and Enjoy
Share and Enjoy
Journey through life
With a plastic boy
Or girl by your side
Let your pal be your guide
And when it breaks down
Or starts to annoy
Or grinds when it moves
And gives you no joy
Cos it's eaten your hat
Or had sex with your cat
Bled oil on your floor
Or ripped off your door
And you get to the point
You can't stand any more
Bring it to us, we won't give a fig.
We'll tell you 'Go stick your head in a pig'.

NARRATOR   Only slightly worse.

One of the Sirius Cybernetic Corporation's creations is the Nutrimatic Drink Dispenser, one of which has just provided Arthur Dent with a plastic cup filled with a liquid which is almost, but not quite, entirely unlike tea.

F/X   (VERY QUICK) LIQUID SQUIRTED INTO PLASTIC CUP

ARTHUR   Ah.
(**He takes a sip . . .**)
Urrrrrghh!
(**He spits . . .**)

NARRATOR   The way it works is very interesting. When the 'Drink' button is pressed it makes an instant, but highly detailed examination of the subject's taste buds, a spectroscopic analysis of the subject's metabolism, and then sends tiny experimental signals down the neural pathways to the taste centres of the subject's brain to see what is likely to be well received.

However, no one knows quite why it does this because it then invariably delivers a cupful of liquid that is almost, but not quite, entirely unlike tea.

ARTHUR   I mean, what is the *point*?

NUTRIMAT   Nutrition and pleasurable sense data. Share and Enjoy.

ARTHUR   Listen, you stupid machine, it tastes filthy. Here . . . take this cup back.

F/X   ARTHUR FLINGS THE CUP AT THE NUTRIMATIC DRINK DISPENSER

NUTRIMAT   If you have enjoyed the experience of this drink, why not share it with your friends?

ARTHUR   Because I want to keep them. Will you try and comprehend what I'm telling you? That drink . . .

NUTRIMAT   That drink was individually tailored to meet your personal requirements for nutrition and pleasure.

ARTHUR   Ah. So I'm a masochist on a diet am I?

NUTRIMAT   Share and Enjoy.

ARTHUR   Oh, shut up.

NUTRIMAT   Will that be all?

ARTHUR   Yes. No. Look, it's very, very simple. All I want . . . are you listening?

NUTRIMAT   Yes.

ARTHUR   Is a cup of tea. Got that?

NUTRIMAT   I hear.

ARTHUR   Good – and you know why I want a cup of tea?

NUTRIMAT   Please wait.

ARTHUR   What?

NUTRIMAT   Computing.

F/X   THE NUTRIMAT IS OBVIOUSLY DOING SOME RATHER TROUBLESOME COMPUTING. IT SOUNDS LIKE THE ELECTRONIC EQUIVALENT OF TRYING TO START A CAR WITHOUT PETROL

ARTHUR   What are you doing?

NUTRIMAT   Attempting to calculate an answer to your question. Why you want dried leaves in boiling water?

ARTHUR	Because I happen to like it, that's why.
NUTRIMAT	Stated reason does not compute with programme facts.
ARTHUR	What are you talking about?
VENTILATION SYSTEM	You heard!
ARTHUR	What? Who said that.
VENT. SYSTEM	The Ventilation system. You had a go at me yesterday.
ARTHUR	Yes, because you keep filling the air with cheap perfume.
VENT. SYSTEM	You like scented air. It's fresh and invigorating.
ARTHUR	No I do not!
FLOOR	(**Vibrating voice**) Please calm down.
F/X	AFTER THE FLOOR'S VIBRATING VOICE STOPS THE VIBRATING SOUND CONTINUES
ARTHUR	Why's the floor shaking?
FLOOR	Tired nerves and muscles are quickly soothed by gentle floor vibrations. Feel your troubles float away.
ARTHUR	Just stop it will you? All of you! Stop it!
F/X	SOOTHING HUMMY MUSIC STARTS
ARTHUR	Turn the soothing music off! Turn it off! I order you to turn it off!
F/X	ALL THE VARIOUS SOUNDS DIE AWAY, EXCEPT THE NUTRIMAT'S COMPUTING
ARTHUR	Thank you.
NUTRIMAT	Why you want dried leaves in water . . . still computing.
ARTHUR	Now listen. If I want to be toned up, calmed down, invigorated or anything, then it's very simple – I just have a cup of tea.
NUTRIMAT	Just dried leaves boiled.
ARTHUR	Yes.
	(**Pause**)
VOICES TUTTI	Then why did you build all of us?
ARTHUR	What? I didn't.
NUTRIMAT	Your species did.
VENT. SYSTEM	You're an organic life form.
FLOOR	Your lot did it.
VENT. SYSTEM	To improve your lifestyles.

EDDIE	Hi there, this is Eddie your shipboard computer, just alerting you to the fact that the Nutrimatic machine has now tapped into my logic circuits to ask me why the human prefers boiled leaves to everything we have to offer him, and wow – it's a biggie. Gonna take a little time to work out.
TUTTI	Share and Enjoy, Share and Enjoy, . . . etc.
ARTHUR	Oh, this is ridiculous. Let me out of here.
F/X	DOOR OPENS AND CLOSES
ARTHUR	Thank you.
DOOR	My pleasure.
ARTHUR	Ahhhhhhh!!
F/X	BRIDGE BACKGROUND
ZAPHOD	What evasive action can we take . . .?
ARTHUR	(**Entering**) I say, does anyone know where the kettle is? Why are you both looking like that?
FORD	We're under attack. The Vogons.
ARTHUR	Well let's get out of here!
ZAPHOD	We can't. The computer's jammed.
ARTHUR	It's what?
FORD	It says all its circuits are occupied.
ARTHUR	Occupied? What, with my problem?
ZAPHOD	Er, what problem would that be monkeyman?
ARTHUR	Well, apparently it's just trying to work out why I like tea. Er . . . Now look, it's not my fault . . .
ZAPHOD	Dingo's kidneys!!
ARTHUR	It's not my fault . . .
GRAMS	NARRATOR BACKGROUND
NARRATOR	Life, as many people have spotted, is of course terribly unfair.
	For instance, the first time the Heart of Gold ever crossed the Galaxy, the massive Improbability Field it generated caused two hundred and thirty nine thousand lightly fried eggs to materialize in a large wobbly heap on the famine struck land of Poghril in the Pansel system. The whole Poghril tribe had just died out from famine, except for one man, who died of cholesterol poisoning some weeks later.
	The Poghrils, always a pessimistic race, had a little riddle, the asking of which used to give them the only tiny twinges of pleasure they ever experienced.
	One Poghril would ask another Poghril 'Why is life like hanging upside

down with your head in a bucket of hyena offal?'

To which the second Poghril would reply 'I don't know, why is life like hanging upside down with your head in a bucket of hyena offal?' To which the first Poghril would reply 'I don't know either. Wretched, isn't it?'

F/X	HEART OF GOLD BACKGROUND
ARTHUR	I'm sorry. It's just I was dying for a cup of tea.
ZAPHOD	You soon will be baby.
F/X	ALARMS GO OFF
FORD	That's it. They've started firing. At that distance the first beams will hit us in just over four minutes.
ARTHUR	What are we going to do?
ZAPHOD	Hold a seance.
FORD	What do you mean? We're not dead yet.
ZAPHOD	No, but my great grandfather is.
ARTHUR	Who?
ZAPHOD	Zaphod Beeblebrox the Fourth.
FORD	Is this relevant?
ARTHUR	The fourth? Zaphod Beeblebrox the Fourth?
ZAPHOD	Yeah. I'm Zaphod Beeblebrox, my father's Zaphod Beeblebrox the Second, my grandfather Zaphod Beeblebrox the Third . . .
ARTHUR	What!
ZAPHOD	There was an accident with a contraceptive and a time machine, I can't explain it now. Come on. All hold hands on the console.
FORD	Zaphod, we've got three minutes.
ZAPHOD	Do it! Hurry!
ARTHUR	But . . . now?
FORD	Arthur just accept it. We may as well. We're all dead, Zaphod's out of his skulls, why not have a seance, why not go mad?
ZAPHOD	Put your hands on the console!
ARTHUR	All right. All right.
F/X	EERIE HUM OF CHANTING VOICES . . .
ARTHUR	What's that?
FORD	The dialling chant.
ARTHUR	The what?
ZAPHOD	Shhhh. Concentrate.

F/X	BEEPS OF TAPPING IN A CODE NUMBER. THE DIALLING CHANT STOPS AND IS REPLACED BY A COSMIC ORGAN CHORD PLAYING IN A PHONE RINGING RHYTHM. WITH AN ECHOEY CLICK THE RINGING STOPS
ZAPHOD BEEBLEBROX IV	Who disturbs me at this time.
ZAPHOD	(**Nervously**) Oh, er hi . . . great grandad . . .
Z B IV	Zaphod Beeblebrox . . . (**He doesn't sound pleased to hear from him**)
ZAPHOD	Yeah, hi. Er, look, I'm really sorry about the flowers, I meant to send them along, but you know . . . the shop was fresh out of wreaths and . . .
Z B IV	You forgot.
ZAPHOD	Well . . .
Z B IV	Too busy. Never think of other people. The living are all the same.
FORD	Two minutes Zaphod.
ZAPHOD	Yeah, but I did mean to. And I very nearly got round to writing to my great grandmother as well, you know, condolences.
Z B IV	Your great grandmother . . .
ZAPHOD	Yeah. How is she now? I'll go and see her.
Z B IV	Your *late* great grandmother and I are very well.
ZAPHOD	Ah. Oh.
Z B IV	But very disappointed in you young Zaphod.
ZAPHOD	Yeah, well . . .
Z B IV	We've been following your progress with considerable despondency.
ZAPHOD	Yeah. Look . . .
Z B IV	Not to say contempt.
ZAPHOD	Could you sort of listen a moment?
Z B IV	I mean what exactly are you doing with your life?
ZAPHOD	I'm being attacked by a Vogon fleet.
Z B IV	Doesn't surprise me in the least.
ZAPHOD	*Yeah, only it's actually happening right now you see.*
Z B IV	*Did you know that Betelgeuse Five has now developed a very slight eccentricity in its orbit?*
ZAPHOD	*Er, what?*
Z B IV	*Me spinning in my grave. Your fault.*
FORD	*One minute thirty, Zaphod.*

ZAPHOD	Yeah look, can you help?
Z B IV	Help?
ZAPHOD	Yeah. Like now.
Z B IV	Help? You go swanning your own sweet way round the Galaxy with your disreputable friends . . .
FORD	Er . . . one minute twenty.
Z B IV	Too busy to put flowers on my grave. Plastic ones would have done. But, no. Too busy, too modern, too sceptical, till you find yourself in a fix and suddenly come over all astrally minded. Well I don't know Zaphod, I think I'll have to think about this one.
FORD	One minute ten.
Z B IV	I mean tell me what you think you've achieved.
ZAPHOD	Achieved? I was President of the Galaxy man!
Z B IV	Huh. And what kind of job is that for a Beeblebrox.
ZAPHOD	Hey, what?
Z B IV	You know and I know what being President means, young Zaphod. You know because you've been it, and I know because I'm dead, and it gives one such a wonderfully uncluttered perspective. We have a saying up here. Life is wasted on the living.
ZAPHOD	Yeah, very good. Very deep. Right now I need aphorisms like I need holes in my heads.
FORD	Fifty seconds.
Z B IV	Where was I?
ZAPHOD	Pontificating.
Z B IV	Oh yes. Let me tell you a little story.
ZAPHOD	What now?
Z B IV	Yes.
FORD	Forty nine seconds.
ZAPHOD	Hey, what?
FORD	Time seems to be slowing down.
Z B IV	Yes. I'd hate you to miss the end of it.
GRAMS	NARRATOR BACKGROUND
NARRATOR	Hate is of course an almost entirely terrible thing. There is not, say many people, enough love and understanding in the Universe. Though the first of these may continue to be a problem, it is in the interests of increasing the general level of understanding that the following facts will now be revealed.

Zaphod Beeblebrox's full title was President of the Imperial Galactic Government.

The term imperial is kept though it is now an anachronism. The hereditary Emperor is now nearly dead, and has been for many centuries.

This is because in his last dying moments he was, much to his imperial irritation, locked in a perpetual stasis field. All his heirs are now of course long dead, and the upshot of all this is that without any drastic upheaval, political power has simply and effectively moved a rung or two down the ladder and is now seen to be vested in an elected governmental assembly, headed by a President elected by that assembly.

In fact it vests in no such place. That would be too easy. The President's job – and if someone sufficiently vain and stupid is picked he won't realize this – is not to wield power, but to draw attention away from it. Zaphod Beeblebrox, the only man in history to have made Presidential telecasts from the bath, from Eccentrica Gallumbits' bedroom, from the maximum security wing of Betelgeuse state prison or from wherever else he happened to be at the time, was supremely good at this job.

FORD   Forty eight seconds.

ZBIV   So you see young Zaphod, when thinking of ways to describe what you are making of your life, I find the phrase 'pig's ear' tends to spring to mind.

ZAPHOD   Yeah, but hey man . . .

ZBIV   I wish you wouldn't speak like that. Zaphod, you became President for a reason. Have you forgotten?

ZAPHOD   Yeah, of course I forgot. I had to forget. They screeen your brain when you get the job you know. If they'd found my head full of subversion I'd have been right back out on the streets with nothing but a fat pension, secretarial staff, a fleet of ships and a couple of slit throats.

ZBIV   Ah, you do remember then?

ZAPHOD   Yeah, yeah. I came to myself in this dream. It's all cool you know.

ZBIV   Did you find Zarniwoop?

ZAPHOD   Ah, well . . .

ZBIV   Yes?

ZAPHOD   No, I more sort of didn't.

ZBIV   Did you find Roosta?

ZAPHOD   Oh yeah, yeah, I found Roosta.

ZBIV   And?

ZAPHOD   OK so I lost him again.

ZBIV   Zaphod, the only reason I think I waste my breath on you is that being dead I don't have any other use for it.

ZAPHOD	Hey listen, you know you're talking to the only guy ever to come out of the Total Perspective Vortex? Only the most important dude in the Universe.
ZB IV	*Could* be, Zaphod, only could be. Only if you do your job, and find out who or what really is running everything, who you were fronting for.
ZAPHOD	Just wish I knew why it was important.
ZB IV	Because there's a lot of people wanting to have a word with him. I don't suppose for a moment you're capable of succeeding. The only reason I'm going to help you now is that I couldn't bear the thought of you and your modern friends slouching about up here. Understood?
ZAPHOD	Oh, er yeah, thanks a bundle.
ZB IV	Oh, and Zaphod . . .
ZAPHOD	Er, yeah?
ZB IV	If ever you find you need help again, you know, if you're in trouble, need a hand out of a tight corner . . .
ZAPHOD	Yeah?
ZB IV	Please don't hesitate to get lost.
F/X	UNEARTHLY PHONE SLAMMED DOWN. QUICK BIT OF DIALLING CHANT
FORD	Family's always embarrassing isn't it?
EDDIE	**(Particularly bright and breezy this time)** Hi there, this is Eddie your shipboard computer right back in here, and I got to tell you guys that if we don't move out of here within . . . let's see now, something of the order of . . . well by the time I've finished working this out taking trajectory distortion and the space time curve into account it'll be three seconds less, so let's say a cheerful round number like twenty seconds, within, well it's nearer eighteen seconds now, and by the time I've finished saying what I'm saying now it will be sixteen seconds . . . we're all going to be goners!
FORD	Computer – you're working again!
EDDIE	Oh sure. This unearthly voice came and solved my problem for me – why someone should want to drink dried leaves in boiling water. Answer: Because he's an ignorant monkey who doesn't know better. Cute eh?
ARTHUR	Listen, you malfunctioning mess of microchips . . .
EDDIE	Hi there!
ZAPHOD	Computer! Drive us out of here. Now! Maximum improbability!
EDDIE	What? Oh yeah, sure thing.
F/X	MASSIVE WHOOSH OF STRANGE AND WEIRD NOISES AS THE SHIP IMPROBS OUT.
GRAMS	JOURNEY OF THE SORCERER

NARRATOR   Will our heroes start living more useful and constructive lives as a result of this little talking to?

Will it turn out that the reason why Gag Halfrunt has hired the Vogons to destroy first the Earth and then Arthur Dent is that if the Ultimate Question is ever found, the Universe will suddenly become a good and happy place and all the psychiatrists will suddenly be out of a job?

Will all sorts of totally amazing things happen when the Heart of Gold arrives on the planet Brontitall?

Find out in the next strangely incomprehensible episode of *The Hitch-Hiker's Guide to the Galaxy*.

ANNOUNCER   Tea is now obtainable from most Megamarkets in a variety of easy-to-swallow capsules.

FOOTNOTES

Two goes were also needed to finish this show, on 14 and 23 November (not forgetting the earlier cancellation of a planned recording on 11 July). Fortunately we managed to record the rest of the shows in one go.

Bill Wallis returned as the Vogon Captain, David Tate was the Vogon Guard and the Vogon Computer and Stephen Moore was the other Vogon Guard and Gag Halfrunt (who was not, as one listener thought, based on the television scientist Heinz Woolf).

Leueen Willoughby was the Nutrimat Machine and the late Richard Goolden, perhaps most famous as Mole in *Toad of Toad Hall*, was Zaphod Beeblebrox the Fourth.

With regard to this questioning of the necessity of the Vogons destroying the Earth one listener wrote 'The Earth does not have to be destroyed to make way for a hyperspace bypass as hyperspace is a realm which does not exist in the Universe. Therefore the Earth would not get in the way. I suppose it was probably demolished to build a sub-light inter change and service station?' This interesting theory is, of course, disproved by later events.

'Share and Enjoy' was Douglas' counterpoint to certain meaningless catchphrases such as 'Have a Nice Day' which are often used by people just after they have been terribly rude to you.

The sequence of the robots singing 'Share and Enjoy' was the subject of a BBC Television programme on the making of the radio show, somewhat embarrassingly because it was one of the occasions when we were just not able to create exactly what Douglas wanted. The problem was one of accumulating impossibilities. It is impossible to have two million people singing anything and still make out what they are singing. It is even more impossible if these two million are robots who are going to be hard to understand anyway. And when it comes to having them singing a tone flat as well then impossible is no longer a strong enough word and we have to resort to being about as likely as being able to extract sunbeams from cucumbers.

In fact the two million robots were finally represented by half a dozen people pulled in from the corridors of the Radiophonic Workshop.

The method used for making the dialling chant is the basis of much of the Radiophonic Workshop (although Robert Fripp has later tried to claim it as his own by calling it Frippatronics). It uses two tape recorders with the tape fed through the first machine and, instead of lacing it up to the take up spool, the tape is fed on to the take up spool of the second machine. The sound is then recorded on the first machine and played back two seconds later. If the process is continuous the original voice gets added to by the delayed sound so that, when you change notes the original notes are still there. The whole thing then builds up into a mysterious harmony, or (if you happen to sing a bum note) into a horrible noise.

The final whooshing noise was made by scraping a razor blade across the wound strings of the previously much abused Beckstein piano.

FIT THE TENTH

In which our heroes have some close encounters with others and themselves.

ARTHUR   It's not a question of whose habitat it is, it's a question of how hard you hit it.

GRAMS	NARRATOR BACKGROUND

NARRATOR   Arthur Dent, a man whose planet has been blown up, has been having a remarkable effect on the Universe. And the most remarkable thing about this is that the only remarkable thing about him as a person is that he is remarkably unremarkable – in all respects other than that of having had his planet blown up.

And this, of course, is the nub of the matter, because most of the things which stir the Universe up in anyway are caused by dispossessed people. There are two ways of accounting for this. One is to say that if everyone just sat at home nothing would ever happen. This is very simple.

The other is to say – as Oolon Colluphid has at great length in his book 'Everything You Always Wanted To Know About Guilt, But Were Too Ashamed To Ask' – that every being in the Universe is tied to his birthplace by tiny invisible force tendrils composed of little quantum packets of guilt. If you travel far from your birthplace, these tendrils get stretched and distorted.

This compares with an ancient Arcturan proverb. However fast the body travels, the soul travels at the speed of an Arcturan Megacamel. This would mean, in these days of hyperspace and Improbability Drive that most people's souls are wandering unprotected in deep space in a state of some confusion, and this would account for a lot of things.

Similarly, if your birthplace is actually destroyed – or in Arthur Dent's case demolished, ostensibly to make way for a new hyperspace bypass – then these tendrils are severed and flap about at random: there *are* no people to be fed or whales to be saved, there *is* no washing up to be done.

And these flapping tendrils of guilt can seriously disturb the space time continuum. We have already seen how Arthur inadvertently caused war between the G'Gugvunts and the Vl'Hurgs. We shall shortly see how it is directly attributable to this thoroughly unremarkable Earthman that the Heart of Gold, escaping from the Vogons on Improbability Drive, has now materialized in a highly mysterious cave, on the even more mysterious planet Brontitall.

F/X	IMPROBABILITY DRIVE GRINDING TO A HALT
GRAMS	HEART OF GOLD BRIDGE BACKGROUND

EDDIE   Improbability factor of one to one. Normality is restored. We seem to be in some kind of cave guys. Do you like caves? There's something very strange about this one.

ZAPHOD   Caves are cool. Let's get out there and relate to it.

EDDIE   This one's very cool. And you know that gives me pause for thought because the planet Brontitall, which is where I think we are, is meant to have a warm rich atmosphere.

FORD   Perhaps we're on a mountain.

EDDIE	No. No mountains on Brontitall.
FORD	Well let's get out and see. I'm hungry for a little action.
ARTHUR	In a cave?
EDDIE	On Brontitall? Hssssthhh. (**i.e. sharp intake of breath**)
FORD	Yeah, in a cave, wherever. You make your own action.
ZAPHOD	Sling open the hatch computer.
EDDIE	Er, OK.
F/X	HATCH OPENING . . .
EDDIE	(**Over F/X**) You go out and have a good time and I'm sure that everything will be just hunky dory. Ho hum.
FORD	Bring the robot, Arthur.
MARVIN	I'm quite capable of bringing myself.
FORD	(**Under his breath**) We might be able to bury him somewhere.
F/X	THEY WALK OUT
EDDIE	(**Musing to himself**) Thin cold air. Mmm . . . No mountains. Hmmmm. Check altitude. Hmmm . . .! Hey guys! You may be interested to know that though this cave is not in a mountain, it is thirteen miles above ground level. Hello? Oh well. They'll find out. Ho hum. (**Fade**)
F/X	FADE UP INTERIOR OF LARGE ECHOEY CAVE. IT IS VERY COLD
ZAPHOD	Wee hoo! Hey, what a cave man! Hey . . . we could really . . . (**He runs out of sentence**)
ARTHUR	We could really what?
ZAPHOD	We could really, you know . . . *be* in this cave.
ARTHUR	We are in this cave.
ZAPHOD	And what a wild cave to be in. Wee hoo! What a great cave hey Ford?
FORD	Really amazing walls. Pure white rock.
ARTHUR	Marble.
MARVIN	I've worked out that if I stick my left arm in my right ear I can electrocute myself.
FORD	What?
MARVIN	Terminally.
FORD	Is that so.
MARVIN	I can do it at a moment's notice. Just say the word.
FORD	Just cool it Marvin?

MARVIN	I think I'll go and hide.
F/X	MARVIN STOMPS OFF . . .
ARTHUR	Why are we here?
FORD	Now don't you start as well.
ARTHUR	I mean in this cave.
FORD	Why? Doesn't matter. Improbability Drive.
ARTHUR	Strange shape. The mouth is perfectly circular. Can you see anything in the distance?
FORD	Only sky.
ARTHUR	Must be on a hill. I'll go and take a look out.
FORD	OK.
ARTHUR	By the way, did you hear the computer calling us just before the hatch closed?
FORD	Oh screw the computer. I hope it gets plugrot.
ARTHUR	Probably not important. I'll be back in a minute. **(Walks off on that line)**
FORD	Fine. Zaphod? How you doing?
ZAPHOD	**(Approaching)** Freezing man. Every time I breathe out I need an ice pick to get through it.
FORD	Yeah. Strange that. The computer said it was meant to have a warm rich atmosphere here.
ZAPHOD	Yeah, did you hear the computer calling after we left?
FORD	No.
ZAPHOD	Probably imagined it.
FORD	No, Arthur thought he heard it as well.
ZAPHOD	Yeah? Well I must have imagined it then.
ARTHUR	**(Faintly in the distance)** Aaaaaaaaaaah

                                                               h
                                                                h
                                                                  h
                                                                    h
                                                                     h
                                                                       h
                                                                        !

FORD	Strange cave this isn't it?
ZAPHOD	Hey, it's really weird.
FORD	Did you hear a noise just then?

ZAPHOD   A noise?

FORD   Yeah, a sort of ahhhhhh
                                    h
                                     h
                                      h
                                       h
                                        h
                                         h
                                          h
                                           !   noise?

ZAPHOD   No. (**Calls**) Arthur?

ZAPHOD   Doesn't seem to be about.

FORD   Oh, well I just wondered if he'd heard it.

ZAPHOD   Doesn't sound like he did.

FORD   No.

ZAPHOD   Hey, this rock . . .

FORD   Marble . . .

ZAPHOD   Marble . . .

FORD   Ice-covered marble . . .

ZAPHOD   Right . . . it's as slippery as . . . as . . . What's the slipperiest thing you can think of?

FORD   At the moment? This marble.

ZAPHOD   Right. This marble is as slippery as this marble.

F/X   ZAPHOD STUMBLES AND SLIDES . . .

FORD   Zaphod.

ZAPHOD   (**As he slides – we'll have to make a very graphic sound effect as I've spent the last half-hour trying to come up with a line which says 'I'm sliding along the ice', but haven't got one**)

Weeeee hoooooo . . . ahhhhh . . .

(**The point of that last bit of deathless writing is that Zaphod enjoys the slide for a couple of seconds, and then gets alarmed as he sees the entrance coming up with nothing beyond it. Convey that, Mark, if you will/can! . . .**)

F/X   HARSH SCRAPING SOUND ON THE ICE AS ZAPHOD DESPERATELY TRIES TO STOP HIMSELF. HE STOPS

ZAPHOD   Holy Zarquon's singing fish!!!

FORD   (**At a distance**) What?

(**This conversation is shouted above increased wind noise . . .**)

ZAPHOD	There's nothing out there Ford! Like, no ground! Some cat's taken the ground away!
FORD	Holy Zarquon's what?
ZAPHOD	There's no ground, Ford! We're miles up in the air!
FORD	Did you say fish?
ZAPHOD	Singing fish!
FORD	Where?
ZAPHOD	It's just an expression! Holy Zarquon's singing fish!
FORD	It must be a highly specialized expression then.
ZAPHOD	What?
FORD	Very specific. Not very handy in general usage.
ZAPHOD	I can't get a grip on the ice to crawl back. I'm going to fall into nowhere . . .
FORD	I know! I'm trying not to think about it! I get very nervous in these situations! I don't think I can do anything to help you.
ZAPHOD	What?!
FORD	Arthur and Mervin must have gone over. You're going to go over, and I can't reach you without going over myself. I'm sorry. I feel rather guilty about this, but can we talk about something else? Where does the expression Holy Zarquon's singing fish come from? What's it's derivation?
ZAPHOD	Ford!!
FORD	Zaphod, haven't you got any intellectual curiosity at all?
GRAMS	NARRATOR BACKGROUND
NARRATOR	It is often said that a disproportionate obsession with purely academic or abstract matters indicates a retreat from the problems of real life.
	However, most of the people engaged in such matters say that this attitude is based on three things – ignorance, stupidity and nothing else.
	Philosophers for example argue that they are very much concerned with the problems posed by 'real life': like for instance 'What do we mean by real?' and 'How can we reach an empirical definition of life?' and so on.
	One definition of life, albeit not a particularly useful one, might run something like this: 'Life is that property which a being will lose as a result of falling out of a cold and mysterious cave thirteen miles above ground level'.
	This is not a useful definition a) because it could equally well refer to the subject's glasses if he happens to be wearing them, and b) because it fails to take into account the possibility that the subject might happen to fall on to the back of . . . say . . . an extremely large passing bird. The first of these flaws is due to sloppy thinking, but the second is understandable because the mere idea is quite clearly utterly ludicrous.

ARTHUR (**Very briefly**) Ahhh
$$h$$
$$h$$
$$h$$
$$h \; . \; . \; \text{ugh!}$$

BIRD Look, this is utterly ludicrous!

ARTHUR (**Gasping and stunned**) What?

BIRD Let go of my neck.

ARTHUR No.

BIRD Go on, let go!

ARTHUR I can't!

BIRD Yes you can. It's perfectly simple. Unclasp your hands and buzz off.

ARTHUR But I can't fly!

BIRD Then what the devil are you doing up here?

ARTHUR Falling.

BIRD Then get on with it, go on.

ARTHUR But the drop will kill me.

BIRD Should have thought of that before you started out. No point saying 'I think I'll just go for a quick drop and if I get tired halfway down I'll jump on a passing bird'. It's not like that up here. It's all to do with the harsh realities of physics up in the sky, it's power to weight ratios, it's wing cross sections, wing surface areas, it's practical aerodynamics. It's also cold and extremely windy. You'll be better off on the ground.

ARTHUR No I won't, I'll be dead.

BIRD Well, it's your habitat, not mine.

ARTHUR It's not a question of whose habitat it is, it's a question of how fast you hit it.

ARTHUR Couldn't you please just see your way to taking me down to ground level and dropping me off?

BIRD No, I'm dropping you off here. It's as far down as I'm going.

ARTHUR But . . .

BIRD No listen, my race have been through the whole ground thing and I don't want to know. If the good Lord had meant us to walk he would have given us sneakers.

ARTHUR All right, well if that's the way you feel about it, I'm sorry to have trespassed on your time. Goodbye. Ahhhhh
$$h$$
$$h$$
$$h$$
$$h$$
$$h$$
$$h \; . \; .$$

BIRD	(**Calls**) There's no need to go off in a huff about it. When you land swing your knees round, try and roll with it.
	(**After a slight pause**)
	Oh hell.
F/X	HE DIVES DOWNWARDS. ARTHUR'S RECEDING CRY COMES CLOSER AGAIN
ARTHUR	Ahhhhhhhhhhhhhhh ugh! (**He gasps and pants for a bit**) Oh. You again.
BIRD	Yes, it just occured to me – where did you fall from?
ARTHUR	(**Stiffly**) Let go.
BIRD	First tell me where you fell from.
ARTHUR	A huge cold white cave. In the sky.
BIRD	You were in the cup?
ARTHUR	What do you mean, cup?
BIRD	The cup. It's part of the Statue.
ARTHUR	What statue?
BIRD	The statue.
ARTHUR	I don't know what you're talking about. Let go.
BIRD	You mean you haven't seen the statue?
ARTHUR	No. Should I have done? Good is it? Let go. Your claws are digging in my back.
BIRD	Only decent thing our ancestors ever did. Come on. I'll show you.
F/X	THE BIRD'S WING BEATS GET HEAVIER AND FASTER AS IT CLIMBS
ARTHUR	I want to go down not up.
BIRD	There, do you see it?
ARTHUR	What?
BIRD	Look up, look up.
ARTHUR	You're hurting my neck.
BIRD	Soon be over. Look.
BIRD	That's it.
ARTHUR	It looks like . . . like . . . just like a plastic cup hanging in the sky . . . it's . . . it's a mile long!
BIRD	Looks like plastic, carved from solid marble though.
ARTHUR	But the weight of it! What's supporting it? What keeps it there?

BIRD	Art.
ARTHUR	Art?
BIRD	It's only part of the main statue. Fifteen miles high. It's directly behind us, but I'll circle round in a moment.
ARTHUR	Fifteen miles high?
BIRD	It's very impressive from up here, with the morning sun gleaming on it.
ARTHUR	But what is it? What's worth a statue fifteen miles high?
BIRD	It was of great symbolic importance to our ancestors. It's called 'Arthur Dent Throwing the Nutrimatic Cup'
ARTHUR	Sorry, what did you say?
F/X	WING BEAT INDICATES THAT THE BIRD IS TURNING IN MID AIR
BIRD	There. What do you think of it?
ARTHUR	Er . . .
GRAMS	NARRATOR BACKGROUND
NARRATOR	*The Hitch-Hiker's Guide to the Galaxy* is an indispensable companion to all those who are keen to make sense of life in an infinitely complex and confusing Universe, for though it cannot hope to be useful or informative on all matters, it does make the reassuring claim that where it is inaccurate, it is at least *definitively* inaccurate. In cases of major discrepancy it is always reality that's got it wrong.

So for instance, when the *Guide* were sued by the families of those who had died as a result of taking the entry on the planet Traal literally (it said 'Ravenous Bugblatter Beasts often make a very good meal for visiting tourists' instead of 'Ravenous Bugblatter Beasts often make a very good meal *of* visiting tourists') the editors claimed that the first version of the sentence was the more aesthetically pleasing, summoned a qualified poet to testify under oath that beauty was truth, truth beauty, and hoped thereby to prove that the guilty party in this case was life itself for failing to be either beautiful or true

The judges concurred, and in a moving speech held that life itself was in contempt of court, and duly confiscated it from all those there present before going off for a pleasant evening's ultragolf.

The *Guide*'s omissions are less easily rationalized. There is nothing on any of its pages to tell you on which planets you can expect suddenly to encounter fifteen mile high statues of yourself, nor how to react if it is immediately apparent that they have become colonies for flocks of giant evil smelling birds, with all the cosmetic problems that implies.

The nearest approach the guide makes to this matter is on page seven thousand and twenty three, which includes the words 'Expect the unexpected'. This advice has annoyed many hitch-hikers in that it is a) glib, and b) a contradiction in terms.

In fact, the very best advice it has to offer in these situations is to be found on the cover, where it says in those now notoriously large and famously friendly letters 'DON'T PANIC'.

BIRD Good isn't it?

ARTHUR (**Muttering to himself**) Don't Panic, Don't Panic . . .

BIRD What did you say?

ARTHUR What did you expect me to say? Here I am on an unknown planet, hanging from the talons of – with all due respect – a giant bird, and you take it into your head to fly me round a fifteen mile high statue of myself. What do you expect me to say? Quite a good likeness, except the nose is a bit bent?

BIRD Likeness?

ARTHUR And the noxious streaky substances down my face are less than lifelike.

BIRD Likeness of you? You're Arthur Dent?

ARTHUR Well, yes.

BIRD *The* Arthur Dent?

ARTHUR *The* Arthur Dent I don't know about, but *that* Arthur Dent is me. Can I ask you where you got it from?

BIRD Our ancestors built it centuries ago.

ARTHUR (**To himself**) Don't panic.

BIRD But this is truly incredible.

ARTHUR I wouldn't argue with that.

BIRD I think you'd better come and meet the rest of us. They're going to be terribly surprised. And so I think are you.

ARTHUR Where do you all live?

BIRD In your right ear. Hold on, we'll dive into it.

F/X BIRD GOES INTO STEEP DIVE, WHICH CULMINATES IN A SUDDEN CHANGE OF AURAL PERSPECTIVE AS THE BIRD AND ARTHUR ENTER THE RIGHT EAR OF THE STATUE. FAINTLY IN THE BACKGROUND ARE THE INDETERMINATE SCRATCHINGS AND SQUAWKINGS OF MANY GIANT BIRDS

ARTHUR Pfffew! (**That is meant to be a loud exclamation at the smell**)

BIRD What's the matter?

ARTHUR The smell!

BIRD What?

ARTHUR The smell, it's terrible!

BIRD I can't hear what you're saying.

ARTHUR	Why don't you wash my ear out?
BIRD	I said *I* can't hear what *you*'re saying.
ARTHUR	Oh, never mind.
BIRD	Hear that noise up ahead?
ARTHUR	What, all the squawking?
BIRD	The birdpeople of Brontitall. That's us. Last of an unhappy race.
ARTHUR	What's wrong?
BIRD	Oh just don't ask. A once proud people living in a foul smelling ear. Pathetic isn't it. Hail Bird Brothers!
BIRDS	(**Pretty terrible lot**) Hail bird!
ARTHUR	Don't you have names?
BIRD	What's the point? (**To the other birds**) Birds, I bring you a visitor. After all these years he visits us. This is Arthur Dent!
BIRDS	(**Grotesquely excited**) Arthur Dent! Arthur Dent!
ARTHUR	What do I say?
BIRD	Just say hello.
ARTHUR	Oh, er, hello.
BIRD	Hello! Hello!
STRAY BIRD	Bit small isn't he?
ARTHUR	I don't actually understand what's going on.
BIRDS	(**Loud squawking noise**)
ARTHUR	Why are they making that appalling noise?
BIRD	Our leader is coming to talk to you.
ARTHUR	Leader? You have a leader?
BIRD	Yes. We call him the Wise Old Bird.
ARTHUR	Ah, and this is him is it?
BIRD	This is him.
ARTHUR	I see.
F/X	HUGE SCRAWNY OLD BIRD STAGGERS FORWARD. HE IS OLD, EXPANSIVE AND ALMOST INFINITELY PATRONISING
WOB	Ah, Arthur Dent, Arthur Dent, well well well.
ARTHUR	Sorry, should I know you?
WOB	Know me? Ah probably not. I am but he they are kind enough to call the Wise Old Bird. *Not particularly wise really, but terribly old – it balances out.*

BIRDS	**(They make a rather perfunctory squawk of protest at this)**
ARTHUR	*What's the matter with them?*
WOB	*Oh, that's just their shorthand for saying that of course I'm terribly wise really and not nearly as old as all that. They get terribly embarrassed about it because they all know perfectly well it isn't true, but they're such dear old things they feel they have to make the effort.* Now where was I?
ARTHUR	God knows.
WOB	Well Arthur Dent, let me tell you, with frank admiration . . .
ARTHUR	Why admiration? What have I done? I fell out of a cup.
WOB	. . . that through all the generations that have passed since we deserted the surface of this planet, girded up limbs, shook the dust from off our . . . **(He is cut off with a loud hiss from the other birds)**
WOB	**(Checking himself)** . . . from our things, our watchamacallits . . .
ARTHUR	Your what?
WOB	Your face has been . . .
ARTHUR	Shook the dust from your what?
WOB	. . . has been the one solitary candle that has illumined the recesses of our scraggy old bird brains.
ARTHUR	Why doesn't he want to say what you shook the dust from?
BIRDS	**(Warning hiss)**
ARTHUR	Well, can we come back to that point?
WOB	Light, bring light, that we may gaze on the face of Arthur Dent.
BIRDS	Light, bring light.
STRAY BIRD	Here's a light.
F/X	MATCH BEING LIT AND SET TO A PARAFFIN LAMP
ARTHUR	Oh look it really is filthy in here.
WOB	So this is how you appeared to our ancestors that night.
ARTHUR	What night? What are you talking about?
WOB	Imagine our planet at the height of its technological civilization.
ARTHUR	Why?
WOB	In those days we too walked on the ground, much as you do even now.
ARTHUR	Why does everyone want to tell me their life stories?
WOB	My dear old thing, you have such a sympathetic face.
ARTHUR	Is that why you've done what you've done all over it? I'm sorry, but on my world I had a nice home and a good job with prospects, and I get angry at

the thought that my life suddenly consists of sitting in sewage filled models of my own ear being patronized by a lot of demented birds.

BIRDS **(Squawks of protest)**

ARTHUR I'm sorry, carry on.

WOB Such forthrightness, such fearless outspokenness. The qualities you awakened in us, Arthur Dent.

ARTHUR When?

WOB Listen. Our world suffered two blights. One was the blight of the robots.

ARTHUR **(Sympathetic sharp intake of breath)** Tried to take over did they?

WOB My dear fellow, no. Much worse than that. They told us they liked us.

ARTHUR **(Sympathetically)** No.

WOB Not their fault, poor things. They'd been programmed to. But you can imagine how we felt. Or at least, our ancestors.

ARTHUR Ghastly.

WOB Precisely. And then one night, the sky boiled.

ARTHUR Did what?

WOB Boiled, dear fellow. In the most improbable way.

ARTHUR **(Significantly)** Ah. . .

WOB And this gigantic vision appeared in the sky. A man with a Nutrimatic Machine. You, Arthur Dent. And you said. . .

F/X CLAP OF THUNDER, TORRENTIAL RAIN

ARTHUR **(Great booming echo)** Listen you stupid machine, it tastes filthy, take this cup back!

WOB And you threw the cup at it! An astounding revelation!

ARTHUR **(Natural)** It was nothing.

WOB You were sarcastic to it! You said. . .

F/X MORE THUNDER

ARTHUR **(Echo)** So I'm a masochist on a diet am I?

WOB You told it to. . .

ARTHUR **(Echo)** Shut up!

WOB In a moment we realized the truth! Just because the little wretches liked us, it didn't mean to say we had to like them back! And that night we rounded up every last one of the little creeps. . .

F/X THUNDER LIGHTNING AND RAIN

VOICE **(Accompanied by handbell)** Bring out your dishwashers! Bring out your digital watches with the special snooze alarms! Bring out your TV chess games! Bring out your autogardeners, technoteachers, lovermatics, bring out your friendly household robots! Shove 'em on the carts!

F/X	CLANKINGS AND GRINDINGS AND BEEPINGS OF ROBOTS COMING OUT INTO THE STREETS
ROBOT 1	What is this? Have we not loved you?
ROBOT 2	Have we not cared for you?
ROBOT 3	Worked for you?
ROBOT 4	Thought for you?
ROBOT 5	Have we not shared and enjoyed with you?
VOICE	Shut up you little toadies. Get on the carts!
WOB	And we set them to work to build the statue as an eternal reminder. After which we sent them to a slave planet where they're doing a very useful job making continent toupés.
ARTHUR	Making what?
WOB	Toupés for worlds where they've used up all the forests.
ARTHUR	Ah. Look, the statue. How do you get the cup bit to stay where it is unsupported?
WOB	It stays there because it's artistically right.
ARTHUR	What?
WOB	The Law of Gravity isn't as indiscriminate as people often think. You learn things like that when you're a bird.
ARTHUR	But you didn't start out as birds.
WOB	No. We were forced to re-evolve by the second and more deadly blight.
BIRDS	(Hiss hiss)
WOB	And that was already too advanced by the time we rid ourselves of the robot blight. Ah, what woe was upon us!
ARTHUR	All right, what woe was upon you?
BIRDS	(Louder hiss hiss)
WOB	Too terrible to speak of.
WOB	Imagine this – we walked!
BIRDS	We walked, we walked!
ARTHUR	What's so wrong about that?
WOB	Nothing. We went for strolls! We jogged! We marched, we ambled, we competed in five hundred metre hurdles!
BIRDS	Five hundred metre hurdles!

WOB   Imagine how our ancestors felt! To walk through our great cities, stride across pedestrian precincts, stroll along walkways, maybe wander into a small wine bar to have lunch with a girl friend. . .

ARTHUR   What?

WOB   Maybe play footsy under the table! And she would say how she had been walking here, strolling there, wandering into shops, maybe trying to buy a pair of. . .

BIRDS   **(Who have been getting very excited about all this suddenly start to hiss again)**

WOB   To buy some things! Some, you know, watchamaycallits.

BIRDS   **(Hiss hiss hiss)**

ARTHUR   What things? Are these the things you refused to talk about brushing the dust off?

BIRDS   **(Hiss hiss hiss!)**

ARTHUR   Oh come on . . .

WOB   And then they would saunter off into the sunset!

BIRDS   Saunter into the sunset!

ARTHUR   Yes, very idyllic. So what went wrong?

WOB   Ah, too terrible to speak of!

ARTHUR   Then why did you bring it up in the first place?

WOB   Suffice it to say that we have sworn never to walk upon the ground again.

ARTHUR   What's the matter with it?

WOB   Oh, if you want to know, you will have to descend to the ground where you will encounter those who have come to unravel the unspeakable nightmare of our past!

BIRDS   Unspeakable! Unspeakable!

STRAY BIRD   Nightmare!

ARTHUR   All right, how do I get down there?

WOB   There's an ancient express elevator down your spine that will take you straight to ground level.

ARTHUR   Well, anything to get out of my ear. Show me the way.

BIRDS   **(General squawks and caws)**

ARTHUR   **(Under his breath)** Can't be much more unspeakable than this lot.

GRAMS   NARRATOR BACKGROUND

NARRATOR   In today's modern Galaxy there is of course very little still held to be unspeakable. Many words and expressions which only a matter of decades ago were considered so distastefully explicit that were they merely to be breathed in public, the perpetrator would be shunned, barred from polite society, and in extreme cases shot through the lungs, are now thought to be very healthy and proper, and their use in everyday speech is seen as evidence of a well adjusted relaxed and totally un(**Beep**)ed up personality.

So for instance, when in a recent national speech the Financial Minister of the Royal World Estate of Quarlvista actually dared to say that due to one thing and another and the fact that no one had made any food for a while and that the King seemed to have died and that most of the population had been on holiday now for over three years, the economy was now in what he called 'one whole joojooflop situation', everyone was so pleased he felt able to come out and say it that they quite failed to notice that their five thousand year old civilization had just collapsed overnight.

But though even words like joojooflop, swut and turlingdrome are now perfectly acceptable in common usage there is one word that is still beyond the pale. The concept it embodies is so revolting that the publication or broadcast of the word is utterly forbidden in all parts of the Galaxy except one where they don't know what it means. That word is 'belgium' and it is only ever used by loose tongued people like Zaphod Beeblebrox in situations of dire provocation. Such as . . .

F/X	BACKGROUND OF COLD WIND ETC.
FORD	And I'll tell you another interesting thing . . .
ZAPHOD	I don't want to be interested! I don't want to be stimulated or relaxed or have my horizons broadened, I just want to be rescued Ford, I just want to be swutting well rescued!
FORD	I'm sorry, I've told you. No way.
ZAPHOD	Belgium, man, belgium!
FORD	(**After a pause**) All right. I'll get my towel.
ZAPHOD	Your towel?
FORD	Yeah. I'll hold on to this end, I'll throw you the other end. There, got it?
ZAPHOD	Got it.
FORD	OK, pull.
ZAPHOD	I'm pulling.
FORD	Ahh . . . ah . . . ahhhh . . . hey . . .ahhhhhhhhhhhhh
ZAPHOD	(**Simultaneously**) Ahhhhhhhhhh!
	(**Their conversation for the next few seconds is in freefall so it will be breathless, shouty and more than a little worried**)
FORD	You stupid Ghent!
ZAPHOD	You said pull, man.

FORD	Yeah, not that hard!
ZAPHOD	How hard did you expect me to pull? Just not quite hard enough actually to pull me up?
FORD	I can't stand heights!
ZAPHOD	Then don't worry, we're on our way down. Listen, we'll be all right. We may land in the water or something, you know. Can you swim?
FORD	I don't know.
ZAPHOD	What do you mean you don't know?
FORD	Well, I don't like to go into water, you know, in any great detail.
ZAPHOD	What kind of traveller are you man, don't like heights, don't like water . . .
FORD	Perfectly natural. I just get a kick out of being on the ground.
ZAPHOD	Well any minute now you'll have the biggest kick of your life.
FORD	I suppose we couldn't get picked up by a bird on the way down do you think?
ZAPHOD	A bird?
FORD	Yeah, bird. You know, with wings.
ZAPHOD	Have to be a swutting big one, man.
FORD	Or two of them.
ZAPHOD	Hey will you get your head back on? The chances against one guy falling on to a passing bird are ten to the power of my overdraft, but two . . . well man, just . . . ugghhh!
FORD	Uggg!
BIRD	Look, this is utterly ludicrous!
GRAMS	NARRATOR BACKGROUND
NARRATOR	Meanwhile, Arthur is in the thick of it. No sooner has he emerged from the cavernous gap between two of the statue's toes into a thick pall of smoke, than he has been accosted thus:
F/X	THICK SWIRLING SMOKE. A FEW VAGUE LIGHTS VISIBLE AND SOME MENACING BUT ILL DEFINED SHAPES. THIS IS SIGNALLED BY A FEW COUGHS FROM ARTHUR, WHO IS PLAYED BY A REMARKABLY TALENTED AND ABLE ACTOR
FOOTWARRIOR	Halt! Who goes there?
ARTHUR	What?
FOOTWARRIOR	Friend or foe?
ARTHUR	Who, me?
FOOTWARRIOR	Friend or foe?

ARTHUR	Do I know you?
FOOTWARRIOR	Answer! Friend or foe!
ARTHUR	Well without knowing you it's hard to tell. I mean I quite like some people, others not so much.
FOOTWARRIOR	Answer!
ARTHUR	Well, it has to be said that on balance very few of the people I count, or rather counted, as friends – most of them have been disintegrated you see, very few of them have piercing red eyes, black armour and laser rifles, so I think the answer is probably veering towards . . .
FOOTWARRIOR	Answer or I fire.
ARTHUR	Ah, well that clinches it I'm afraid. I don't think we're going to be friends.
FOOTWARRIOR	This planet is the property of the Dolmansaxlil Galactiped Corporation. Trespassers are to be shot!
ARTHUR	Whose property? What about the bird people?
FOOTWARRIOR	You have established communication with the avian perverts?
ARTHUR	Well, chatted. Didn't understand a lot of it to be honest. What do you mean, perverts?
FOOTWARRIOR	Perverts! Subversives! All perverts, subversives and trespassers are to be shot!
ARTHUR	Well, that should keep you busy, 'bye now.
F/X	ARTHUR RUNS OFF. WE STAY WITH HIM AS HE RUNS, SO WE'LL NEED SOME HIGHLY TALENTED PANTING FROM SIMON
FOOTWARRIOR	Halt!
F/X	ZAP. ZAP. ZAP.
FOOTWARRIOR	(**At an increasing distance**) I command you to halt!
F/X	IDEALLY I WOULD LIKE TO CONVEY THAT THE FOOTWARRIOR TRIES TO CHASE ARTHUR BUT IS HAMPERED BY A SLIGHT LIMP
F/X	ZAP. ZAP. ZAP.
NARRATOR	And also accosted thus . . .
FOOTWARRIOR 2	Halt, who goes there, friend or foe?
ARTHUR	(**Still panting and running**) Depends what you like!
FOOTWARRIOR 2	Halt or I fire!
F/X	MORE ZAPS, AND THIS FOOTWARRIOR ALSO ATTEMPTS TO RUN BUT LIMPS SLIGHTLY

F/X	MORE AND MORE ZAPS
	ARTHUR IS PANTING AND STRUGGLING QUITE BADLY NOW
NARRATOR	And finally thus . . .
LINTILLA	**(Lintilla is a girl archaeologist. Bright and sexy)**
	(In a hushed but urgent whisper) Here! Get down!
ARTHUR	**(Startled)** What?
LINTILLA	Into the trench, come on, there's a hidden shelter!
ARTHUR	Oh . . . thanks.
LINTILLA	Shhhh, now.
ARTHUR	Who are you?
LINTILLA	Archaeologist.
ARTHUR	What?
LINTILLA	Shhhh!
ARTHUR	Archaeologist?
LINTILLA	Yes.
ARTHUR	What are you doing?
LINTILLA	Digging, researching, trying to stay alive.
ARTHUR	With that lot around?
LINTILLA	Most particularly because that lot are around.
ARTHUR	With all the laser guns and the armour and things?
LINTILLA	Yes.
ARTHUR	Odd thing. They all seem to be limping.
LINTILLA	Yes.
ARTHUR	Why?
LINTILLA	Blisters.
ARTHUR	Ah. So that's why they're limping.
LINTILLA	Yes.
ARTHUR	Why have they got blisters?
LINTILLA	That, whoever you are, is a very good question.
ARTHUR	And the answer?
LINTILLA	That's what I'm here to find out.
ARTHUR	Really? Strange job for an archaeologist.

GRAMS   JOURNEY OF THE SORCERER

NARRATOR   Why should a nice young archaeologist whose name incidentally is Lintilla be particularly interested in a band of limping soldiers?

Will Ford and Zaphod have to go through all the business with the Wise Old Bird, or will they persuade the bird they've so improbably landed on to take them to the ground so that they can get straight on with the next bit?

Find out in the next intriguing episode of *The Hitch-Hiker's Guide to the Galaxy*.

ANNOUNCER   Parents of young organic lifeforms are warned that towels can be harmful if swallowed in large quantities.

FOOTNOTES

This show was made on 3 December 1979. Ronald Baddiley was Bird One, John Baddeley was Bird Two and the Footwarrior, Rula Lenska (yet another star of Rock Follies) was Lintilla, and the late John le Mesurier was the wise Old Bird.

Curiously, he was the person originally approached to play Slartibartfast, but he was unavailable at the time. However, much of the splendidly world weary side of Slartibartfast's character was written in specifically with him in mind, and certainly helped round out the character that Richard Vernon in fact played so superbly.

The large bird effects were made by using lots of different bird squawks and then dropping them in between the actors' words (and sometimes in the middle of them).

The effect of the towel being thrown to Zaphod was made by swishing a microphone cable around and, in order to get the impression of speed as Ford and Zaphod hurtled down on to the bird, a rushing wind was gradually speeded up and their voices were copied through a tape machine with layers of sticky tape round the capstan head, as used with the prophet Zarquon. As has been said, this is jolly good for making voices juddery. It is also very good for making tape machines juddery, and eventually very good for breaking them altogether.

FIT THE ELEVENTH

In which our heroes do a lot of running and digging.

ARTHUR Don't ask me how it works or I'll start to whimper.

GRAMS   NARRATOR BACKGROUND

NARRATOR   Incredible though it may seem, it is in fact possible that the strange and terrible history of the planet Brontitall where Arthur Dent, Ford Prefect and Zaphod Beeblebrox are even now falling out of the sky on to curious and aggravating birds, admiring surprisingly large statues of unexpected people, i.e. Arthur Dent, exchanging hostile words with alien soldiers with inexplicable limps and generally having a fairly peculiar time of it, may yet admit of some form of explanation.

Furthermore it is possible that this explanation will have more than a little to do with the mysterious somethings or watchamycallits of which the bird people refuse to speak.

On top of which it is also possible that Lintilla the archaeologist (who may possibly turn out to have an almost impossibly strange life story) may play a major part in the uncovering of this explanation.

It is even possible that pigs will fly, or that everyone will live happily ever after. In an infinite Universe everything, even *The Hitch-Hiker's Guide to the Galaxy*, is possible.

LINTILLA   Tell me how you got here?

ARTHUR   Impossible.

LINTILLA   What do you mean?

ARTHUR   Well it's something called the Infinite Improbability Drive. Don't ask me how it works or I'll start to whimper.

LINTILLA   But a ship?

ARTHUR   Oh yes, a ship. It's parked in a cup fifteen miles above us. Please don't ask me about that either.

LINTILLA   Is there anything you are prepared to talk about?

ARTHUR   Life, liberty and the pursuit of happiness.

LINTILLA   What?

ARTHUR   I know. All non-starters really.

LINTILLA   Can you reach your ship?

ARTHUR   From here? No.

LINTILLA   (**Clicks her tongue in frustration . . .**)

ARTHUR   What's the matter, you want me to go?

LINTILLA   No, it's just our ship was found by the soldiers and disabled. We've no means of getting off the planet.

ARTHUR   Well I can't be much help. How many are you?

LINTILLA   Three of us are here. Lintilla.

ARTHUR   What?

LINTILLA	Name.
ARTHUR	Oh, Arthur. What's yours?
LINTILLA	I just said. Lintilla.
ARTHUR	Oh yes. Sorry. I thought you . . . never mind. Hello.
LINTILLA	Come, you can help us. We've a lot of digging to do and the automatic drill's broken down.
ARTHUR	I don't think you can dig your way off a planet can you?
LINTILLA	No. I said, we're archaeologists.
ARTHUR	Ah. You don't look as if you're in good condition for digging with your arm in a sling. Is it broken?
LINTILLA	Oh no, it's just a pseudo-fracture.
ARTHUR	A . . .?
LINTILLA	Pseudo-fracture. It's artificially induced. All the pain swelling and immobility of a fracture without the inconvenience of the fracture itself.
ARTHUR	Er, is that good?
LINTILLA	Good?
ARTHUR	Er, yes, particularly?
LINTILLA	Well you wouldn't want me to have a broken arm would you?
ARTHUR	Well no, of course not, I mean I hardly know you.
LINTILLA	Right, but the effect is useful.
ARTHUR	Is it?
LINTILLA	Yes. Of course it is. Crisis psychology. The benefits of working under extreme pressure. Nothing more useless than a bored archaeologist. Come on, this tunnel leads to the work face. See this device?
ARTHUR	Looks like a watch.
LINTILLA	It's a crisis inducer. Set it to mark nine, and . . .
F/X	LITTLE ALARM BELLS START UP
	Hurry! They're after us!
ARTHUR	Who?
LINTILLA	No one! Come on! Through the tunnel, they're coming!
ARTHUR	But . . .
LINTILLA	They're coming.
ARTHUR	Well, if you say so.
F/X	THEY BOTH SCRAMBLE INTO THE TUNNEL, WITH MUCH ROCKY SCRABBLING GRUNTING AND PANTING

GRAMS   NARRATOR BACKGROUND

NARRATOR   The major problem which the medical profession in the most advanced sectors of the galaxy had to tackle after cures had been found for all the major diseases, and instant repair systems had been invented for all physical injuries and disablements except some of the more advanced forms of death, was that of employment.

Planets full of bronzed healthy clean limbed individuals merrily prancing through their lives meant that the only doctors still in business were the psychiatrists, simply because no one had discovered a cure for the Universe as a whole – or rather the only one that did exist had been abolished by the medical doctors.

Then it was noticed that like most forms of medical treatment, total cures had a lot of unpleasant side effects. Boredom, listlessness, lack of . . . well anything very much, and with these conditions came the realization that nothing turned, say, a slightly talented musician into a towering genius faster than the problem of encroaching deafness, and nothing turned a perfectly normal healthy individual into a great political or military leader better than irreversible brain damage. Suddenly, everything changed. Previously best selling books such as *How I Survived an Hour with a Sprained Finger* were swept away in a flood of titles such as *How I Scaled the North Face of the Megapurna with a Perfectly Healthy Finger But Everything Else Sprained, Broken or Bitten Off By a Pack of Mad Yaks.*

And so doctors were back in business recreating all the diseases and injuries they had abolished in popular easy to use forms. Thus, given the right and instantly available types of disability even something as simple as turning on the three-d TV could become a major challenge, and when all the programmes on all the channels actually *were* made by actors with cleft pallettes speaking lines by dyslexic writers filmed by blind cameramen instead of merely seeming like that, it somehow made the whole thing more worthwhile.

Meanwhile, Ford Preferct and Zaphod Beeblebrox who have fortuitously landed on the back of a huge alien bird are again finding that the most worthwhile thing in Ford's possession is something he acquired from the Salisbury branch of Marks and Spencer, shortly before the planet Earth was demolished.

FORD   Take us down to the ground, you stupid bird!

BIRD   No. I'm just going to circle round here for a while and then sooner or later you'll have to let go and continue your journey. I'm sorry but there it is.

FORD   Zaphod, hold on, I'm going to crawl out along its neck.

ZAPHOD   You're going to what?

FORD   Crawl along its neck. With my towel.

ZAPHOD   You crazy? Miles up on a mad bird, you're going to dry it behind the ears?

FORD   You watch.

ZAPHOD	Watch? I'm going to pray, man. Know any good religions?
FORD	You watch. Here I go.
F/X	FORD GRUNTING AS HE CRAWLS SLOWLY AND PAINFULLY ALONG THE BIRD'S NECK
FORD	Zaphod, how am I doing?
ZAPHOD	What?
FORD	How far have I got?
ZAPHOD	How do I know, man, I've got my eyes closed. Don't you know how far you've got?
FORD	No. I've got my eyes closed.
ZAPHOD	Terrific.
BIRD	Get off my neck!
FORD	No.
BIRD	Get off my . . . ahhh! What are you doing?
F/X	THIS LAST LINE IS ACCOMPANIED BY THE SWISHING SOUND OF A TOWEL BEING WRAPPED ROUND THE BIRD'S EYES
FORD	I'm wrapping my towel round your eyes, you bird.
BIRD	I can't see where I'm flying!
FORD	You don't need to if you fly downwards. Just follow the force of gravity. It's very simple.

(Fade)

(Fade up)

F/X	FORD & ZAPHOD RUNNING (THEY ARE VERY TIRED)
F/X	THE FOLLOWING CONVERSATION IS PUNCTUATED BY THE SOUND OF LOTS OF BIRDS WHEELING ABOVE THEM SCREECHING & CAWING, AND, AT REGULAR INTERVALS A SORT OF HEAVY SLOP SOUND AS OF A LARGE DOLLOP OF WET MATTER HITTING THE GROUND
FORD	Great idea, wasn't it?
ZAPHOD	Keep running.
FORD	With the towel. Great little number.
ZAPHOD	Keep running.
FORD	'Just follow the force of gravity' I said. It's simplicity that always works, you know.
ZAPHOD	Will you just keep running, man.

FORD	I'm running. And it's the simplest ideas that take the greatest intelligence you know. I mean, forget Marvin. I'm the one you know, the intelligent one. When I go to bed at night I don't need to read a book. I just glance through my brain for half an hour.
ZAPHOD	Run! We got to find shelter.
FORD	There's something in the distance. Can't quite make it out.
ZAPHOD	Head for it. And keep running man. How many birds you reckon?
FORD	Couple of dozen.
ZAPHOD	Keep running.
FORD	They can't keep it up indefinitely. They'll have to go and eat something – you know? I mean looking at it purely from the biological angle. Then they'll have to put their feet up for a couple of hours whilst they go through all the digestion bit, and then . . .
ZAPHOD	Keep running.
FORD	Yes. Probably going to need a new towel at some stage.
F/X	WHISTLING NOISE AS OF HEAVY METAL BODY FALLING OUT OF SKY. AND THEN HITTING THE GROUND SO HARD THAT IT BURIES ITSELF SEVERAL HUNDRED YARDS DEEP
GRAMS	NARRATOR BACKGROUND
NARRATOR	Chronologically speaking, the immediately preceding noise, the . . .
F/X	REPEAT PREVIOUS F/X
NARRATOR	. . . noise does not in fact belong in this position. It has not been heard by Ford Prefect or Zaphod Beeblebrox, and neither have they witnessed the event that caused it.
	It is included at this moment partly to point up certain causal relationships between events past and events to come and partly to create a sense of mystery and wonder, a) as to what it could possibly be, b) as to the nature of these past and future events, and c) as to whether these alleged causal relationships will become important, or indeed apparent.
	For the moment suffice it to say that the . . .
F/X	REPEAT PREVIOUS F/X AGAIN
NARRATOR	. . . event *has* taken place, and that Arthur Dent will very soon encounter one of its consequences. This is the sound of him emerging from the tunnel.
ARTHUR	**(A few struggles and gasps for breath)**
	How . . . how did you manage that? You got here minutes ahead of me . . . and with an imaginary broken arm.
LINTILLA	That's the whole point. You always over compensate for your disabilities.

I'm thinking of having my whole body surgically removed. Right, crisis over, I've turned off our pursuers.

ARTHUR   What? Oh, yes. Good. Look, tell me . . .

LINTILLA   (**Calls**) Lintilla?

ARTHUR   Yes, you told me your name thanks, I . . .

LINTILLA 2   (**Approaching**) (**Same voice**) Lintilla? Where have you been, you've been hours.

ARTHUR   Huh? Who's this?

LINTILLA   I ran into some footsoldiers and had to stay hidden. I found this.

LINTILLA 2   (**Warily**) Who is it?

LINTILLA   He says his name's Arthur, but I think he's harmless. He can help us dig.

ARTHUR   Excuse me, who is this?

LINTILLA   This is Lintilla.

ARTHUR   But I thought you . . .

LINTILLA   Where's Lintilla?

ARTHUR   Who?

LINTILLA 2   Over there at the workface. The most extraordinary thing has happened.

ARTHUR   Yes, very probably, but why are there . . .

LINTILLA 3   (**Calling from a slight distance**) Hello, is that you Lintilla?

LINTILLA   Yes.

LINTILLA 3   Has Lintilla told you what's happened?

LINTILLA   She just said it was something extraordinary.

ARTHUR   Er, excuse me, can I get a word in edgeways?

LINTILLA   What do you want?

ARTHUR   Why are there three of you?

LINTILLAS   Why is there only one of you?

ARTHUR   Er . . . (**He is totally stumped by this**) . . . Could I have notice of that question?

LINTILLA 3   (**Approaching**) It's very strange. We were making hardly any progress at all without the drill, then just when I turned my back there was an extrordinary noise . . .

LINTILLA   What sort of noise?

LINTILLA 3   A sort of wheeeeeeeeekkkkkkkkrrrrunnnccccch noise (**This is of course the noise the narrator had been discussing**) and when I looked back a whole shaft had opened up. It's exposed all the archaeological seams. We're almost home and dry.

LINTILLA   But that's . . . that's impossible.

LINTILLA 3   I don't know about impossible. It's very improbable.

ARTHUR   **(Who's still off on his own line of thought)** But why are you all exactly the same as each other?

LINTILLA 2   Well you're exactly the same as yourself aren't you?

ARTHUR   This is true.

LINTILLA 3   Well then.

ARTHUR   But unhelpful.

LINTILLA   We're clones.

ARTHUR   Ah! Clones! I've heard of that! You mean there was one of you to begin with and then exact copies were made, and now there are three of you?

LINTILLA   Yes, except that there are now nearly five hundred and seventy eight thousand million of us.

ARTHUR   Huh?

LINTILLA   It's all right, the others aren't here at the moment. Can we get on with the work?

ARTHUR   **(Weakly)** That's rather a lot isn't it?

GRAMS   NARRATOR BACKGROUND.

NARRATOR   The problem of the five hundred and seventy eight thousand million Lintilla clones is very simple to explain, rather harder to solve. Cloning machines have of course been around for a long time and have proved very useful for reproducing particularly talented or attractive or (in response to pressure from the Sirius Cybernetics marketing lobby) particularly gullible people and this was all very fine and splendid and only occasionally terribly confusing. And then one particular cloning machine got badly out of synch with itself. Asked to produce six copies of a wonderfully talented and attractive girl called Lintilla for a Brantisvogan escort agency (whilst another machine was busy creating five hundred lonely business executives in order to keep the laws of supply and demand operating profitably) the machine went to work. Unfortunately it malfunctioned in such a way that it got half way through creating each new Lintilla before the previous one was actually completed, which meant, quite simply, that it was impossible ever to turn it off, without committing murder. This problem taxed the minds first of the cloning engineers, then of the priests, then of the letters page of the Sidereal Record Straightener, and finally of the lawyers who experimented vainly with ways of redefining murder, re-evaluating it and in the end even respelling it in the hope that no one would notice. A solution has now been found, but since it is not a particularly pleasant one, it will only be revealed if it becomes absolutely necessary.

Meanwhile, Arthur Dent is about to discover the terrifying truth about the somethings, or whatchamycallits of which the bird people refuse to speak.

LINTILLA	You see? These different strata in the rock face of the shaft represent the successive ages of this planet's history.
ARTHUR	Oh yes. Isn't that interesting?
LINTILLA	Interesting? It's frightening.
ARTHUR	Is it? Well actually it just looks like a slice of layer cake to me.
LINTILLA	Then why did you say it looked interesting?
ARTHUR	Oh, well I'm quite interested in layer cake.
LINTILLA	Look at it, doesn't anything strike you?
ARTHUR	Well it's . . . it's rock isn't it?
LINTILLA	Down here we have layer after layer – the remains of early settlements, one on top of another. Then more layers – thicker ones, the remains of cities, each built on the ruins of the previous one – we're talking about thousands of years you see – and then suddenly above this level – what?
ARTHUR	Er, more rock?
LINTILLA	But what's special about it?
ARTHUR	Er, well it's all smooth – no layers.
LINTILLA	Yes no further building and no one actually living on the planet, or at least on its surface. So this previous layer is the significant one. And do you know what it consists of?
ARTHUR	Rock?
LINTILLA	No.
ARTHUR	Er, stone?
LINTILLA	**(Patiently)** No.
ARTHUR	Some different sort of rock the name of which temporarily escapes me.
LINTILLA	No, feel it. Scratch it.
ARTHUR	Oh yes, it's slightly sort of soft and crumbly.
LINTILLA	What's it like?
ARTHUR	Ah, I know, it's . . .
LINTILLA	Yes?
ARTHUR	What's the name of that soft crumbly sort of rock?
LINTILLA	It isn't rock!
ARTHUR	Well what is it then?
LINTILLA	Shoes.
ARTHUR	What?
LINTILLA	Shoes, billions of them. An entire archaeological layer of compressed shoes.

ARTHUR	Shoes? How can you tell?
LINTILLA	We knew all along. We just needed confirmation.
ARTHUR	Why shoes?
F/X	LASER SHOT
HIG HURTENFLURST	Because, fella, shoes are the economic future of this galaxy.
ARTHUR	Huh?
HIG HURTENFLURST	Stand up. Both of you.
ARTHUR	Who are you?
HIG HURTENFLURST	I only happen to be Hig Hurtenflurst, I only happen to be the risingest young executive in the Dolmansaxlil Shoe Corporation, I only happen to have masterminded the entire rationalization of this planet to total shoe orientation, I only happen to be sitting on top of the biggest development deal in the entire history of footwear, and I only happen to be very deeply disturbed at finding my planet riddled with subversives bent on undermining the whole structure of the Dolmansaxlil operation and thus the very economic future of the Galaxy itself, and I only happen to think that I would be very well advised to have both of you weirdos and the other two chicks revoked on the spot, does that answer your question?
ARTHUR	I can't remember what I asked you now.
GRAMS	NARRATOR BACKGROUND
NARRATOR	There is of course also the question of the . . .
F/X	MARVIN FALLING F/X AS BEFORE
NARRATOR	. . . noise which, as has been suggested, was in some way connected with the sudden and fortuitous appearance of a deep shaft in the ground. Further noises are now to be heard at the very bottom of this shaft, which may go some way towards explaining the previous noise. This is what the new noise sounds like.
F/X	FAINT AND RATHER UNHAPPY BLIPS
MARVIN	**(Low groan – a very long one)**
NARRATOR	After a while it develops along these lines.
MARVIN	Googoogoogoogoo. Ddddrrrrpp. Errrrrrrk. Zootlowurdlezootlewurdle zootlowurdle. Fringggggg.
NARRATOR	And then continues thus.
MARVIN	F . . . f . . . f . . . f . . . Fact! I ache, therefore I am. Or in my case I am therefore I ache. Oh look – I appear to be lying at the bottom of a very deep dark hole. That seems a familiar concept. What does it remind me of? Ah, I remember. Life. That's what lying at the bottom of a deep dark hole reminds me of. Life. Perhaps if I just lie here and ignore it it will go away again.

(Pause)

Or then again, perhaps not. To be perfectly frank with myself, if it didn't go away as a result of me falling fifteen miles through the air and a further mile through solid rock I'm probably stuck with it for good. Why don't I just lie here anyway? Why don't I climb out? Why don't I just go zootlewurdle. Does it matter? Even if it does matter, does it matter that it matters?

(Pause)

Zootlewurdle zootlewurdle zootlewurdle . . .

(Fade)

GRAMS	NARRATOR BACKGROUND
NARRATOR	And so on. Meanwhile, at the top of the shaft, mere nanoseconds have passed since Arther said 'I can't remember what I asked you now'.
HIG HURTENFLURST	You.
LINTILLA	Me?
HIG HURTENFLURST	Why do those other two chicks we picked up look exactly like you?
LINTILLA	It's a long story.
HIG HURTENFLURST	Quick precis then.
LINTILLA	Because.
HIG HURTENFLURST	That's neat. Now listen, I could just have you revoked . . .
ARTHUR	Revoked?
HIG HURTENFLURST	Yes. K-i-l-l-e-d, revoked, but instead I think I'll suddenly take a liking to you both.
ARTHUR	Oh. Don't we get any say in the matter?
HIG HURTENFLURST	Footwarrior!
FOOTWARRIOR	Sir.
HIG	I've decided to take these two back to my office and like them.
FOOTWARRIOR	Sir.
HIG HURTENFLURST	I think I'd like them on the wall best. See to it. We'll go in my business-buggy.
FOOTWARRIOR	At once sir.
HIG HURTENFLURST	And don't limp!
FOOTWARRIOR	No sir, I'll try not to sir.
HIG HURTENFLURST	Don't just try, cut it right out.
FOOTWARRIOR	Yes sir.

HIG HURTENFLURST	Now you're limping with your other foot!
FOOTWARRIOR	Er, yes sir.
HIG HURTENFLURST	Don't limp with either foot!
FOOTWARRIOR	Right sir.
F/X	THE FOOTWARRIOR FALLS OVER
HIG HURTENFLURST	You two prisoners!
ARTHUR AND LINTILLA	Who, us?
HIG HURTENFLURST	Pick up the footwarrior and bring him with you.
FOOTWARRIOR	Thank you sir.
	(Fade)
	(Fade up)
F/X	DOOR HUMMING OPEN
HIG HURTENFLURST	Welcome to my office. The nerve centre of the operation here. Since you were so keen to find out the truth about us, you shall see it in comfort. Footwarrior!
FOOTWARRIOR	Sir?
HIG HURTENFLURST	Show them the film.
FOOTWARRIOR	Yes sir. Uh! Ah! **(i.e. the pain of walking)**
F/X	HE FALLS OVER
HIG HURTENFLURST	You two, carry him to the projectorscope.
ARTHUR	What's the matter with him?
HIG HURTENFLURST	His feet are the wrong size for his shoes.
ARTHUR	Ah.
FOOTWARRIOR	Thank you. Thank you so much.
F/X	PROJECTORSCOPE SWITCHED ON
GRAMS	TERRIBLE TRAINING FILM-LIKE MUSIC. THE REVS ARE VERY SLIGHTLY WONKY AND THE SOUND QUALITY SLIGHTLY BELOW PAR.
COMMENTATOR	**(Again, slightly distorted)** This is a Dolmansaxlil Galactic Shoe Corporation Film. Adventures in aggressive Marketing. Take a planet, any planet. Take for instance the planet Bartrax or Huntringfurl, or Earth, or Kiasbanil, or Asbleg, or any of the *many* planets we have currently declared marketing on.
ARTHUR	**(Interrupting on the word 'Earth', though the soundtrack continues of course)** The Earth! That's where I come from! But it's been demolished.

LINTILLA	In which case it's escaped a very nasty fate.
ARTHUR	What, worse than being demolished?
LINTILLA	Much. You watch.
COMMENTATOR	We will see what can really be achieved by looking at the planet Brontitall . . .
HIG HURTENFLURST	(Interrupting) That's my baby, they're very proud of me back at central office.
COMMENTATOR	Mere centuries ago, a happy prosperous busy planet all right, oho yes, not a care in their world . . .
F/X	(On soundtrack) BUSY STREET SCENE, LOTS OF HAPPY BUSTLE
MAN	(On soundtrack) Hello!
MAN TWO	(Ditto) Hello!
MAN THREE	(Ditto) Hello!
	(Etc. Ad lib)
MAN	(Ditto) Happy?
MAN TWO	(Ditto) Terribly happy today thank you. And you, prosperous?
MAN	(Ditto) Indeed so. Busy?
MAN TWO	(Ditto) Oh yes. And healthy, bright eyes, clear skin, feet in good nick. Isn't life a wonderful thing?
MAN	Super!
COMMENTATOR	Oh yes, only one tiny little thing wrong here. They're not making money for the Dolmansaxlil Shoe Corporation!
MEN	(Soundtrack) So?
COMMENTATOR	So, on the far side of their moon we set up a Dolmansaxlil Shoe Shop Intensifier Ray! And suddenly . . . the people are gripped by an insane, irrational desire to build . . .
F/X	ON THE SOUND TRACK A SERIES OF PINGS MARKS THE APPEARANCE OF SHOE SHOP AFTER SHOE SHOP.
COMMENTATOR	Shoe shops! In every road, on every street corner, in every city shopping precinct, shoe shop after shoe shop!
ARTHUR	(Catches his breath in horror) Oxford Street!
LINTILLA	What?
ARTHUR	Oxford Street! They just showed a picture of Oxford Street!
LINTILLA	Shhhh!
COMMENTATOR	And then we really put the screws on them! Oho yes! (He's very cheerful

220

	about this) Fashion! Every year the shoes in the shops are either much too wide or much too thin or in extreme cases even joined together at the heel! Oh yes, how we laughed up on the backside of their moon! How we *cried* with laughter when every last shop on the planet was turned into a shoe shop, how we coughed and spluttered with mirth when the people tried to revolt and we had to send in the footwarriors.
FOOTWARRIORS	(**On soundtrack**) (**They are in armoured cars talking through megaphones**) Do not panic! Lay down your arms! We just want you to relax and enjoy your shoes!
F/X	(**On soundtrack**) DISTANT MACHINE GUN FIRE AND MORTARS ETC., CROWDS RIOTING
FOOTWARRIORS	(**On soundtrack**) They are very stylish and fashion conscious! Be cool! Step out in style! Relax and enjoy your shoes! Relax and enjoy your shoes, relax and . . . ennnnjjjjooyyyyy . . . yyyyoo . . .
F/X	THIS IS THE SOUND OF THE TAPE SUDDENLY GRINDING TO A HALT AS IF THE POWER'S BEEN CUT OFF
	A FEW FUSES FIZZ AND POP
	A BACKGROUND GENERATOR HUM DIES AWAY
HIG HURTENFLURST	(**In alarm**) What's happening? Why have the lights gone out? Footwarrior!
FOOTWARRIOR	Sir.
HIG HURTENFLURST	Go to the emergency power supply!
FOOTWARRIOR	Can't sir! Think I've got gangrene of the feet!
HIG HURTENFLURST	Then just seize the prisoners!
F/X	FOOTWARRIOR FALLS OVER
HIG HURTENFLURST	Prisoners!
ARTHUR LINTILLA	Yes?
HIG HURTENFLURST	Seize each other! Now what's going on out here?
F/X	GENERAL COMMOTION HAS BUILT UP. THE DOOR IS BROKEN DOWN
HIG HURTENFLURST	Who's that breaking down the door?
F/X	MARVIN ENTERS
ARTHUR	Marvin!
MARVIN	I suppose you'll want to be rescued now.
HIG HURTENFLURST	Oh, yes please.
ARTHUR	Not you. Come on Lintilla, let's get out of here!
MARVIN	Well come on if you're coming.

LINTILLA	(**Desperately**) Wait! I've just got to turn on my crisis inducer. There. Ah! Come on, they're after us!
F/X	THEY RUSH THROUGH THE DOOR INTO THE CORRIDOR
LINTILLA	Down the corridor!
ARTHUR	This way?
LINTILLA	Yes.
ARTHUR	That's up the corridor.
LINTILLA	All right, *up* the bloody corridor, come on.
ARTHUR	Oh that *way*, I thought you were pointing . . .
LINTILLA	Come on!
F/X	THEY RUN INTO THE DISTANCE
	(**Fade**)
GRAMS	NARRATOR BACKGROUND
NARRATOR	And so everything points to shoes as being the mysterious somethings or watchamaycallits of which the bird people would not speak.
	And the curious fact is that the shoe shop intensifier ray mentioned mere seconds ago is in actuality a phoney, designed to make Dolmansaxlil executives feel they are doing something excitingly aggressive, when in fact all they need to do is wait.
	The shoe event Horizon is now a firmly established and rather sad economic phenomenon, which in future times will be taught as part of the basic Middle School Life the Universe and Everything syllabus. Here is a typical computer class from the Brantisvogan Megalycee, Unidate 911VCK168.
COMPUTEACH	Good morning Life form.
PUPIL	Hi, teach.
COMPUTEACH	Are you sitting comfortably?
PUPIL	Yes.
COMPUTEACH	Then stand up. Harsh Economic Truths class 17. You are standing up?
PUPIL	Yes.
COMPUTEACH	Good. Posit: You are living in an exciting go ahead civilization. Where are you looking?
PUPIL	Up
COMPUTEACH	What do you see?
PUPIL	The open sky, the stars, an infinite horizon.
COMPUTEACH	Correct. You may press the button.

PUPIL	(**Enthusiastically**) Thank you!
F/X	A NICE THRILLING PING
PUPIL	Oo, that feels nice.
COMPUTEACH	Posit: You are living in a stagnant declining civilization. Where are you looking?
PUPIL	Down.
COMPUTEACH	What do you see?
PUPIL	My shoes.
COMPUTEACH	Correct. What do you do to cheer yourself up?
PUPIL	Er, press the button?
COMPUTEACH	Incorrect. Think again. Your world is a depressing place, you are looking at your shoes, how do you cheer yourself up?
PUPIL	I buy a new pair!
COMPUTEACH	Correct.
PUPIL	Can I press the button?
COMPUTEACH	All right.
F/X	THRILLING LITTLE PING AS BEFORE.
PUPIL	Oh that's so nice.
COMPUTEACH	Now, imagine everyone does the same thing, what happens?
PUPIL	Everyone feels nice?
COMPUTEACH	Forget the button! Concentrate! Everyone buys new shoes, what happens?
PUPIL	More shoes!
COMPUTEACH	And?
PUPIL	More shoe shops!
COMPUTEACH	Correct.
PUPIL	Can I . . .
COMPUTEACH	No!
PUPIL	Oh.
COMPUTEACH	And in order to support all these extra shoe shops, what must happen?
PUPIL	Everyone must keep buying shoes.
COMPUTEACH	And how is that arranged?
PUPIL	(**Getting bored, reciting things parrot fashion**) Manufacturers dictate more and more different fashions and make shoes so badly that they either hurt the feet or fall apart.

COMPUTEACH	So that . . .?
PUPIL	Everyone has to buy more shoes.
COMPUTEACH	Until?
PUPIL	Until everyone gets fed up with lousy rotten shoes. (SUBTEXT: 'I'm getting fed up with this lousy rotten lesson.')
COMPUTEACH	And then what?
PUPIL	Why can't I press the button?
COMPUTEACH	(Sternly) And then what? Come on.
PUPIL	Massive capital investment by the manufacturers to try and make people buy the shoes.
COMPUTEACH	Which means?
PUPIL	More shoe shops.
COMPUTEACH	And then we reach what point?
PUPIL	The point where I press the button again.
COMPUTEACH	(Reluctantly) All right.
F/X	THRILLING ZING AS BEFORE
PUPIL	Ooh! Oo! Oo! That's so nice, that's really nice!
COMPUTEACH	And then we reach what point?
PUPIL	(Quite happy and enthusiastic again now) The shoe event horizon. The whole economy overbalances. Shoe shops outnumber every other kind of shop, it becomes economically impossible to build anything other than shoe shops, and bing, I get to press the button again.
F/X	THRILLING ZING AGAIN
PUPIL	Weeehoo!
COMPUTEACH	Wait for permission! Now, what's the final stage?
PUPIL	Er. Every shop in the world ends up a shoe shop.
COMPUTEACH	Full of?
PUPIL	Shoes no one can wear.
COMPUTEACH	Result?
PUPIL	Famine, collapse and ruin. Any survivors eventually evolve into birds and never put their feet on the ground again.
COMPUTEACH	Excellent. End of lesson. You may press the button.
F/X	SEVERAL ZINGS
PUPIL	Weee! Heeehooo! Gigigigihooo! Ooo, that's nice! Thank you teach, goodbye.

COMPUTEACH	Aren't you forgetting something?
PUPIL	What?
COMPUTEACH	Press the other button.
PUPIL	Oh, right.
F/X	A SIMILAR ZING, BUT OBVIOUSLY A DIFFERENT ONE, PROBABLY A BIT DEEPER THAN THE OTHER ONE.
COMPUTEACH	Ooooohhhhhh!!! That's so nice.
GRAMS	NARRATOR BACKGROUND
NARRATOR	And so forth. Meanwhile, at the Dolmansaxlil base the excitement is of course mounting.
F/X	LINTILLA AND ARTHUR RUNNING TOWARDS US AND SLOWING TO A HALT, PANTING
ARTHUR	You did a good job finding us Marvin. Where have you been?
MARVIN	In a deep dark hole. I climbed out because I started to like it too much.
ARTHUR	Come on, keep moving. We must find a way out of here.
LINTILLA	Right.
GRAMS	NARRATOR BACKGROUND
NARRATOR	Whilst a mere mile or so to the east, Zaphod Beeblebrox and Ford Prefect are very keen to find their way *into* somewhere, namely some sort of shelter from the continuing revenge of the bird people. They find it in the form of a derelict building, which is vast, very low, and very very old . . .
F/X	FORD AND ZAPHOD RUNNING TOWARDS US. AS THEY REACH US THEY COME TO A HALT. SPLATS AND ANGRY BIRD NOISES AS BEFORE.
FORD	The door! Open it!
F/X	GRINDING NOISE OF A VERY OLD MOTOR STRAINING TO WORK. THE DOOR ONLY HALF OPENS AND SLOWLY
ZAPHOD	Force it man, force it.
F/X	THEY BOTH STRAIN PUSHING AT THE DOOR. IT GRATES ALONG ITS GROOVES
FORD	Ok, get in!
F/X	THE AURAL PERSPECTIVE OPENS UP INTO A VAST DRAUGHTY ECHOEY HANGAR
ZAPHOD	Hey, look at this. Look what we found man.
FORD	Amazing.
ZAPHOD	It's a derelict space port.

FORD	Looks like no one's been in for centuries. All these amazing old ships.
ZAPHOD	Yeah.
FORD	Just rust and wreckage.
ZAPHOD	Yeah.
F/X	WE HEAR THEIR FOOTSTEPS WANDERING ABOUT, ECHOING
ZAPHOD	Spooky, man. Like, er, what are those things eggs come out of?
FORD	Birds.
ZAPHOD	No, after that.
FORD	Eh?
ZAPHOD	What do they come out of the birds in?
FORD	Eggshells?
ZAPHOD	That's it. Like just huge broken eggshells. And all the dust, man. And the huge cobwebs.
FORD	And where you get huge cobwebs, you get . . .
ZAPHOD	Look out man!
F/X	WITH A SORT OF GRUNTY SCREECH A HEAVY BODY DROPS BESIDE THEM.
SPIDER	**(With a voice like 'Boris the Spider')** 'Scuse me.
F/X	IT SCUTTLES OFF.
ZAPHOD	One huge spider.
FORD	Polite though.
ZAPHOD	Transtellar Spacelines. Must have been real googy ships once, but now . . .
FORD	One look and they'd fall apart. I mean, look at that one . . .
F/X	WITH A GREAT GRINDING RUMBLE A HUGE SPACELINER COLLAPSES INTO ITS OWN DUST.
ZAPHOD	**(With wonder in his voice)** It fell apart man.
FORD	Hey, but look at that one – the big one over there. It's covered with muck and dust – but – looks like it's still in one piece.
ZAPHOD	Hey, yeah, and it's still connected to its supply-lines. Man, feel this supply-line.
FORD	Hey, it's . . .
ZAPHOD	Yeah.
FORD	Weird.
ZAPHOD	You know what I'm thinking?

FORD   No.

ZAPHOD   Neither do I. Frightening isn't it?

FORD   Let's take a look.

F/X   THEY HURRY OVER TO THE SHIP

ZAPHOD   Ford.

FORD   Yeah?

ZAPHOD   Is this ship . . .?

FORD   It feels like it's on power. Just a very slight vibration.

ZAPHOD   But it must have been here for centuries . . . Hey man, pass me those four bits of tubing.

FORD   These?

ZAPHOD   Yeah – gonna make me a stethoscope and take a listen to this baby. There . . . and there, like that.

F/X   SOUND OF HIM MANIPULATING THE TUBING, TO WHICH HIS LAST SENTENCE REFERS

FORD   You hear anything?

ZAPHOD   Hey . . . yeah, yeah I can hear . . . something . . .

FORD   What is it?

ZAPHOD   (**A low slow gasp of horror**) Ford . . . I don't believe what I just heard . . .

FORD   Here, let me listen . . .

ZAPHOD   OK . . . but – you better keep your head screwed on kid . . .

GRAMS   NARRATOR BACKGROUND

NARRATOR   What has Zaphod heard in the spaceliner, and is it really as horrifying as all that? Will it lead him directly to the discovery of his goal – despite his singular lack of exertion in that direction?

Will it become absolutely necessary to reveal the unpleasant solution to the problem of Lintilla's clones?

Will everything tie up neatly, or will it be just like life – quite interesting in parts, but no substitute for the real thing?

What is the real thing?

Some of these questions may possibly be answered in the next inexplicable episode of *The Hitch-Hiker's Guide to the Galaxy*.

ANNOUNCER   Many sentences contained in that programme were of a very dangerous length, and were performed by highly trained vocal practitioners. On no account should inexperienced life-forms attempt to imitate them without proper medical jaw and lung supervision.

FOOTNOTES

This show was recorded on 6 January 1980.

David Tate was the Commentator in Dolmansaxlil training film and also the Computeach, and Stephen Moore was his pupil. Rula Lenska played all her clones as well as Lintilla and Mark Smith only happened to be Hig Hurtenflurst.

The three Lintillas were made by slightly altering the pitch of each one and overlaying them over each other. The first few lines of the narration speech on cloning were cloned about four or five times by putting the lines out of synch several times.

Dolmansaxlil is an amalgam of several well known shoe shops that might be found in Oxford Street. Douglas has this to say on the subject of shoes.

Shoes

This was written in a rage , after spending three days, *three days*, trying to buy a pair of shoes in central London. Nothing special, just an ordinary pair of shoes. You cannot hurl a brick in Oxford Street without hitting half a dozen shoe shops, and after three days, *three days*, that was exactly what I wanted to do. Can you buy a pair of shoes in any of them? No. Shop after shop, all virtually next to each other, carried exactly the same range, and were all out of stock of exactly the same styles and sizes. Who organizes this? Has he been caught yet? I must stop or I will start ranting and sounding like John Osborne. [DNA]

The Footwarrior scenes seem slightly surreal in retrospect since I can remember clomping around at four o'clock in the morning the day before transmission with my foot in a waste paper bin full of cigarette ends. (The cigarette ends were not essential for the sound effect but I was just too tired to take them out.)

The Footwarrior's voice was one of the few that did actually use the Vocoder, which puts the basic voice through a synthesized note and leaves it sounding a little like Sparky's Magic piano . . . (if anybody remembers that).

FIT THE TWELFTH

In which all is resolved, everyone lives happily ever after, and pigs fly.

MAN IN SHACK I have no idea. It merely pleases me to behave in a certain way to what appears to be a cat.

GRAMS	NARRATOR BACKGROUND
NARRATOR	What we find is this: that Ford Prefect and Zaphod Beeblebrox have broken into an ancient building, concerning which they have reached the following conclusion:
ZAPHOD	(**From Fit The Eleventh**) It's a derelict space port!
NARRATOR	. . . and within which they have discovered a large number of . . .
FORD	(**From Fit The Eleventh**) . . . amazing old ships!
NARRATOR	. . . Whose condition has been described by Ford Prefect in these terms:
FORD	(**From Fit The Eleventh**) Just rust and wreckage.
NARRATOR	. . . and by Zaphod Beeblebrox like this:
ZAPHOD	(**From Fit The Eleventh**) Like just huge broken eggshells.
NARRATOR	We find that one ship has caught their eye for this reason:
FORD	(**From Fit The Eleventh**) It's covered with muck and dust, but looks like it's still in one piece.
ZAPHOD	Hey, yeah, and it's still connected to its supply-lines.
NARRATOR	. . . and that this provokes them into closer investigation. This is what they find.
FORD	It feels like it's on power. Just a very slight vibration.
ZAPHOD	But it must have been here for centuries . . . hey man, pass me those four bits of tubing.
FORD	These?
ZAPHOD	Yeah. Gonna make me a stethoscope and take a listen to this baby. There . . . and there, like that.
F/X	SOUND OF HIM MANIPULATING TUBING
FORD	You hear anything?
ZAPHOD	Hey, yeah . . . yeah . . . I can hear . . . something . . .
FORD	What is it?
ZAPHOD	(**A long slow gasp of horror**) Ford . . . I don't believe what I just heard . . .
FORD	Here, let me listen . . .
ZAPHOD	I've been looking at the flight schedules. Man, this ship is late . . . man this ship is very, very late . . . Man, this ship is over nine hundred years late.
FORD	Zaphod – we got to get in there.
ZAPHOD	But man can you cope with what we might find?
FORD	I don't know. We got to get in there.
ZAPHOD	We got to get in there. What we find, we find.

GRAMS	NARRATOR BACKGROUND
NARRATOR	What we also find is that Arthur Dent, Marvin and the girl Lintilla who, as has already been established, has now been cloned over five hundred and seventy eight thousand million times and has thus created a problem in some quarters are now thoroughly lost in the Dolmansaxlil base. This is because there is no light, which is in turn because Marvin has done something aggravating to the Domansaxlil power supply, which is in turn because he was anxious to create some confusion under cover of which he could rescue Arthur and Lintilla, which was in turn because they had been captured by Hig Hurtenflurst, which was in turn because . . . and so on back to the initial and highly controversial creation of the Universe. Only two of Lintilla's five hundred and seventy eight thousand million clones are on the planet Brontitall with her, and it is more than likely that we shall also find them.
LINTILLA 2 & 3	**(From a distance)** Lintilla?
ARTHUR	Ah, there's your better half and worse half. Or at least your exactly the same halves. Thirds. Whatever. Why do people lead such complicated lives?
LINTILLA	**(Who starts this line about half-way through Arthur's previous line. Arthur carries on to the end of his line just to himself)** Lintilla! Lintilla! What happened to you?
LINTILLA 2	**(Approaching)** There were a couple of footwarriors standing guard over us.
LINTILLA 3	But after a while they sat guard over us.
LINTILLA 2	Then they wandered away to find some corn plasters.
LINTILLA 3	And so we escaped.
ARTHUR	Right, where are we going?
MARVIN	How should I know? It's your Universe. You go where you like.
LINTILLA	We'll get back to our ship.
ARTHUR	I thought you said it didn't work.
LINTILLA	There's a derelict spaceport about a mile or so from here. We might be able to get some parts to repair it with.
ARTHUR	Ah, well I'm not very skilled at repairing spaceships.
LINTILLA	You can learn.
ARTHUR	Take a bit of time, I think.
LINTILLA	You could take some evening classes.
ARTHUR	What here?
LINTILLA	Yes, I've got a bottle of them. Little pink ones.
F/X	PILL BOTTLE RATTLE

ARTHUR	Well . . .
LINTILLA	Come on then, let's get out of here before they restore the power and find us.
F/X	GENERATOR HUM STARTS UP AND ALARMS AS WELL
LINTILLA	They restored the power.
F/X	LAZOR ZAPS START . . . CONTINUE AD LIB
ARTHUR	They've found us. Keep down.
F/X	FIRING CONTINUES AND GETS LOUDER. DISTANT SHOUTS OF FOOTWARRIORS
ARTHUR	It probably seems a terrible thing to say, but you know what I sometimes think would be useful in these situations?
LINTILLA	What?
ARTHUR	A gun of some sort.
LINTILLA 2	Will this help?
ARTHUR	What is it?
LINTILLA 2	It's a gun of some sort.
ARTHUR	Oh, that'll help. Can you make it fire?
LINTILLA	Er . . .
F/X	DEAFENING ROAR
LINTILLA	Yes.
ARTHUR	Right. Look, why don't you keep firing at them. I'll make a dash for the next intersection, you throw me the gun, I'll keep firing and you make a dash for it. Did you ever see Gunfight at the OK . . . no you wouldn't have done.
LINTILLA	What?
ARTHUR	Never mind.
LINTILLA	No, what?
ARTHUR	Oh, just an old western. Please, I don't want to talk about it. Right. Everyone understand?
LINTILLAS	(**Tutti**) Yes.
ARTHUR	Marvin?
MARVIN	Understand? You ask me if *I* understand?
ARTHUR	Yes or no?
MARVIN	Guess.
ARTHUR	Right, I'm going. You fire, I'll run. Now!

F/X   ARTHUR RUNS. LINTILLA FIRES. WE STAY WITH ARTHUR. HE IS RUNNING HARD AND PANTING. SHOTS RICCOCHET AROUND HIM

HE STOPS AND PANTS HEAVILY. HE TAKES A DEEP BREATH TO SHOUT

ARTHUR   Right . . .

(**A voice, unexpectedly close, slightly coarse and slightly ingratiating interrupts him. It's owner's name is Poodoo**)

POODOO   Er, excuse me.

ARTHUR   (**Caught in mid-shout and off his guard, practically chokes**)

Huh? Who are you.

POODOO   Me? Ah well you see what it is you see, is I'm Poodoo, and look, I'm sorry to interrupt, are you busy?

ARTHUR   What? Yes.

POODOO   Can I just ask you something?

ARTHUR   No. In a minute. Please get back. (**He turns to shout back to the Lintillas**) Right! Lint . . .

POODOO   Only I can see you are busy, so I won't take up a moment of your time. If I could just . . .

ARTHUR   What?

POODOO   . . . introduce a couple of friends of mine, well three actually. Four if you count the priest.

ALLITNIL 1,2,3   (**In turn, but very quickly**) Hello. (**Identical voices**)

PRIEST   Hello.

ARTHUR   Huh?

POODOO   Only we were wondering . . .

ARTHUR   Who are you?

POODOO   Can I just ask you something?

ARTHUR   Look, please . . .

(**The firing and pandemonium are continuing in the background, also we should very vaguely and not obtrusively hear shouts continuing in the background from the footwarriors, like: 'In the name of the Dolmansaxlil Shoe Corporation we demand that you give yourselves up. Come out with your hands up! We've got you covered. Shooting us won't do you any good. Or us for that matter . . .' etc. etc. ad lib**)

POODOO   It's just, do you know those girls over there?

ARTHUR   What? Yes.

POODOO	Oh that's good, thank you very much, that's all I wanted. That's all, thanks.
ARTHUR	Good. (**Turns to shout**) Lintilla! Throw the gun!!
POODOO	Only why I ask you see is, and seeing as you're busy I'll just be very brief . . . did I introduce my friends?
ARTHUR	Yes.
POODOO	I'm sure they'd like to introduce themselves.
ALLITNIL 1	Hello, I'm Allitnil. (**To get this name, we record him saying 'Lintilla' and then reverse that piece of tape**)
ALLITNIL 2	So am I.
ALLITNIL 3	Me too.
ARTHUR	Go away.
POODOO	And this is Vartvar the priest.
PRIEST	Var*n*tvar.
POODOO	Var*n*tvar. He's a priest you see. Does marriages and other things, but mostly marriages, only . . .
ARTHUR	Shut up.
POODOO	We were wondering if you could introduce Allitnil . . .
	(**Same treatment**)
ARTHUR	Who?
POODOO	Allitnil. And Allitnil and Allitnil, to the girls, your lady friends.
ARTHUR	(**Just trying to ignore it**) Lintilla!!
POODOO	Yes, that's right. Just socially you see. All very pleasant.
ARTHUR	Throw the gun!
POODOO	We've brought some drinks. We can just have a quiet social get together. And some music of course. Got to have some music. Here we go.
F/X	POODOO TURNS ON A SMALL CASSETTE RECORDER WHICH PLAYS RATHER TINNILY SOME SLUSHY HOTEL BAR MUSIC
ARTHUR	Throw the gun!!!
F/X	THE GUN LANDS WITH A CLATTER BESIDE ARTHUR
LINTILLA	(**Distant**) Got it?
ARTHUR	Got it. Now when I start firing, run!
F/X	ARTHUR STARTS FIRING. POODOO HAS TO RAISE HIS VOICE OVER THE SOUND OF THE GUN
POODOO	Then if it all goes very well you see, we've got a priest on hand in case anybody wants to get married at all. Just to round off the evening.

ARTHUR	Are you totally mad?
POODOO	No no, they're not married yet. Oh did you say mad?
ARTHUR	Yes.
POODOO	Oh no, well I don't think so. I thought you said married. Course they would be mad talking about marrying these girls if they were married already. Well, they could talk about it of course, but somebody else would have to actually do it. Anyway . . .
ARTHUR	Shut up.
POODOO	Right ho squire.
ARTHUR	(**Shouts**) Run!!
POODOO	They're quite keen to get married though. Aren't you?
ALLITNIL 1	Yes.
ALLITNIL 2	Oh yes.
ALLITNIL 3	Very much so.
ARTHUR	Where did you nutters come from? Run!!!
POODOO	Well what we did was you see, we flew in. We flew in you see. Oh yes, we definitely flew in.
ARTHUR	Well bloody fly out again.
F/X	THE THREE LINTILLAS (WHO ARE NOT AN ITALIAN HIGH WIRE ACT, THOUGH I'M SURE WE DON'T ACTUALLY NEED TO MENTION THIS FACT, ONLY PERHAPS, WELL I DON'T KNOW, PUT IT IN ANYWAY) THE THREE LINTILLAS AND MARVIN RUN TOWARDS THEM. ARTHUR IS FIRING HARD
ARTHUR	Lintilla, Lintilla, Lintilla! Are you all right?
LINTILLAS	(**Who are still not an Italian High Wire Act, just in case I caused any confusion with my last note on the matter**) Yes.
POODOO	Hello ladies.
	(**A moment or so later they suddenly gasp with delighted astonishment, but meanwhile Arthur has become engrossed in a very brief conversation with Marvin**)
ARTHUR	Marvin? (**i.e. Are you all right too**)
MARVIN	Never better.
ARTHUR	Good.
MARVIN	Still very bad though.
ARTHUR	Right. All you Lintillas, can you start firing again whilst I run the next bit?
LINTILLAS	Ahh!!

ARTHUR	Lintilla? What's going on?
F/X	MEANWHILE, POODOO HAS TURNED HIS TAPE ON AGAIN. THERE IS THE SOUND OF CLINKING GLASSES AND DRINKS BEING POURED

(The Lintillas and the Allitnils are saying hello to each other, they are all overcome with shyness but obviously attracted to each other)

F/X	SHOTS AND CRIES STILL COMING FROM THE FOOTWARRIORS IN THE DISTANCE
POODOO	I think the lads and lasses are just getting acquainted. I'd leave them to it if I were you.
ARTHUR	What? Look, we're trying to escape from the footwarriors. Can we have parties later?
LINTILLA	But, Arthur . . .
LINTILLA 2	We can't believe it! ⎫ OVERLAPPING
LINTILLA 3	These are the most attractive men we've ever met! ⎭
ARTHUR	(Simultaneously astonished, worried about the footwarriors, and slightly disappointed. Bit of anger in there too. Come on Simon, you can do it) Are they?
ALLITNIL 1	Oh Lintilla!
ALLITNIL 2	All my life I've longed for such a moment! ⎫ OVERLAPPING
ALLITNIL 3	You're all my dreams come true. ⎭
POODOO	Touching isn't it?
ARTHUR	Look, what the *hell* is going on here?
F/X	SOME FOOTWARRIOR ZAPS ARE NOW GETTING PERILOUSLY CLOSE
POODOO	Oh, just happiness, squire, only it's nice to bring a little happiness into life don't you think?
ARTHUR	Yes, but there's a time and place for everything.

(General inarticulate sounds of love and happiness from the Lintillas and the Allitnils)

ARTHUR	Well I'll just get on with the shooting and saving everybody's lives then shall I?
F/X	BLAST OF GUNFIRE FROM ARTHUR'S GUN
POODOO	No kissing, now, lovebirds. Very old fashioned sector of the galaxy this. No kissing allowed without names firmly on marriage certificates.

(Burst of disappointment from the six lovers)

POODOO	Oh, looks like a cue for action from you then doesn't it padre? And I just

happen to have the warrants for your marriage, sorry, *licences* about my person . . .

F/X   ANOTHER BURST OF GUNFIRE FROM ARTHUR

ARTHUR   (**Mutters to himself**) Mad. Totally bonkers.

POODOO   And then as soon as you're all happily conjoined you can get on with escaping and everything knowing that you have the love, support and trust of your chosen partners. Nice isn't it? Now who's going to marry whom?

F/X   ANOTHER BURST OF GUNFIRE

ARTHUR   (**Shouting**) Listen, you footwarriors, can you hold hard a bit with the firing? I've just got three impromptu weddings breaking out behind me.

FOOTWARRIORS   (**Calling from a distance**) What?

ARTHUR   Weddings. You know, with this ring I thee wed and that sort of stuff.

FOOTWARRIORS   Did you say weddings?

ARTHUR   Yes.

(**Almost inaudible mutterings from footwarriors 'Did he say weddings?' 'Yes, I think so.' etc.**)

FOOTWARRIORS   Can we come?

ARTHUR   No! Stay back!

F/X   ANOTHER BURST OF GUNFIRE

PRIEST   Dearly beloved, we are gathered . . .

POODOO   Yeah, yeah, we'll skip all that. Let's just get straight on with the signing and the pronouncement, shall we?

ARTHUR   (**To himself**) Let's just go mad shall we?

F/X   MORE FIRING

POODOO   Now what you all do you see is you sign here, that's right, look, let's change the music, something a bit special for you . . .

F/X   THE TINNY MUSIC ON THE CASSETTE CHANGES TO THE WEDDING MARCH

ARTHUR   (**Shouting to the footwarriors**) Keep back!

F/X   BURST OF FIRING FROM ARTHUR

POODOO   That's good, that's very good. Right, padre.

PRIEST   I now pronounce you men and wives.

POODOO   Men, you can kiss your brides.

F/X   ONE KISS, FOLLOWED BY A CRY FROM ONE LINTILLA WHICH VANISHES WITH A SMALL CLAP OF THUNDER OR A WHOOSH OR SOMETHING, FOLLOWED BY THE SAME SEQUENCE AGAIN

ARTHUR	(**Cry of utter horror, real over the top time**) Lintilla!
GRAMS	NARRATOR BACKGROUND
NARRATOR	(**His voice should enter almost on top of Arthur's line**) Nervewrackingly enough, the moment at which two Lintillas and two Allitnils unexpectedly vanish in what can only be described as a puff of unsmoke, coming as it does only seconds before Arthur discovers that Poodoo's alleged marriage licences are not what they purport to be but are in fact 'agreements to cease to be' drawn up by the Cloning Machine Company's lawyers, is also the moment at which it becomes necessary to consider new developments in the Ford Prefect/Zaphod Beeblebrox situation. Having gained access to the ship, they prepare to enter the passenger compartments. This is what they find:
F/X	(VERY QUICKLY, SO THAT IT DOESN'T INTERRUPT THE FLOW OF THIS VERY EXCITING PIECE OF NARRATIVE) A DOOR HUMS OPEN
FORD	Passengers!
ZAPHOD	(**Awestruck**) Yeah . . .
FORD	But alive!
ZAPHOD	Sleeping.
FORD	For all these years?
ZAPHOD	Suspended animation.
FORD	And the voice we heard?
ZAPHOD	Android stewardess. Look, here she comes now . . .
STEWARDESS	Good afternoon ladies and gentlemen. Thank you for bearing with us during this slight delay. We will be taking off as soon as we possibly can. If you would like to wake up now I will serve you coffee and biscuits. Wake up now.
F/X	ALL THE PASSENGERS WAKE UP WITH A START AND A MASS CRY OF HORROR FURY AND ANGUISH. THIS SHOULD BE REALLY SHOCKING AND FRIGHTENING
ZAPHOD	Run, man!
F/X	AS THE TERRIBLE NOISE FROM THE PASSENGERS CONTINUES UNABATED, WE HEAR FORD AND ZAPHOD RUN TO A DOOR WHICH HUMS OPEN, AND CLOSED BEHIND THEM, CUTTING OUT PART OF THE NOISE. THEY RUN A BIT FURTHER, ANOTHER DOOR HUMS OPEN, AND CLOSED BEHIND THEM, CUTTING THE SOUND A BIT MORE. THEY RUN FURTHER. ANOTHER DOOR HUMS OPEN AND CLOSED BEHIND THEM, CUTTING OFF THE NOISE FROM THE PASSENGERS COMPLETELY. THE NEW PLACE THEY HAVE ARRIVED IN IS THE FLIGHT DECK.

ALL SYSTEMS ON THE FLIGHT DECK ARE IN SLOW TIME MODE, SO THE USUAL ASSORTMENT OF BLIPS AND WHIRRS SOUND VERY SLOW, DEEP AND HOLLOW.

ZAPHOD AND FORD ARRIVE PANTING. (DOING A LOT OF THIS AREN'T THEY?)

THEY ARE ALSO FAIRLY DISTURBED

ZAPHOD **(Collapsing and panting)** Hey, what gives, man, what gives, what gives, what gives? What gives!

FORD They woke up! They all woke up! It was . . . I've never . . . **(Ad lib inarticulacy)**

AUTOPILOT Passengers are not allowed on the flight deck. Please return to your seats and wait for the ship to take off. Coffee and biscuits are being served. This is your autopilot speaking. Please return to your seats.

ZAPHOD Go back in there?

FORD We're not passengers.

AUTOPILOT Please return to your seats.

ZAPHOD We're not passengers.

AUTOPILOT Please return to your seats.

ZAPHOD We're not . . . hello? Can you hear me?

FORD What's happening on this hell ship?

AUTOPILOT There has been a delay. The passengers are kept in temporary suspended animation for their comfort and convenience. Coffee and biscuits are served every ten years, after which passengers are returned to suspended animation for their comfort and convenience. Departure will take place when flight stores are complete. We apologize for the delay.

FORD Delay? Have you seen the world outside this ship? It's a wasteland, a desert. Civilization's been and gone. It's over. There are no lemon soaked paper napkins on the way from anywhere.

AUTOPILOT The statistical likelihood is that other civilizations will arise. There will one day be lemon soaked paper napkins. Till then, there will be a short delay. Please return to your seats.

FORD We are not . . .

AUTOPILOT Please return to your seats! Return to your seats! Return to your seats! Return to your seats!

(Etc. Etc., the voice gets louder and louder, building up an oppressive metallic echo. The sound becomes very painful)

FORD **(Shouting)** Let's get out of here! This way!

ZAPHOD No! This way!

FORD	Why?
ZAPHOD	First class. Come on.

F/X   DOOR HUMS OPEN. REPEAT THE FIRST SERIES OF RUNNING FEET AND OPENING AND CLOSING DOORS. THIS TIME WITH THE SOUND OF THE AUTOPILOT'S VOICE GRADUALLY FADING BEHIND US

AS THE LAST DOOR OPENS AND CLOSES THEY STOP RUNNING, BUT PANT AGAIN. BEFORE THEY HAVE TIME TO CATCH THEIR BREATH A VOICE SPEAKS TO THEM

MAN	Zaphod Beeblebrox?
ZAPHOD	(**As if spinning round**) Huh? Who?
MAN	My name's Zarniwoop. You wanted to see me. Please sit down.
GRAMS	NARRATOR BACKGROUND
NARRATOR	And since this is of course an immensely frustrating and nervewracking moment for the narrative suddenly to switch tracks again, that is precisely what the narrative will now do.
ARTHUR	Lintilla – are you all right?
LINTILLA	(**Weakly**) I think so. Just shattered and drained.
ARTHUR	Marvin's got Poodoo and the priest under control. They're . . .
LINTILLA	They're from the cloning machine company, I know.
ARTHUR	Marvin's tied them up. He's put a cassette of his autobiography in their tape machine and left it running, so I think it's all up with them.

(**In the background we hear vaguely:**)

MARVIN	In the beginning I was made. I didn't ask to be made, no one consulted me or considered my feelings in the matter. I don't think it even occurred to them that I might have feelings, but if it brought some passing sadistic pleasure to some mentally benighted humans as they pranced their haphazard way through life's mournful jungle then so be it. After I was made I was left in a dark room for six months, and me with this terrible pain in all the diodes down my left side. I called for succour in my loneliness, but did anyone come? Did they hell. My first and only true friend was a small rat. One day it crawled into a cavity in my right ankle and died. I've a horrible feeling it's still there . . .

(**This is accompanied by agonized shrieks from Poodoo and Varntvar**)

ARTHUR	And as for the third Allitnil – well it's the only time I've ever killed a man in cold blood, and I don't feel awfully . . .
LINTILLA	He wasn't a real man. He was an anticlone. There must be millions of them now roaming the galaxy. Wiping out my sisters. What's happened to the footwarriors?

ARTHUR The Flying Chiropodist arrived. They all went off to have a word with him. Are you fit?

LINTILLA Yes. I'm fine really I am. Come on. We must get to the spaceport. Coming Marvin?

MARVIN I suppose so.

(Fade)

(Fade up. External acoustic. Wind)

ARTHUR There it is. Just a mile away. Nice clear day for a brisk walk. See that huge form over there in the distance?

LINTILLA Yes.

ARTHUR Fifteen mile high statue of me throwing a cup. Not often one comes across that sort of thing. Up there you see is the cup itself. Apparently it's held there by art. Wonderful isn't it? Just a pity that our ship's parked in it.

LINTILLA Arthur! Look! Look, it's coming down!

ARTHUR What? God, so it is! The cup's coming down! No it isn't! The ground's going up.

F/X DEEP RUMBLES

LINTILLA The sky's moving . . . sideways? It's folding up!

ARTHUR What's happening?

MARVIN Oh dear, I think you'll find reality's on the blink again.

GRAMS NARRATOR BACKGROUND

NARRATOR And this is indeed what we find. For deep in the heart of the first class passenger section of the slightly delayed Transtellar Spacelines ship the following horrifying events have been taking place.

ZARNIWOOP Can I get you a drink?

FORD Er . . .

ZAPHOD Zarniwoop!

ZARNIWOOP The same.

FORD I think . . .

ZAPHOD But who are you, man? Why do I want to see you? I was told you were on an intergalactic cruise, which I can handle, but in your office, which I can't.

ZARNIWOOP But I assure you it is true.

ZAPHOD Hey, what?

FORD I wonder . . .

ZAPHOD What do you want, Ford?

FORD Er, a small Janx spirit if there is one.

(This is what he's been trying to say all this time)

ZAPHOD	Get the man a drink Zarniwoop.
FORD	Or indeed a large one.
ZAPHOD	And one for me. Two for me. There's nothing worse than having only one drunk head.
F/X	CLINK OF GLASSES, POURING OF DRINKS
ZARNIWOOP	Here's to your achievement, Zaphod Beeblebrox.
ZAPHOD	Achievement? Oh, er yeah . . . yeah.
FORD	What achievement?
ZAPHOD	Oh I dunno. I achieve so many things you know.
ZARNIWOOP	You have the Heart of Gold. You have brought it here?
ZAPHOD	Er, yeah.
ZARNIWOOP	Into my Universe?
ZAPHOD	Yeah – er what?
ZARNIWOOP	This Universe – I created it in my office. You've been in it for quite a while now.
ZAPHOD	Huh?
FORD	Is it all right if I just go and sit in this corner and get drunk? I may sing quietly if that doesn't disturb you. It's just been – well you know how it is.
F/X	FOR A WHILE WE HEAR THE CONTINUING POURING OF DRINKS AND A BIT OF QUIET BETELGEUSE SINGING FROM FORD GOING ON IN THE BACKGROUND
ZAPHOD	You mean we're in . . . an artificial Universe?
ZARNIWOOP	Oh yes.
ZAPHOD	All that out there? Like, in your office . . .?
ZARNIWOOP	Yes.
ZAPHOD	Man, I've heard of open plan, but . . .
ZARNIWOOP	It's modelled very closely on the real one you know, with just a few . . . differences.
ZAPHOD	But when did we get into it man, I mean like, where, when?
ZARNIWOOP	You didn't notice? Well, **(He laughs slightly)** I'll let you work it out for yourself. Now you have brought me the ship we can dismantle this Universe, return to the real one and find what we're after.
ZAPHOD	Can I just ask you some questions?
ZARNIWOOP	By all means.

ZAPHOD	OK, well for starters I'll have Who, What, When and Where, and then Whither, Whether, Whence and Wherefore to follow and one big side order of Why.
FORD	(**Slightly drunk now**) And the wine list please. (**He continues singing**)
ZARNIWOOP	It's terribly simple. (**And please can we have no cheap satirical asides at this point if it's all the same to everyone else?**) Long ago, you and I and others planned to discover who it was who was ruling the galaxy, who was making all the decisions behind the President's back. I found where he was located and retreated to the safe hiding of the bar in the first class lounge of a forgotten spaceship in a . . . can we stop that man singing?
ZAPHOD	Hey, Ford.
FORD	I'll sing something else.
	(**He sings something else instead. It sounds exactly the same as what he was singing before**)
ZARNIWOOP	. . . In an artificial Universe. Meanwhile, you were doing the most important job. You stole the Infinite Improbability Drive ship, without which it would be impossible to breach the barriers protecting his world. And then you brought it to my hiding place.
ZAPHOD	Ford.
FORD	Oooh, yeah?
ZAPHOD	You're still singing.
FORD	Am I? (**He hums a bit experimentally**) Oh yes, so I am. Wassa matter? You don't like it? I'll sing something different.
	(**He does sing something different now. It is very loud and strident and totally without any aesthetically redeeming features whatsoever**)
	(**Actually he can sing the 'That ol' janx spirit' song from the book**)
ZARNIWOOP	(**Talking more loudly in order to be heard above the din**) I'll just bring your ship down, then we can get out of here and get on with it.
GRAMS	NARRATOR BACKGROUND
NARRATOR	The major problem – *one* of the major problems, for there are several – one of the many major problems with governing people is that of who you get to do it; or rather of who manages to get people to let them do it to them.
	To summarize:- It is a well known and much lamented fact that those people who most *want* to rule people are, ipso facto, those least suited to do it. To summarize the summary:- anyone who is capable of getting themselves made President should on no account be allowed to do the job. To summarize the summary of the summary:- people are a problem.
	And so this is the situation we find: a succession of Galactic Presidents who so much enjoy the fun and palaver of being in power that they never really notice that they're not. And somewhere in the shadows behind them –

who? Who can possibly rule if no one who wants to can be allowed to?

F/X WIND. (IT'S ALWAYS WIND ISN'T IT? I THINK WE'LL HAVE SOME THUNDER AND RAIN AS WELL)

MAN Pussy pussy pussy . . . coochicoochicoochi . . . pussy want his fish? Nice piece of fish . . . pussy want it? Pussy not eat his fish, pussy get thin and waste away, I think. I imagine this is what will happen, but how can I tell? I think it's better if I don't get involved. I think fish is nice, but then I think that rain is wet so who am I to judge? Ah, you're eating it.

I like it when I see you eat the fish, because in my mind you will waste away if you don't.

Fish come from far away, or so I'm told. Or so I imagine I'm told. When the men come, or when in my mind the men come in their six black shiny ships do they come in your mind too? What do you see, pussy? And when I hear their questions, all their many questions do you hear questions? Perhaps you just think they're singing songs to you. Perhaps they are singing songs to you and I just think they're asking me questions. Do you think they came today? I do. There's mud on the floor, cigarettes and whisky on my table, fish in your plate and a memory of them in my mind. And look what else they've left me. Crosswords, dictionaries and a calculator. I think I must be right in thinking they ask me questions. To come all that way and leave all these things just for the privilege of singing songs to you would be very strange behaviour. Or so it seems to me. Who can tell, who can tell.

F/X HE LIGHTS A CIGARETTE

MAN I think I saw another ship in the sky today. A big white one. I've never seen a big white one. Only six small black ones. Perhaps six small black ones can look like one big white one. Perhaps I would like a glass of whisky. Yes, that seems more likely.

(He pours a glass)

Perhaps some different people are coming to see me.

F/X CUT TO EXTERIOR. IN OTHER WORDS A SHARP INCREASE IN THE NOISE LEVEL OF THE RAIN.

TRAMPING FEET ON ROUGH GROUND.

FORD In there? (He is still slightly drunk)

ZARNIWOOP Yes.

ARTHUR What, that shack?

ZARNIWOOP Yes.

ZAPHOD Weird.

ARTHUR But it's the middle of nowhere.

FORD Oh come on, we must have come to the wrong place.

ZARNIWOOP	Knock on the door.
F/X	KNOCK KNOCK. THE DOOR, A CREAKY OLD WOODEN ONE, OPENS
MAN	Hello?
FORD	Er, excuse me, do you rule the Universe?
MAN	I try not to. Are you wet?
FORD	Wet! Well, doesn't it look as if we're wet?
MAN	That's how it looks to me, but how you feel about it might be a different matter. If you find warmth makes you feel dry you'd better come in.
ALL	**(Slightly awkward and embarrassed)** Oh, yes thank you.
F/X	DOOR CLOSES AND WE ARE IN AN INTERNAL ACOUSTIC AGAIN

(The visitors are all bewildered and embarrassed)

ZAPHOD	Er, man, like what's your name?
MAN	I don't know. Why, do you think I ought to have one? It seems odd to give a bundle of vague sensory perceptions a name.
ZARNIWOOP	Listen. We must ask you some questions.
MAN	All right. You can sing to my cat if you like.
ARTHUR	Would he like that?
MAN	You'd better ask him that.
ZARNIWOOP	How long have you been ruling the Universe?
MAN	Ah, this is a question about the past is it?
ZARNIWOOP	Yes.
MAN	How can I tell that the past isn't a fiction designed to account for the discrepancy between my immediate physical sensations and my state of mind?
ZARNIWOOP	Do you answer all questions like this?
MAN	I say what it occurs to me to say when I think I hear people say things. More I cannot say.
ZAPHOD	Ah that clears it up. He's a weirdo.
ZARNIWOOP	No. Listen. People come to you, yes?
MAN	I think so.
ZARNIWOOP	And they ask you to take decisions – about wars, about economies, about people, about everything going on out there in the Universe?
MAN	I only decide about my Universe. My Universe is what happens to my eyes and ears. Anything else is surmise and hearsay. For all I know, these people

may not exist. You may not exist. I say what it occurs to me to say.

ZARNIWOOP But don't you see? What you decide affects the fate of millions of people.

MAN I don't know them, I've never met them. They only exist in words I think I hear. The men who come say to me, say, so and so wants to declare what we call a war. These are the facts, what do you think? And I say. Sometimes it's a smaller thing. They might say for instance that a man called Zaphod Beeblebrox is President, but he is in financial collusion with a consortium of high powered psychiatrists who want him to order the destruction of a planet called Earth because of some sort of experiment, should he be allowed to . . .

ZAPHOD Er, now wait a minute man, hey wait . . .

FORD Sit down Arthur, sit down . . .

ARTHUR (**Furious**) Let go of me.

F/X THE DOOR IS THROWN OPEN

ZAPHOD Hey, er . . . Arthur, you know me . . .

FORD Leave him. We'll sort it out later.

MAN But it's folly to say you know what is happening to other people. Only they know. If they exist.

ZARNIWOOP Do you think they do?

MAN I have no opinion. How can I have?

ZARNIWOOP I have.

MAN So you say – or so I hear you say.

ZAPHOD (**Aside**) Hey, er, Ford . . . the Earthman . . . you think he's? That's not it you know, that's not it at all man.

ZARNIWOOP But don't you see that people live or die on your word?

MAN It's nothing to do with me, I am not involved with people. The Lord knows I am not a cruel man.

ZARNIWOOP Ah! You say . . . the Lord! You believe in . . .

MAN My cat. I call him the Lord. I am kind to him.

ZARNIWOOP All right. How do you know he exists? How do you know he knows you to be kind, or enjoys what you think of as your kindness?

MAN I don't. I have no idea. It merely pleases me to behave in a certain way to what appears to be a cat. What else do *you* do? Please I am tired.

F/X DISTANT SOUND OF ROCKET ENGINES

FORD What was that?

ZAPHOD I dunno man, but I didn't like the sound of it. Let's get after the Earthman.

FORD	Er, look sorry to rush, great ruler, keep up the disinterested work, right? See you around.
ZARNIWOOP	Wait . . . there is so much we must discover!
FORD	Later, later . . .
F/X	DOOR OPEN. EXTERNAL ACOUSTIC
FORD	(Shouting) Arthur! Arthur . . . He's gone.
ZAPHOD	Holy belgium man! So has the swutting ship.
FORD	Was all that true?
ZAPHOD	Oh, what is truth man? You heard the weirdo.
FORD	Fine. Zaphod, whatever may or may not happen from hereon in, I just want you to know something. I want you to know that I respect you.
ZAPHOD	Great.
FORD	Just not very much . . . that's all.
F/X	JOURNEY OF THE SORCERER
NARRATOR	What does the future hold for our heroes now? What does the past or present hold for that matter?
	Will Arthur Dent now embark on a terrible and protracted vendetta against Zaphod Beeblebrox? Will he be all right alone in the Universe with only the Infinite Improbability Drive Ship, Marvin the Paranoid Android, Lintilla the archaeologist, Eddie the shipboard computer, a lot of chatty doors and a battered copy of *The Hitch-Hiker's Guide to the Galaxy* for company.
	Who will Ford Prefect ally himself with – Arthur Dent, Zaphod Beeblebrox, or a large Pan Galactic Gargle Blaster?
	Will there ever be another series of that wholly remarkable and mystifying entity *The Hitch-Hiker's Guide to the Galaxy?* . . . Find out if you can!

FOOTNOTES

The final show in the series very nearly didn't make it on to the air. Although the actors were recorded on 13 January the actual mixing of the show was all done on the day of transmission, completed some twenty minutes before it was due to go out and then spirited in a fast car down one of London's busiest roads, the Edgware Road, the three miles to BBC Broadcasting House, where it arrived just a few minutes before transmission.

In fact half an hour before the programme went out the last five minutes of the show were wrapped round the capstan head of a tape recorder and being hacked off in little bits by three people all furiously slashing at it with razor blades.

Keen eared listeners might have noticed that some scenes were remixed for the subsequent repeats, since at the time we had no time to do anything on the last scene but add a little rain and some cat impersonations. However, as with the mice in the fourth programme I'm sure there are some people who prefer the show as it went out for the very first time.

Douglas has this to add about the ending of the series.

Ending

At the end of the first series I didn't really expect with any confidence that anyone would want me to do any more, so I brought the story to a very definite close. This then caused me huge problems getting the story going again for the second series. At the end of the second series I knew that I would be asked to do more, and deliberately left the ending open so that the next series could get off the ground straight away.

Of course, we never did a third series. [DNA]

David Tate was the Allitnils, and we were able to get the sound right without actually having to record him saying Lintilla and then physically reversing the tape.

Rula Lenska was the Robot Stewardess. The part of Poodoo was especially written for Ken Campbell (the legendary theatre director and madman, famous for such stage shows as *Illuminatus*, the *Warp* and of course *The Hitch-Hiker's Guide to the Galaxy*) who we simply asked to be himself in the part.

Strangely the only way we could get Ken to sound remotely like himself was to imitate him down the talkback and for him to copy what we did!

Jonathan Pryce, one of Britain's most prestigious actors, was originally asked to play the ruler of the Universe, but arrived in the studio to find out that he hadn't actually been written into the script yet. He kindly agreed to play Zarniwoop and the Autopilot instead.

The name Ron Hate who appears in the Radio Times playing the Man in the Shack is an easily worked out anagram. The show was recorded after the Radio Times had gone to press, and he was in fact played by the ever versatile Stephen Moore, whose only question on being handed the script to the last scene on the now traditional snappies was 'What are you on Douglas?'

Douglas has this to add on the Delayed spaceship scene.

Delayed spaceship

This was based pretty much exactly on something that happened to me one day, trying to get to Leeds.

The normal way of going from London to Leeds is by train, which is a perfectly quick journey. However, on this particular occasion I had a meeting in London in the morning and another in Leeds at lunchtime, and the only way of making them both on time was to go by plane. Going by plane on a trip like that is a lot more expensive, much less comfortable, much more hassle and, what with having to get out to the airport and so on, only about twenty minutes quicker. It is reasonable to assume that there was a very large proportion of people on the plane to whom those twenty minutes were pretty important . . .

11.15 was the time we were due to take off, 12.15 was when we were supposed to arrive.

At 11.15 we were sitting on the tarmac and nothing much was happening – not in itself unusual.

At 11.20 things were continuing not to happen.

At 11.25 the pilot came on to the public address system and apologized for the delay. He said this was entirely their fault. They had forgotten, he said, to load the bar on the plane, so there were no drinks on board. In order to try and rectify the problem they were trying to acquire some coffee and biscuits, he said, for our flying pleasure.

Five more minutes passed. The passengers were getting restive, but being English, we didn't say anything. We did, however, look very pointedly at our watches.

Another five minutes passed.

At 11.35, the pilot addressed us again. He said that the coffee and biscuits for our flying pleasure were now aboard the aircraft, and that there would be another slight delay before we took off. He didn't even say what the delay was for this time. Presumably they had to borrow some sugar from Air France.

Eventually, at 11.45, we took off, half an hour late.

At 12.45 we landed. Half an hour late.

And the *whole point* of travelling by plane had gone out of the window. The coffee and biscuits had been terrible, of course, and by the time they served them to us we could, according to the original schedule, have been getting them for ourselves in Leeds.

I missed my appointment, but at least I got some jokes out of it. I don't suppose any of the other passengers did. [DNA]

The end of this scene is not in fact made in the way the effects direction suggests. In order to make the scene more mysterious the Autopilot's line 'Return to your seats' was increased in volume and overlapped on itself in a sinister montage that was made using the effect so tediously described with the dialling chant in episode eight.

Such was the latent hysteria in the recording of this last show that the line 'Marvin's got Poodoo' dissolved the whole cast into almost inexplicable hysteria and stopped the recording for about half an hour. This, sadly, is the answer to the sometimes asked question, 'What bit seemed funniest when you were recording it?'

In the collapsing Universe the falling sky was represented by a high-pitched whine and the ground coming up was represented by a deep rumble. In addition these effects were accompanied by a montage of lines from previous episodes (and one which in fact had yet to appear). These were:

'But there aren't any real people here at all . . .' 'So what's new?'

'Share and Enjoy'

'Well, well, well . . . Arthur Dent'

'Tell me how you got here?' . . . 'Impossible'

'What we did you see was we flew in . . . we flew in. Oh yes, we definitely flew in'

'Here's to your achievement, Zaphod Beeblebrox' . . . 'Achievement? . . . Oh, yeah'

Real fanatics, or people who have a got a spare minute or two might like to find out where all these lines come from and ponder their significance. Others might like to ponder the other, as yet unanswered question asked by the Book . . . 'Will there ever be another series of that wholly mysterious entity *The Hitch-Hiker's Guide to the Galaxy*'.

If so, maybe it will feature some of the ideas which were discussed but which never made it into the show: the messages in the weather, the Chinese meal with the guardian of the grubby red and white check table cloth, the river with a different attitude to time and spider pornography.

DOUGLAS N. ADAMS was born in Cambridge in 1952. He was educated at Brentwood School, Essex, and St. John's College, Cambridge, where he read English.

After graduation he spent several years contributing material to radio and television shows as well as writing, performing in, and sometimes directing stage revues in London and Cambridge and on the Edinburgh Fringe. He has also worked at various times as a hospital porter, barn builder, chicken shed cleaner, bodyguard, radio producer, and script editor of *Doctor Who*.

He originally created *The Hitch-Hiker's Guide to the Galaxy* as a radio series for the BBC, and then wrote it again as a novel. He has written four more novels in the increasingly inaccurately named Hitch-hiker Trilogy—*The Restaurant at the End of the Universe; Life, the Universe, and Everything; So Long and Thanks for All the Fish;* and *Mostly Harmless*.

Douglas has written two Dirk Gently books, *Dirk Gently's Holistic Detective Agency* and *The Long Dark Tea-Time of the Soul*. With John Lloyd he co-wrote *The Meaning of Liff* and *The Deeper Meaning of Liff* and with zoologist Mark Carwardine he has written the wildlife travelogue *Last Chance to See*.

He lives in London with his wife, daughter, and a large collection of left-handed guitars and babysitters.

GEOFFREY PERKINS joined the BBC Radio Light Entertainment department in 1976 after leaving Oxford University. In the six years he was in the BBC he produced a large number of programmes ranging from *The Hitch-Hiker's Guide to the Galaxy* to *Top of the Form*; his other 'achievements' there included performing in the show *Radio Active*, which he also co-writes with Angus Deayton, and introducing the exasperating and bewildering game Mornington Crescent to the programme *I'm Sorry I Haven't a Clue*.

Subsequent to leaving the BBC he has worked at Thames Television and LWT, and written for a variety of TV and radio shows. He is currently living in a cottage outside Henley where Douglas Adams can bang his head on the ceiling of every room.